Lincolnshire
COUNTY COUNCIL

COMMUNITIES, CULTURAL SERVICES
and ADULT EDUCATION

**This book should be returned on or before
the last date shown below.**

To renew or order library books please telephone 01522 782010
or visit www.lincolnshire.gov.uk
You will require a Personal Identification Number.
Ask any member of staff for this.

EC. 199 (LIBS): RS/L5/19

LARGE PRINT

B·BAK

L 5/9

3

THE CENTRE OF THE BED

Joan Bakewell was born in 1933, in an era when most women were expected to stay at home. She became a wife and mother, but also one of the first women journalists on television. The programme *Late Night Line Up* made her a sixties icon and, with series such as *Heart of the Matter*, she has remained an influential presence on our screens.

In this intimate account of her life, she retraces the paths she has taken and the choices she made. She describes her BBC television debut during the Cuban missile crisis; being the only woman on *Late Night Line Up*; and being dubbed 'the thinking man's crumpet'. Here too, is how it felt to see her affair with Harold Pinter transmuted into his play Betrayal.

Throughout, Joan Bakewell provides a fascinating overview of the changes in British society and culture over the last seventy years, from the perspective of an astute observer whose own experience exemplifies the transformation in women's lives.

THE CENTRE OF THE BED

Joan Bakewell

BBC
LARGE
PRINT

First published 2003
by
Hodder and Stoughton
This Large Print edition published 2004
by
BBC Audiobooks Ltd
by arrangement with
Hodder and Stoughton

ISBN 0 7540 9550 9

British Library Cataloguing in Publication Data available

Printed and bound in Great Britain by
Antony Rowe Ltd., Chippenham, Wiltshire

For Harriet and Matthew,
with love

CONTENTS

	Prologue	ix
1.	Roots	1
2.	Mother Love	15
3.	Other Shores	29
2 4.	Being a Girl	40
5.	Wartime	48
6.	Certainties	72
7.	Cambridge Days	102
8.	The Big Wide World	138
9.	The Party	160
10.	Late Nights	193
11.	Family and Friends	243
12.	The Secret	263
13.	Television Times	290
14.	Arts Matters	318
15.	The Heart of Things	355
16.	Veteran	378
	Epilogue	395
	Acknowledgements	401

PROLOGUE

The room in which I am sitting is white. White as a blank, a fresh sheet of paper. The room is also empty. Indeed, emptiness is its prevailing characteristic. Echoing, without life. There are big spaces in all directions, across to the long french windows, which open not on to green lawns but on to a balcony, which surveys great swathes of London to the south and east, stretched out across the sky, the London Eye and Canary Wharf winking in the distance. The sun comes in through the windows. An empty sunlit room with me in it. Blank as a sheet of paper.

There has been furniture here, lots of it. Once there were children's cots and furry toys. Then there were beds, rumpled blankets and Airfix planes swinging from the ceiling. Later there were discreet furnishings, tasteful and neutral, made up of items surplus to other rooms and claiming to be for guests. Decades on, it became 'the office': not mine, someone else's. Overcrowded, hectic, filled with office equipment, and the paraphernalia of television sets and recording machines, phones, lots of them, mobile phones and answering machines, each with its separate plug or jack. Plenty of wires. Machines humming. Desks too, loaded with computers and photocopiers. The desks were black. The machines were black. The phones were black. There was a brightly coloured carpet on the floor in front of the mock fire. But the coals were black and the fender was black as well. Pretty, though.

Everywhere paper. Heaps of it—intended heaps, heaps that meant something. But not to me. Letters everywhere, many unanswered, some unopened. Files spilling on the desks, lolling against the machines. CDs on the chairs where cushions should have been. A dirty coffee cup, a mislaid set of photographs. Another life. Another's life.

That has all gone now. Scooped up and stacked efficiently by young men in jeans used to doing this sort of thing. An everyday matter to them. But for me a wrench, a raw wound. The walls are scarred, bearing the shadows of removed pictures and charts. Blu-tack splodges and Rawlplugs clog or eat into the plaster. But to my eyes the empty room is white and full of sunlight. A good place to begin.

A daytime place to begin.

*　　　*　　　*

Nights are different. There have been changes there, too. It's what happens when you are divorced. Or widowed. Or alone. I have moved into the centre of the bed.

I am reminded of St Ursula and her dreaming. Not the saint herself, but a painting of her. Indeed, how would I imagine her unless prompted by a painting? Paintings are among my transactions with the world. They guide and shape how I see skies, rivers, rooms, people. Sometimes they sit in my mind waiting, even for decades, to stir an idea. As St Ursula and her dreaming does now.

Women have done much dreaming, and men have painted them doing so. Dreaming themselves into significance, perhaps. Even into the company of saints. St Helena dreamed a dream, woke, set off on her journey and, as the dream had foretold, found what she declared to be the True Cross in Jerusalem. She was the mother of the Emperor Constantine so people were inclined to believe her. I see her as Veronese painted her, hand on brow, the gorgeous Renaissance dress suggesting she had fallen asleep by some noonday window rather than between the sheets.

St Ursula, on the other hand, is definitely between the sheets, neat, tight sheets, the kind favoured by hospitals. But she is not in hospital. She lies, taut and tidy, in a sumptuous Venetian bedchamber. Venetian because the man who put her there is Carpaccio, one of Venice's greatest painters, although by rights she should be in Cologne where she had the dream.

I saw her when I was day-dreaming at my girls' high school in Stockport. Morning assembly was a time that inclined young girls to fidget. But mine was a strict, old-fashioned school, and fidgeting was an offence. So I fidgeted with my mind and my eyes. It was the tradition in our grammar school for the rostrum from which the headmistress presided to be graced by two large easels on which sat two paintings, large reproductions of some of the world's great art that had been bequested to the school by some unremembered benefactor. It was an inspired gift. Each week the pictures were changed and every Monday morning an announcement from the platform told us what the newly displayed ones were called and who had painted them. No explanation was offered. Odd Italian names and strange subjects jumbled into my child's mind and have stayed there ever since.

The Dream of St Ursula was one of a series of nine painted by Carpaccio in the late fifteenth century. Her high-ceilinged Renaissance room is dominated by a tall four-poster bed where she lies under a scarlet blanket. Her cheek rests on her hand, her slender body lies stiff and straight, and her pert little feet make a bump in the coverlet. The scene is one of domestic calm: there are plants in pots, a book, perhaps the Bible, left open at the table where she was reading; a small dog rests at the foot of the bed. It is at the right of the picture that dramatic action blazes into life: beyond the foot of the bed the door stands open and a shaft of light declares the presence of a magnificent angel.

He has come to tell Ursula of her destiny, which, given its violence, makes the serene smile on her lips already saintly. For Ursula, supposedly betrothed to a British prince, will lead a pilgrimage to Rome of some eleven thousand virgins who, on their return, will be massacred by marauding Huns somewhere outside Cologne. Set aside the improbable logistics of getting eleven thousand virgins across Europe and keeping them in that condition, this is one of the great fables of the medieval Church. It was already current in the eighth and ninth centuries, and was to underpin the foundation of the Ursuline order. Ursula gave her name to the most formidable teaching order—women teaching girls—in the Catholic Church. As such we might claim her as an early feminist. But none of that is in the painting.

What *is* in the painting, and seemed strange to me at the age of eleven, is a domestic detail that caught what for me at the time seemed the essence of a woman's life. Perhaps, even then, I was beginning to question it. For Ursula—dreaming of sainthood—is, none the less, sleeping in only one half of the large double bed. The other half, by its vacancy, implies the presence of another. In Renaissance Italy, as everywhere else, a woman's life is to be shared: without a man she is not complete. Without a man Ursula still behaves as though this were the accepted distribution of space and comfort.

I wonder now whether we are destined to share our lives, as I have shared most of mine. What is this thing—destiny? And how much is mine conditioned by those other destinies that have gone before, defined by family, endorsed by religion, shaped by tradition? It doesn't suggest much room for manoeuvre. But, then, sharing at its best is a fine condition: it is generous, open-hearted, supportive. It creates children, and communities. It fosters happiness and provides the nearest insight we have into the heart of another.

But it seems to be getting harder. Around four in ten adults in Britain now live alone; their numbers are increasing. The sharing seems to run out: it begins to require tolerances and acquiescences that were not bargained for at the outset. It inhibits and restrains, it chafes and provokes. It presents a new conundrum for many women in the modern West: the single or the shared life? How to reconcile the interdependencies of love with the independence of spirit that, for over half a century, we have been struggling to gain?

St Ursula went on to meet her own particular destiny. In the last in the series, Carpaccio paints the massacre of the virgins and, finally, the carrying of her body to the mausoleum bearing her name, once again under the red blanket, but with a slightly more fancy pillow, the same beatific smile, the same hand under cheek. Is Carpaccio suggesting it was all a dream—a dream of escape from the matrimonial bed? This time, however, there is no space beside her. Here, she is on her own. Death shares no beds.

*   *   *

As I write this book I shall move between the centre of the bed and the white room. And I shall reinhabit the past. Every family has its cupboards and its boxes, some records kept, arbitrarily, many discarded, some of it regretted later but not much. 'These fragments I have shored against my ruins'— against the quirks and loss of memory, more like, encouraging the notion of pinning down what the past was really like, how things actually happened. But these remnants are the only scaffolding I have, dates and appointments that have left a trace. And they are scattered, in disorder, in different rooms and corners, to be retrieved and unfolded. Can I expect them to disclose anything much except perhaps in myself an unwillingness to move on and discard the past? And that I own up to.

As I begin, I shall have to rely on two not entirely reliable contributors to this story: my memory and my sense of who I am. Both are highly selective, self-regarding and inclined to wool-pulling over the eyes. I shall have to make the memory work hard, using the props from the boxes, then let the mind spin away, chasing after a scent on the wind and snatches of old song. I shall leave the white room to walk old streets, visit familiar houses, dawdle by a familiar river, 'And know the place for the first time'. I shall consult with cousins rarely met about the piecing together of family trees. Will I find what I expect or a new self, different from the one I thought I was? And what then? Some sadness, perhaps, loss. And discovery.

Already I have a sense that what has happened to me is shared by many women of my age. Born when people had a rigid notion of a woman's place and expectations, I have seen all that change. Sometimes I have felt part of the changes, sometimes swept along by them, sometimes overtaken. It has been an era in history unique in the convulsive speed with which women's lives have been reconfigured. And mine has been one of them.

As I grew I made choices. I tried to make free ones. Much of today's genetics and evolutionary psychology would have it that we are more circumscribed than we believe in the exercising of free will, our choices predisposed since birth. The vague concept of 'destiny' has been transmuted into something more absolute, already hard-wired into our brains. Yet I can't help feeling fully responsible for who I am, unwilling to blame my genes but interested in examining the play of different forces in my background. I made some choices and I neglected to make others, letting options drift away on the wind like a balloon let go, wished back, out of reach. My life, when I look back on it here, will be a story of selections made and lived with, some nurtured, some abandoned, moving towards a synthesis, some kind of resolution: the person I am today. What follows is how and why I made the choices I did.

CHAPTER ONE

ROOTS

I was born on 16 April 1933 at Hooley Range Nursing Home, Heaton Moor in Stockport. I had been conceived in mid-Atlantic as my parents sailed home on the SS *Deseado* from three years in Buenos Aires. Within another three years they had moved into a new house in Bakewell Road, Hazel Grove, on the outskirts of Stockport, named after a village in neighbouring Derbyshire. It would be eighteen years before the name meant more to me than that. I was Joan Dawson Rowlands.

The announcement of my birth in the local paper gave no name. My parents were still undecided. It was to be Joan or Jacqueline. They came from families crowded with Hetty and Lottie, Polly and Betty, Peggy and Sally. In the end they chose Joan so that no one would be able to abbreviate it. Jackie would have been slovenly and not correct. My parents were like that. Joan Bennett and Joan Crawford were glamorous film stars at the time; perhaps that counted too. Given their exactness about my name I never had the courage to change it. Later, when I read *Little Women*, I longed to abbreviate it to Jo; now when I survey the roll call of actresses I wish I'd lengthened it to Joanna. Might my life have been different if I had? They tell me 'Joan' is due for a revival.

I was born on Easter Sunday and christened six weeks later on Whit Sunday. I have always thought

1

of it as a sort of blessing, to arrive on the most joyous day of the Christian year, and to be baptised on its most triumphant. Whitsuntide is largely neglected now, but as a child I took part in the local Whit Walks—new clothes for the occasion, smart white gloves, the entire community turned out in its best. I am no longer devout, but I carry the legacy of that sort of faith, simple, full of the celebration of something good. I still wake happy on Easter Sunday, just as I wake sad on Good Friday.

*   *   *

I was born into my parents' happiness and I grew to share it. My earliest memory confirms as much. I must have been no more than eighteen months old. The two people who mattered most were standing above me, before the living-room fire. I could see the flickering of flames, glimpsed briefly now and then between them, as the hem of my mother's skirt met my father's trousers, obscuring the heat. The trouser legs were wide. I could pull on them. Close beside them, very close, were my mother's strapped shoes, and her soft skin in pale stockings. There was laughter and whispering above me, confiding, loving. The two people in my life speaking softly to each other. I wanted to be a part of it.

Of course I knew I was already a part of it. Or, rather, I sensed I was. After all, I knew nothing else. I knew no one else. Peripheral family members were shadows, noises that came and went, adding their voices. But here was the quiet, whispering heart of all that mattered. And I was there. But not at its heart, not quite at its centre.

I must have wriggled, squealed, tugged the cloth. I don't remember how I broke into their love for each other but the talk erupted into laughter and the four shoes separated into two pairs. My father stooped and scooped me into his arms, his tobacco smell including me as I was lifted between them and admitted to their charmed circle. The laughter was mine too now, and the happiness. I was where I wanted to be. Within my parents' circle, loved by both. I hug this to me, my earliest significant memory. As I trace my life forward, I need to remember, as I pass judgement on myself as well as others, describe hurts as well as triumphs, that fleeting moment, which defined something about my life and possibly my temperament: I was born into happiness.

The memory is mine, of course. And therefore an authentic memory. But is it, in any absolute sense, true? Was that really what happened? Perhaps what my parents experienced was a child whining for attention while they had a furtive discussion over some payment they couldn't afford. Perhaps their laughter marked the point at which they agreed to give in to my bullying. Perhaps they were irritated that I wanted to be at the centre of things. If this were, indeed, their experience, does that invalidate my memory? Or should I stick to my guns and insist that that was how it was?

I have been teased all my life by this quandary. To what extent does my account—my account of anything—tally with that of others? And how can any of this be verified? Suddenly the whole tenuous business of recollection and the given account threatens to tumble around me. Perhaps this is a fiction I am writing. If so, what constitutes my memory of events? Wishful thinking, self-justification, or a story-teller's longing that things should have been so? I press forward, salvaging evidence as I go.

*   *   *

My parents both came from respectable working-class families in inner-city Manchester. The Welsh clan to which my father belonged—the Rowlandses—had flocked out of the modest mid-Wales town of Aberystwyth around the turn of the century seeking work and finding it in the industrial heart of Salford. My mother's tribe, the Blands, had come up from Wolverhampton around the same time, also driven by the need for jobs. They'd found them in the equally grim inner-city settlement of Gorton. Both sets of grandparents converged on the sprawling mass of factories, foundries and warehouses that then constituted the mercantile heartland of one of the greatest cities of the empire.

Aberystwyth, too, had once had an industry of its own. For centuries the lead ore of the Welsh hills had been mined and exported from its busy port to destinations as far away as Spain. Indeed, by the eighteenth century the harbour was so busy that the town petitioned Parliament for its own Customs House, where an ancestor of mine was clerk in the 1840s, and in 1855 my great-grandfather, Rowland Thomas Rowlands, was born in Customs House Street. They all lie buried in the churchyard of Llanbadarn Fawr, among generations of Hugheses, Morgans and

4

Rowlandses, my distant relations who lived out their lives in both Welsh and English. Snatches of Welsh phrases remained lilting through my childhood.

Working the mines in the hills of the Ystwyth Valley was tough. The ore lay deep, sought out along a network of treacherous shafts and dug out in the darkness by crouching men. They lived in dormitory shacks built on the hillsides, bleak and raw, battered by the wind with no trees to offer shelter. Their womenfolk and children were away from this rough male place. They made their homes in the villages and towns, and only met their men at weekends. Generations later I would come with a television crew and film the ruined mines, the rusting doors creaking on broken hinges, the narrow dormitories broken down to nothing more than heaped slates. I probably learned more then than my family knew when the mines were working. How the Rowlands menfolk escaped such hardship I don't know. But escape it they did.

The television venture sent me in search of my ancestry, and in the municipal record offices I opened up large neat books whose entries, in the copperplate writing of the nineteenth century, designate my forebears as gardener, polisher and such, artisans in modest work, but cosier and easier on the hands than mining. They would have lived with their families in modest homes, hardly aware of the harshness and poverty of the hills.

The reason they moved to Lancashire was the same reason all migrations happen: thriving industrial cities have a relentless pull for the rural poor. They promise not just jobs but a different world, a world where things seem possible, where exciting things happen, and where new choices open up before you. In the late nineteenth and early twentieth centuries nothing expressed such a prospect more than the vigour and success of industrial Manchester. Manchester, Cottonopolis, the first industrial community in the world: its pride, its radicalism, its unrelenting passion for hard work, enterprise and achievement were imprinted on me from the start.

On the other side of the family, the Blands, the men had been coopers for three generations, making barrels to carry everything from beer and chemicals to sugar. They were skilled artisans, and my grandfather was one of the best. He did the job with a cheerful dedication to his craft and he brought his skills home, making stools and tables as the family needed. I recall his rickety shed with its bench of tools, where I wandered waist high in sweet-smelling wood shavings, the open stove glowing red beside them—a treacherous fire hazard. But I don't remember ever being warned away from it. People were more casual then.

In the early days of the last century it was the practice in the cooperage trade for journeymen to be sent from towns that were suffering a slump to others that were more prosperous. The Coopers Society looked after its own. Many industries did. Long before there were formal trade-union agreements, there existed a fluid network of mutual support among workers, moving skills to where they were needed and to where families could find an income. When there were slack times in the Midlands, the Coopers Society found my grandfather a job in Manchester at the Burton cooperage in Ardwick. The family moved to where the work was. His son Bill, my uncle, was to follow him into the trade.

*   *   *

The earliest record of the Rowlands family in Manchester is a photograph, a copy provided at someone's request from the archives of the Church Army. It was once sepia but has been painted in with washy colours that, with the years, have faded oddly: the faces have turned slightly blue. Some fifty people align themselves for the camera: the men wear shirts without collars, some have flat caps, some bowlers; the others are bare-headed. The women without exception wear hats, mostly wide straw boaters with a broad buckram band. The wearing of hats was the rule for women when out of doors. To go bare-headed was the equivalent of going half dressed. The girls wear boaters too, and smocked dresses with high necklines. Sitting at the centre of the group, indeed the only man to be sitting, is my great-grandfather, Rowland Thomas Rowlands. The group is posed before a large tent of striped canvas calico upon which a banner proclaims: 'Come and Hear Pioneer Rowlands, the Happy Little Welshman, tonight.' Pioneer Rowlands holds at his knees a large display card on which the heading 'The Work of the Church Army' is just legible. He was a captain in the Church Army, a strand of muscular Christianity within the Church of England that competed with its more famous rival, the Salvation Army, in doing good to the poor.

I remember him spoken of with honour and respect among the others who shared his name.

7

And, being Welsh, there were many called Rowlands, and Morgan. It was pointed out to me proudly, 'Your grandfather'—or was it great-grandfather?—'was a captain in the Church Army.' It was spoken as though his rank was as impressive as the life it indicated of devotion to Christian duty. Yet on scouring my family's records, the desultory selection of the births, marriages and an occasional golden wedding recorded in yellowing newspaper cuttings, I have difficulty tracing him. There are several Rowlandses whose names are included without any mention of a job. He must have been one of them. But how did the photograph come to be in these papers, tucked away among numerous attempts at a family tree, none of which is complete or exact in its detail, various hands adding corners of knowledge that don't coincide? They have left an incoherent mess of papers. And again I have a sense of vertigo, as though the familiar stories, the comfortable family legends, are tilting away from me and vanishing into the maw of verifiable history. Did the story repay the telling so often that who exactly and where exactly this life was lived now eludes my searches? Perhaps all memory is like that. Even history itself.

But then the pieces fall into place. Out of the mist comes a figure I can identify as Captain Rowlands. Helpful papers arrive from Rowlands cousins: I meet with one, my virtual contemporary John Rowlands. He is a former keeper of drawings at the British Museum so he knows about records and such things. We pore over the evidence together, and decide that although Rowland Thomas Rowlands is down in the census records of 1881 as a polisher aged twenty-five, he might have

8

joined the Church Army later when he heard the call from God. This tallies with the date of Captain Rowlands's death at the age of sixty-three in 1917, after twenty-five years of service. Good. I have him nailed. My great-grandfather, evangelist, public orator, referred to even in the death notices from the records of today's Church Army, as 'the happy little Welshman'.

Certainly his cheeriness and Christian feeling were both to be found in the Salford house I knew. Like my maternal grandparents' home in Gorton, it seemed to me a cave of wonder and delight. The Salford house—in Crescent View—was demolished in the late 1960s in what was probably called slum clearance. I have a problem with the word 'slum': the origins of the term are obscure but it is thought to come from slumber, and was used to refer to 'sleepy and unknown alleys' in the choked overcrowding of Victorian cities. At their worst these places were hovels scarcely fit for animals. Those who witnessed them sought to bring the scandal of their existence to public attention. Back in 1844 Friedrich Engels had famously described Salford as 'the classic slum' and he knew what he was talking about. Four years later, Mrs Gaskell, wife of a Unitarian minister, shocked her nineteenth-century contemporaries with her novel *Mary Barton*, which gave an equally harsh and brutal picture of the Manchester poor.

But there was something else here too. The word 'slum' tended to be used by concerned outsiders, deploring the squalor, and pushing for change. Engels, after all, was a factory owner, so had no first hand experience of poverty. How could they know that in many of the overcrowded alleys, courts and streets there existed less than destitute, respectable families managing to keep respectable homes? The overarching designation 'slum' neglects the great variety of working-class life that went on in such places, and the security and steady pattern of that life. Probably the skilled artisans, a group to which both my families belonged, would have been at the top of this hierarchy. Their homes had no bath and the lavatory was outside, across the yard, but they were neat and clean. And as long as things went well they were in steady employment, paid a steady rent and lived by a routine so established it was possible to predict exactly what they would be having for tea each day of the week, when the scones would be baked, the rentman call and the knocker-up—the local 'alarm clock'—tap on the bedroom window each morning.

However, when things went wrong, as they did in my father's home, there was suddenly no security, no money, no means to live and no help. In 1909 my grandfather, John Morgan Rowlands—the records call him an 'iron turner', a term understood in his own day but obscure to us—died at the age of thirty-three, leaving a widow of twenty-eight, Emily, and four children below the age of six: John Roland, my father, who was the eldest, then Arthur, aged four, Mona, two and a half (her twin brother Thomas had died at seventeen months) and Walter, ten months. This was the sort of plight that could presage the downward spiral of a family into destitution and starvation. The evidence was all around.

It is probable that Captain Rowlands came to the rescue: he had contacts with local clerics, Salford worthies like Canon Peter Green and

Bishop Hicks. No doubt guided by him, the family decided that the best solution for the fatherless Rowlands boys—John, Arthur and Walter—was to get them places in Chethams Hospital, then a charity school for the deserving poor. But there was heavy competition, and strings would have to be pulled. My grandmother—Emily—had useful connections: she knew the Entwistle family, headed by a former old boy of the school who was now a governor. His influence was invoked to present a petition to the school on my father's behalf. The string-pulling worked and my father was sent for.

Chethams Hospital had a long history, as did Manchester's mercantile strength. As long ago as the seventeenth century the city was exporting cloth to the continent, and George and Humphrey Chetham, two bachelor brothers, became prominent wool merchants. They also became rich, very rich, but they kept their money to themselves. This was the period of the English Civil Wars and they were anxious to avoid allegiances. It was expected that every owner of land worth more than forty pounds should buy himself a knighthood. Humphrey Chetham refused. In 1635 he refused to become high sheriff. After being obliged to serve a short time as treasurer of the county, he again refused the top job, this time offered him by the victorious Parliamentarians. His stubbornness kept him out of politics and in the money. His motto was appropriately 'Quod tuum tene'—hold on to what is yours. The wily old miser retreated into ill-health and began writing his fifth and final will, which would perpetuate his name and earn him a benign statue in Manchester Cathedral representing him as the assiduously dutiful citizen he clearly was not.

Chetham's legacy provided for the purchase of a disused earlier religious foundation, to be made into a library and college, the latter to provide for forty boys to be brought up 'in learning and labour' in the towns of Manchester and Salford. Each boy must be the son of 'honest, industrious and painful parents and not wandering or idle beggars and rogues and . . . not a bastard, nor lame, infirm nor diseased'—the deserving as opposed to the undeserving poor. Two hundred and fifty years later, my father was one of those poor boys.

By today's standards, the interview was rigorous: at the age of seven my father had to read from the Bible, recite by heart the Catechism, the Ten Commandments and the Apostles' Creed. He passed. But no one told his brothers and sister at home until suddenly he was no longer there. My uncle Arthur, who recorded all this in a manuscript written when he was an old man, recorded how they wept when they were told where their missing brother had gone. Bereavement, examination, separation. There was no space for more than cursory tenderness, it seems. Concerns for a child's feelings weren't the priority they are today. It was universally understood that boys had to be toughened up for the world. It was a way of facing reality.

My father's stories of Chethams Hospital told of a place both Spartan and wonderful—a cross between Eton and Dotheboys Hall. 'Learning and labour' Humphrey Chetham had proclaimed as the destiny of his poor boys, and there was plenty of both. Early rising, daily chores, meagre food and hardy living—the regime of many schools at that time. But there was also Humphrey Chetham's splendid library of books, still one of the oldest and unacknowledged enclaves of historic Manchester. Tall theology books, with ancient parchment pages, books of record, biblical and secular, legal books, books of local history; leather bindings protecting the frail pages, shelved and locked away behind lattice frames; the library stacks shuttered behind fine wooden gates. These were not the books the boys read: they enjoyed Rider Haggard, Robert Louis Stevenson, Harrison Ainsworth. But the awe in which this treasure trove of scholarship was held conveyed the message that learning was among the highest, most cherished of man's pursuits.

Some two hundred and fifty years after Humphrey Chetham's time, another bachelor, a collector of rents, would make his way around Salford, the factories, the metal foundries and dyeworks—the dark satanic mills demonised by Blake and built by the dedicated industry and mercantile genius of nineteenth-century England. He would pause and lean against a wall to make notes that had nothing to do with rents. The squalor and poverty that then ravaged the landscape would pass into the paintings of L. S. Lowry, whose drawings and canvases chronicle the last years in the great industrial experience. He would people his streets and alleys, his factory approaches and city bridges, with teeming crowds of individuals, together but apart. They were the fiction of his imagination, not real people, but somehow real humanity. My parents took it personally, feeling that he sentimentalised their poverty.

Between the Salford of Humphrey Chetham and

L. S. Lowry, swirling millions of poor and struggling, the destitute, the proud, the stubbornly respectable, the threadbare and downtrodden, the talented and the spirited would create the wealth of a great city but not share in it. As such, it was a microcosm of all industrial cities, the very place where the industrial revolution began, a synthesis of wealth and effort, degradation and dogged survival. That was how I dramatised it for myself. When I read Dickens I knew that Manchester was filled with just such life as he describes in his city of London. At the same time as deploring the conditions and wanting them swept away, I also relished the life there, felt a sense of pride and identity with it.

I recall trudging damp pavements as a child and glimpsing, at half-basement level, vast spaces where bolts of cotton of every colour and design were ranked layer on layer waiting despatch to Britain's world markets. Now those spaces host wine bars, Indian restaurants, small commercial enterprises dealing in nothing very much. The skies were always dark, with smoke that settled daily on the city from its factory chimneys and rows and rows of home fires. The red-brick of houses and shops was black. The town hall, built proudly of white stone, had been totally blackened.

Everything is different now. Things began to change in the 1960s when clean-air legislation transformed the place. Now when I visit, I have the sudden surprise of blue skies looking down at a city bristling with grand architectural enterprise. I attend the Lowry Arts Centre to see a play by Michael Frayn, who began his writing life as a journalist on the *Manchester Guardian*. It sits beside canals devoted to pleasure rather than trade. Lowry also lends his name, uninvited, to a glittering, spacious hotel, with beds the size of his front room. Chethams, too, is transformed: it is now an internationally renowned music school, with a woman, Claire Moreland, as its Head. She sees that flowers and pot pourri are set in the guest room where I stay the night, off the still dark and ancient corridors. I'm told one of the teachers has heard a ghostly child crying. I think of my father . . . of many fathers.

The city has softened, losing its bleak toughness for an amorphous, aspirational international style; incongruously, there are palm trees in the elaborate glass railway station, street cafés around the gay enclave of Canal Street. Many hail it as improvement, renewal, and I can see why. But for me, visiting the past, it has the feel of a grafted-on identity, at odds with what actually existed here. For better or worse, the glory days of its industrial past are gone. But before it went, from my child's place in the two homes, with my child's eye for what mattered, I saw in both Salford and Gorton the last days of the industrial North.

CHAPTER TWO

MOTHER LOVE

I want to write lovingly of my mother because I loved her. And I know she loved me. I want to conjure up her kisses as Proust and Nabokov have done; but when I reread what I recall as literature's

15

rapturous moments of childhood, I find them imbued with loss. Proust describes how his mother stooped 'her loving face down over my bed, and held it out to me like a Host, for an act of Communion in which my lips might drink deeply the sense of her real presence . . .' Passionate love, indeed, except that on the same page he speaks of how brief her visit was, her displeasure if he asked for a second kiss, her failure to kiss him goodnight at all when they had guests to dinner. Nabokov, too, conjures a moment of fleeting contact with his mother: 'the touch of reticulated tenderness that my lips used to feel when my lips kissed her veiled cheek comes back to me—flies back to me with a shout of joy out of the snow-blue, blue-windowed (the curtains are not yet drawn) past.'

I, too, want to write rapturously, of candlelight and cushions, of creamy days and the stroking of soft skin. And I would like the feeling of that early happiness to linger, to be all-pervasive, to hover down the years and illuminate my growing self. And, of course, some of it does. If I hold my ear close to the past I can hear the echoes of laughter, of warmth and colour and kindness. The child's earliest comforts.

But in my case there is something more.

For me those early memories are overshadowed now as I look back by my knowledge of what was to come. There is a veil heavy with pain and bewilderment that almost obscures them from sight. Almost. My father, my sister and I didn't know it then. Neither did my mother. None of us sensed it coming. She didn't intend it, nor did she know what it meant, but as she moved through her forties, and I into my teens, my mother was seized

16

increasingly by a profound melancholy.

For me the concept of melancholy has a more historic and spiritual resonance than 'depression', but today depression is what my mother's condition would be called. It is what people have, not what they are. It is referred to doctors and psychiatrists and regarded as a medical condition. And because we expect medical conditions to be treated and, if possible, cured by experts it takes its place neatly in the pigeon-hole of contemporary illnesses. Had we not lived in such inhibited times, when to expose my mother's 'shame' would dishonour all we stood for, then she would have received a doctor's diagnosis, followed by an assortment of drugs, possibly (heaven forbid) ECT and psychiatric help. The family might have been offered counselling. At least something would have been done. Would all this have made her better—made us feel better? I'm not convinced it would, but it might have lifted our ignorance. Instead we lived in stoic resignation to the inexplicable, accepting our lot in ways that would seem irrational now.

Growing up within someone else's unhappiness gives a poignant slant to your own life. It has coloured my outlook ever since. I grew familiar with its vagaries, able to accommodate them, to treat my mother's affliction with respect and negotiate my way round and through her distress. I learned to recognise the signs of a coming storm and step beyond its reach. It hardened my resolve to get away from home. It influenced my choice of career. Perhaps, in some corner of my character, it seeded the empathy I feel for others and the need to understand what they are feeling. Perhaps it made being an interviewer such an appropriate job for me to do. But did it also make me *too* at ease with the condition, so familiar with it, that symptoms of depression seemed part of normal life? And was that why later I sometimes became involved with men who had traces of the same melancholy about them? Was it an old familiar love I was offering them, clinging to old patterns, rather than creating new?

And where did it all begin?

*   *   *

My mother was born in 1902, Rose Bland, the third child of eight and first daughter of William and Charlotte Bland of Gorton. Jack and Bill were the older boys, the first girls named after flowers: Rose, Lily—who died as a baby—and May. Then came the twins Flo and Ted (never known as Florence and Edward) and Ada, the baby of the family.

Bill and Charlotte had married in 1899, moved to Gorton in 1904, living in Sandown Street, and then, from around 1909, at 29 Bright Street. It is the house I visited as a child, and it is still there, though the street, for some inexplicable reason, is now called Brightman Street. In search of the past, I stand outside number twenty-nine, and try to imagine a family of nine occupying its two-up two-down space. Probably the three boys slept in one bed. Did all four girls cram into another? And all in the same room?

I know my grandparents shared a huge double bed, which filled the back bedroom. As a tiny child I was virtually swallowed up in its voluminous feather mattress, and would emerge from its homely smell—embrocation and Yardley's eau-de-

18

Cologne—for Granny to tell me once again the story of the picture over the bed: a poignant Victorian print, grey but vivid, of the execution of Lady Jane Grey. The original painting, by the French nineteenth-century romantic, Paul Delaroche, is huge and hangs in London's National Gallery. Victorians saw her as a Protestant martyr, executed by the Catholic Mary Tudor. That would have satisfied my grandparents. They disapproved heartily of Roman Catholics. There was never any question of their children mixing with them.

There were certain social niceties that attached to working-class homes such as theirs. Even with so great a need for space the front room downstairs was kept entirely unused except for rare, best occasions, major family celebrations and Christmas. Such a haven was usually choked with furniture: tables with chenille cloths, plush armchairs with lace-edged antimacassars to preserve them from smears of masculine hair oil. There was an obligatory aspidistra in a green-glazed pot in the window, a monument to conventional display. When George Orwell called his novel *Keep the Aspidistra Flying* he was referring to just such front-room respectability. The front room of my other grandparents' house in Salford went one better: it had a harmonium. One memorable Christmas we gathered there, my great-uncle on the harmonium, my uncle on his violin, a cousin on his recorder, my father, sister, another cousin, a great-aunt and me supplying the voices, to play and sing our way through the entirety of the *Messiah*. Hailing from Wales, that side of the family liked to celebrate its musicality.

Then there was the front doorstep: two steps, in

fact. For no good reason my grandfather had overlaid the upper one with a sheet of brass, which was kept glittering bright at all times. The lower one was scrubbed daily, then dressed to a flawless yellow with a piece of what must have been a kind of sandstone. Throughout the day people would come and go, scuffing its surface, leaving traces from the street. But that was all right because next day it would get the same treatment all over again. Other homes were judged by whether or not they had 'done' their step. It represented the futile, self-invented traditions of housekeeping to which generations of women were expected to conform.

But my mother had other ideas. Evidently a clever girl, she won a City of Manchester scholarship to go to Ardwick Central School. This was a major departure from anything a woman in the family had done before and set her apart as exceptional and ambitious. Off she went with much pride and eagerness. It soon dissipated. Within a year, at the age of thirteen, she had left. The family story was that, not being able to afford the school uniform, she was exposed to ridicule and humiliation, which was more than she could bear. But my mother would also hint years later that she was needed at home to help bring up the now regularly arriving younger children and her wage was needed too. Thirty years on and she was still resentful.

She took some kind of job at an engineering firm—it was the second year of the First World War and she was among that wave of women given the chance of interesting work by the absence of men. She was even encouraged to go to night school. At Openshaw College she took the second-

20

year technical course, studying experimental maths, practical drawing, mechanics and physics. Later she took a further course in applied mechanics, experimental maths and machine drawing. What surprises me now is not that she found time to study but the subjects she chose. No soft-centred, supposedly female-oriented matters such as domestic science or literature, but tough sciences that, in those days, implied male careers. In the event she became a tracer, to trace and copy the intricate detail of engineering drawings. She worked in the drawing office, and hers was one of the skilled jobs in which women were beginning to work alongside men.

The Ladies Tracing Society, founded in 1880, acknowledged as much. But it was as high up the ladder as any woman keen on architecture and engineering could go. I found this out when, years later, I made a television documentary about the struggle women had to become architects. Early evidence cites two portraits in which Mary Ware and Jane Wren are each painted behind the figures of their renowned architect fathers, Isaac and Christopher, hinting that they were both acknowledged as their father's little helper. But my mother had no such illustrious parentage. Instead she was simply acknowledged as the best tracer in the drawing office.

I know, because it was there she met my father. He would talk proudly of the sassy young woman who would come and go, a large ribboned bow bobbing on her dark hair, delivering the drawings, giving help to others, the one always referred to for a rush job or an exact piece of work. But that was as far as she got. The best tracer of them all. When the job of the head of the drawing office fell vacant she wasn't even eligible to apply. Men only.

Over the years, trying to understand her despair, I have wondered whether she ever considered that being thwarted of a chosen and fulfilling career had any bearing on her later mental state. I doubt it: first, because those caught up in depression don't have the emotional distance to rationalise their plight; and second, because cogent explanations for such depressions, common across a whole generation of women, only emerged when their children engaged with the feminist thinking of the 1970s. In my youth during the late forties and fifties, I judged my mother harshly as a difficult woman. Now I can see clearly that she was clever, she had hopes and training, and it took her nowhere. She, who had access to none of today's open talk of stress and frustration, would have had no option but to accept the inevitability of a woman's lot. Did she instead hug her resentment to herself?

And how much did she notice of the larger world around her? Manchester has always been a radical city: in 1819, fifty thousand people met in St Peter's Fields to urge political reform and were scattered by local yeomanry, leaving eleven dead, four hundred injured: the Peterloo Massacre. In the 1840s John Bright, Manchester's MP, had campaigned against the Corn Laws, seeking to lower the price of bread. In 1838 the Chartists, the first working-class movement for political reform, held one of its earliest and largest rallies there. By the early 1900s Manchester was the crucible of the women's suffrage movement. While my mother was a small child the Pankhurst family was causing mayhem across the city. Emmeline had been born in Moss Side, had married a radical lawyer there and borne the daughters who were to join her in redirecting the campaign for women's suffrage towards its militant tactics. It was at an election meeting in Manchester's Free Trade Hall in 1905 that Christabel Pankhurst and Annie Kenney, the mill girl from Oldham who recruited other working women, persistently heckled Sir Edward Grey, the foreign secretary, and unfurled for the first time the banner 'Votes for Women'. The two of them were thrown out of the meeting, arrested and, having refused to pay the fine, sentenced to seven days in jail. In the same year and another part of the city—Cheetham Hill—Sylvia Pankhurst interrupted a public meeting being held for Winston Churchill, then campaigning for the Liberals, to ask a question about the suffrage. After much clamour she was invited up to the platform to put her question, an apparent courtesy that caught her off-guard. She recorded that, having done so, she turned to go and 'Churchill seized me roughly by the arm and pushed me into a chair at the back of the platform, saying, "No, you must wait here till you have heard what I have to say." Then turning to the audience, he protested that I was "bringing my disgrace upon an honoured name, by interrupting him" and added, "Nothing would induce me to vote for giving women the franchise: I am not going to be henpecked into a question of such importance."'

By the time my mother was a schoolgirl the suffragette movement was at its most assertive. By 1914, the year she won her scholarship, a thousand suffragettes had been imprisoned for destroying public property. Some had been sent to Strangeways in Manchester. Many were force-fed. In my mother's fourteenth year Emily Davison—a woman with an honours degree from Oxford—stepped before the King's horse on Derby Day and died of her injuries. She was wrapped in the suffragette colours. The *Daily Mirror*, like other papers, told a graphic story: 'Anmer [the horse] struck her with his chest and she was knocked over screaming. Blood rushed from her mouth and nose . . .' Her funeral at Morpeth was attended by large crowds, the dramatic cortège led by six children carrying madonna lilies. Did a bright young schoolgirl like my mother ask about such things? Perhaps the young family in Gorton were unaware of them. There was no radio, of course, no television. But even if they didn't buy a newspaper, there must have been gossip, hearsay, word of mouth. Did word go round the small terrace houses of Manchester that women were getting above themselves, being violent and violated in return?

I never asked my mother such questions. By the time I was trying to understand her misery, she was too remote to reach. She certainly didn't want to be called to account. Any feminist talk from me would have put her on the defensive, made her feel a failure. All I have is the evidence of what she did. She studied hard technical subjects with determination against the odds. And stored up disappointment for herself.

*   *   *

My parents came together at a time when both believed they were beginning to make their way as

24

none of their forebears had ever done. As young people they were hard-working, learning skills, expecting to progress in the world. The idea of a single job for life, daily, repetitive, which had been the traditional lot of working people, was changing. Social mobility was a possibility. Now a man might have prospects, the chance of promotion, sustained and rising wages, security in the same company. After they were married, my father would achieve for them both, with my mother creating the home and family, backing his ambition and purpose. They were excited by their future.

What was more, they shared work and interests that had status. Engineering mattered. Britain was still the world's leading industrial power, building the machinery that would drive industries around the globe. And Manchester, with all its smog and pollution, its skies permanently darkened by smoke, its rivers black with effluent, was the powerhouse of engineering. Working side by side, my parents shared the excitement of these enterprises. The company—Simon Engineering— was building huge industrial projects, great grain silos that would handle the transportation of wheat across the world. Together my parents saw the designs develop and go forward. Soon my father was despatched with other young men to remote places to oversee the site constructions. My mother followed. It was a young person's world, calling for initiative, decision-making and independence.

They married on Boxing Day 1928, the former orphan from Chethams who had started his apprenticeship on the foundry floor, and the cooper's daughter who was top of the class in the drawing office, both determined to make their way.

The very next day, after an afternoon's honeymoon in Blackpool, my father sailed for South America to work on a three-year building project in Buenos Aires. Six months later my mother followed, sailing alone from Liverpool, leaving behind a tearful mother who did not expect to see her again. They had escaped.

*   *   *

They always spoke of the early years of their marriage as a golden time: my parents were modest, innocent and unworldly, passionate in their feelings but diffident in expressing them—certainly in print. Recently I came upon a cache of their letters exchanged at this time. Their endearments are formal: 'Dearest Rose', 'your ever-loving Jack'. Nothing more. The implication is that much was left unsaid because even to let the pen put words of passion on to the page was a breach of privacy. Someone—at worst a stranger, at best a sympathetic relation or friend—might read of extravagant affection and pass judgement, finding them too explicit, salacious, or simply not proper. And here I am scouring the frayed pages some seventy years later, searching the lines—the words, even—the very vowels for some indication of the intimacy that must have existed between them.

Their exploits in South America were talked of for ever afterwards: bandits and hold-ups, crazy celebrations to mark the project's progress, whole lambs turning on spits, a black maid who washed in bleach, hopeful of becoming white. Young people's tales of how bold they were, how reckless . . . and

26

how happy. Both of them learned Spanish. Years later I cringed as Spanish waiters, whom my father insisted on addressing in their language, complimented him on his Argentinian accent. My mother, as much as my father, followed the work in hand: all their lives he talked engineering issues with her, often asking her advice. The colleagues who were with them remained friends for life, though contact dwindled to the annual Christmas card, and finally meetings at funerals. But the reminiscences were revisited over and over again. It was their heyday, and nothing would ever match up to it.

*   *   *

The Gorton that my mother knew remains an afflicted area of Manchester. There have been modest individual efforts to give the houses in Brightman Street their own identity: the doors and windows differ slightly now, where people have made an effort with the help of television programmes and chipboard, but the impression is still the same—facing rows of red-brick, an occasional car, trim curtains. I don't think anyone bothers to yellow the front doorstep now. Behind the houses, the alley where I learned to roller-skate looks different. My grandparents' thin spit of garden—where my grandfather's workshop had stood and which reached down towards the railway line where we waved at the steam trains—has gone with all the others and a row of sixties houses has been shoehorned into the space. The area is more densely built now than it was then.

My cousin Sylvia lives three streets away from

my mother's home. I haven't met her for over forty years. On the phone, her round Lancashire vowels have promised a rousing welcome. At first I can't find the doorbell. It lurks behind a cascading basket of bizzie-lizzie. And suddenly there she stands. She is my sister Susan to the life. Susan, who is dead. This is family likeness gone almost too far. I don't just smile and greet, I stare searchingly into her face. At this end of life, those who survive carry coded reminders of those who haven't.

I am treated with special favour: dark brown cups of tea and a three-tier chocolate cake baked in my honour by a neighbour. The house has no garden, but I am shown a backyard where every wall is festooned to its full height with baskets and tiered racks of flowers. Sylvia explains about Gorton, how it has changed. And not for the better. When they had the chance, those residents who could bought their own homes. But now values are plummeting. Five years ago they were worth £49,000, today no more than £15,000. Private landlords buy them up and leave them empty. The housing associations have moved in.

On Ashton Old Road hope is running out. There's a derelict corner full of broken glass and rosebay willowherb, which might have been like that since the wartime bombing. Motorworld, boasting 'all parts for all cars open 7 days a week' is boarded up. There are second-hand shops, discount furniture. Not much trade. An old bank, its marble embellishments shrouded in grime, carries a sign: 'For Sale: re-available due to time-wasters'. There's an Indian restaurant, a Chinese, a pub. Screwy Hughie's promises live entertainment.

When my grandparents lived there, I recall it as

a district teeming with life and energy. In my memory it seems to have had about it vividness and warmth. Certainly neighbours all knew each other: there was time to stop and talk on street corners. Indeed, the fish-and-chip shop on the corner of Brightman Street is still there. But a sense of depression hangs in the air, a sense of being left outside the mainstream. I know that the homes hereabouts now have indoor plumbing and central heating, and there are televisions and video recorders. No one here in my grandparents' time owned a car. All this counts as practical improvement. Of course it does. But was it inevitable that the old sense of community would be lost? I wouldn't wish back the old days of poverty, smoke, sweat and day-long labour to keep a decent home. The paradox seems to be that you can't have both. Relishing the irony, I return to the costly comforts of Manchester's Lowry Hotel, named after the man who made such streets famous.

CHAPTER THREE

OTHER SHORES

Photography has changed the nature of memory. What once lingered only in the mind's eye has now been transmuted into shiny rectangular objects in which we choose to present ourselves to the world. When I was a child the act of taking photographs indicated an event of some significance. My parents were sparing in the way they used the camera. Films were still an extravagance, an indulgence not to be taken too far. One shot of any scene was enough for the record. It didn't do to waste it on any snatched, possibly more truthful, fleeting action picture. That was high risk, unpredictable. Instead people posed rather deliberately for photographs, not as now for a formal record among a cache of more informal images, but as if they believed them to be a definitive history of what had happened, which required orderly assembly in front-facing groups. But history doesn't happen in front-facing groups, so photographs record our vanity, the images of how we want to look. No more so, for me, than in the summer of 1938.

My family album for that year records just one event: an eight-month visit to South America when my father was sent again on business to Buenos Aires and my mother and I went too. The album is frayed now, its tassels dirty but still holding together the heavy grey pages interlaced with decorative yellowing tissue paper, protective of the small sepia photographs glued within. I was five at the time, and throughout the years that followed this album was taken out again and again, to keep fresh the memories, to imprint on my mind how wonderful it all was.

I realise now that they were right to be nostalgic. Like the golden days of Edwardian England, conjured in a hundred memoirs and diaries as the long, dreamy summer before the First World War, this was the last oasis of peace before the Second. My parents must have known what was brewing in Europe. In 1937 Hitler, addressing the massed ranks at Nuremberg, had declared that Germans needed more territory, while in Spain, where Franco's fascists were winning against the elected Republican government, bombers had obliterated Guernica. In Britain, Mosley and his Blackshirts were on the march, and the government had given the go-ahead for air-raid shelters to be built. The omens were bad and people were readying themselves for war. The month before we sailed for South America Hitler marched into his homeland, Austria, to the welcome of cheering crowds.

As we sailed from Southampton I, of course, knew nothing of this, but cheering crowds were there too. As we climbed the gangplank through jostling people, I caught the sense of excitement in the air. We gathered with others along the ship's rail and waved to the swelling throng. Music played, streamers were thrown, crowds surged and waved, screamed and called, the focus of their adulation being the departing passengers above them on the ship. It was my birthday so my own excitement matched theirs and I believed the greetings were all for me. I waved back frantically, delighted to be given such a send-off. My parents didn't disillusion me. In reality one of the top big bands of the 1930s, the Harry Roy Band, was sailing for Argentina in what was proclaimed as a huge celebrity tour of South America and their fans had mobbed the quay.

This was the era of the great liners, the last glory days of the seaways. It was how people travelled from continent to continent. Politicians like Chamberlain might fly to Munich to meet Mr Hitler, but businessmen, and those not beset by crisis, still went by ship. We sailed on RMS *Alcantara*. That and its sister ship RMS *Asturias*, on

31

which we made the return journey, were the pride of the Royal Mail shipping line and the largest motor-driven vessels afloat. Commissioned from Harland and Wolff in 1924, their high-powered diesel engines were seen as the latest advance in engineering technique. Their interiors were lavish: gilded cornices and entablatures in the social hall; a winter garden in Spanish Moorish style, a smoking room panelled in cedarwood carvings copied from Grinling Gibbons, a writing room in Adam style, French Empire in the dining salon, a swimming-pool floored in marble with majolica pillars, and everywhere an abundance of valuable carpets and glass doors—an eclectic mix that was, in its day, the last word in décor, and far more exotic and extravagant then than such flamboyance would seem now. My parents must have been struck dumb with wonder at finding themselves there. And in such company.

When they sailed for South America the Harry Roy Band was the highest paid in the world. This was the era of Ambrose, Geraldo and Ted Heath—bandleaders who were consummate musicians and players in their own right. Harry Roy was primarily a showman: he played the clarinet and the saxophone, and sang a little—scat singing in the style of Cab Calloway. He tagged his style Hotcha, adopted 'Bugle Call Rag' as his signature tune and appeared everywhere—Royal Variety Performances, the universal medium of radio, and the ballrooms of London, the Café de Paris, the Mayfair Hotel.

It was the custom of the day for bandleaders to be to asked to join glamorous guests at their tables for a glass of champagne. It might have been at one such that Harry Roy met his wife: in 1935 he had married Princess Pearl, the daughter of the white Raja of Sarawak. What was I to make of such a name? When I was told that a princess was on board I took the news at its fairytale value and gazed in awe.

Princess Pearl belonged to the last British family to occupy an Oriental throne. Her ancestor James Brooke was a nineteenth-century British adventurer straight out of Conrad. He had captained his own ship and, in 1840, put it at the service of the Sultan of Brunei in a civil war between the Dyaks and the Malays. His reward was the gift of Sarawak, in north-west Borneo. But he died a bachelor and by 1917 the line had passed to Sir Charles Vyner Brooke, whose youngest daughter Elizabeth was nicknamed Princess Pearl by the press. The name stuck—it even suited: she was a lithe, leggy blonde with delicate features and creamy golden skin. And now she was on the same ship as a five-year-old child from Manchester.

We got to know some of the band quite well. My parents were young, good-looking and fancy free. They made friends easily and even shared a flat with the guitarist and his wife when we reached Buenos Aires. I seem to have become a pet, a kind of mascot for them all. Many years later I wrote of the experience for *You* magazine, and received a letter from the daughter of one of the trumpeters, now a middle-aged woman, whose own family album included a photograph labelled—enigmatically until that moment—'little Joan'. There are more such in my own album: the glossy publicity pictures of the individual band players, some of them signed 'for our Joan' and 'to my little sweetheart Joan'.

I think I must have sensed the pleasure to be gained from popularity, and enjoyed the fuss that was made of me. When I hurled a deck quoit overboard, no one frowned, they just roared with laughter and called my mishap to the attention of others. It was different, and rather fun, to transgress and not be reproved. I knew that these people were performers, who had the spirit and flair to put on a show of thrilling sound for the delight of others. Unlike the modest self-consciousness of my parents facing any kind of public situation, these people actually loved it, revelled in it, celebrated themselves and what they could do. That impression sank deep. My own show-off instincts were strong, and I longed to be as bold as them, admiring and envying their bravado and directness in expressing themselves so uninhibitedly. The thought lodged in my mind that performers—dancers, singers, musicians—were blessed with a kind of magic, the ability to put people directly in touch with the joy of life.

Buenos Aires greeted the arrival of RMS *Alcantara* with aeroplanes flying a banner: 'Welcome Harry Roy'. More excitement, more crowds, though this time I didn't believe it was for me. My memories of Buenos Aires are fleeting and jumbled, giving weight to incidentals, with no sense of a wider picture. And one of the most important incidentals was the dolls' shop.

Long before Sindy and Barbie there was something similar but with more class: an exquisitely made doll called Mari-Lu with articulated limbs, a porcelain face and a wardrobe of adult clothes tailored and exact in every detail. The Mari-Lu shop stood in one of the smaller

34

avenidas of Buenos Aires. Each week a new window display would feature Mari-Lu dolls dressed in a particular style—one week they might be doctors and nurses, another teachers, even garage mechanics. I recall in particular a windowful of them dressed as air pilots, climbing in and out of model planes in leather flying jackets and helmets. The previous year Amelia Earhart had gone missing over the Pacific after she had made history as the first woman to fly solo across the Atlantic. She was a celebrated figure, proclaimed an example of what women could do. And here she was as a doll.

Almost daily I pressed my nose against the shop's window. It wasn't acceptable to pester parents for things in those days. But my yearning was obvious. At the close of my stay I was presented with just such a Mari-Lu doll made to my own specification of colouring and hair-style, brown eyes, blonde bob and fringe. Within little more than a year, though, this same precious Mari-Lu was to cause me deep-felt shame. Underneath her blonde hair, written across the back of her neck, was the source of her manufacture: the word 'Germany'. She had been made there by our declared enemy with whom we were now at war. From then on I played with Mari-Lu only when I was alone. I dreaded my friends discovering her origins and turning aside from both her and myself.

Over forty years later I was back in Buenos Aires for the first time since 1938. I was making a programme for BBC 1's *Heart of the Matter* about the children of the 'disappeared'. In a break from filming I casually trawled the *avenidas*, curious to discover whether the Mari-Lu shop still existed.

Almost most by accident I found it. As a child I hadn't registered its impeccably stylish 1930s curving white stone, mock pillars and decorative embellishments straight from a Hollywood set. It didn't sell pilot dolls any longer. Instead, it housed a neat little boutique with its own label. I rushed inside, eager to buy clothes with the Mari-Lu label. As I piled my purchases on the counter I told them I knew it had once been a dolls' shop. The young assistant shrugged, uninterested, but the manageress was intrigued. She fetched coffee and we talked of change and age and how memories linger. The young assistant filed her nails and sighed. Now the linen jacket with the Mari-Lu label and the old German-made doll belong together in my London bedroom, most of the time taken for granted, but occasionally remembered, a ghostly whisper from another country. I hear that the shop itself has since been demolished.

*   *   *

My mother must have taken care to look her best for the trip. I remember her setting out to dine on the ship in flimsy silk dresses cut on the bias that clung to her body. She had just two: one of brown figured flowers, one of navy, each tied with a sash. She wore them on alternate nights. But most of all I remember the fur. Furs were how you measured someone's wealth. Even my Gorton grandmother managed a jacket in grey squirrel. The better off had astrakhan, musquash. Film stars had mink. No one had heard of sable. My mother had a fox wrap, the whole animal. Its head was intact with glass eyes replacing what must have been the wet decay of the dead animal. Its lower jaw had been removed and a hinged grip made of Bakelite replaced it, to close on a limp leg and hold the animal's dead body draped round her shoulders. Snapping the fox's jaws at people's ankles was a great game. Tenderness towards animals just didn't occur to us.

South America yielded two other firsts: I saw my first black person, and I saw my first film, *Snow White*. On the way out, the liner called at Rio de Janeiro and I was taken to one of its dazzling white beaches. The black girl was looking after two white children nearby. She couldn't have been more than twelve, with a white pinafore over a checked dress—a child nursemaid for a well-off white family. My mother asked her to come and join us, but she would do so only for a moment—long enough to have her photograph taken with me. Rio's people have skins of every hue from honey to bronze, from copper to black. And white. But I remember only her: I think she was pointed out to me as a curiosity, her blackness a source of wonder and difference. I hadn't seen black people back in England. There were none where we lived, so blackness was exotic, strange and foreign. We smiled, giggling, at the camera together, she shyly, I with a sort of repressed excitement. Clearly life held extraordinary surprises.

Snow White had been made the previous year and was then on its release in South America. I was taken as a treat, the occasion surrounded, as were all treats, with the need to behave well. But I was overwhelmed. As *Snow White* fled into the forest, whose trees came alive and reached out their branches to trap her, I screamed in panic. There were two terrors here for me: not only was she herself being caught but the thorns on the branches were grabbing at her frock and tearing it. Tearing, breaking and damaging things was forbidden: they cost money, people worked hard to make them, children had a duty to cherish what they were given. Only threats that we would leave quietened me: I hated and loved the fear. We stayed.

After all this fear and treachery, I was well and truly softened up for the seriously hard sell soon to come. And so it was that I bought the myth: 'Some day my prince will come.' Snow White, clothes miraculously mended, having survived a living death, is woken to new life by the man of her—and our—dreams. Here it was, in all its treacherous original form, the stereotype fantasy that would inspire a million love affairs, fuel a film industry around the world and delude generations of women into preposterously romantic expectations.

The artist Paula Rego, born in Portugal of my own generation, told me decades later how much she, too, had been haunted by the film. Her paintings hinting at dark and terrible secrets between people, expose and celebrate the ambiguous power of women. Her sequence about the abused Snow White—swallowing the poisoned apple, riding the prince's horse—shows a woman struggling to assert herself. Rego has been able to externalise her reactions; I hugged mine to me, complicit in the notion of a dashing prince arriving to make all things well.

Years on I recognise how gilded a view of this Argentinian adventure my parents perpetuated, and kept alive in me. The photograph albums were brought out on special occasions: looking at them was considered a treat, sometimes a reward. Whenever my sister and I squabbled about the sharing of parental favours, Susan—born when we were back in England—would tip the balance with 'Yes, but you went to South America!' Too sweet-natured to be jealous, she was none the less made to feel that she had lost out. And I grew to realise I was the favoured one.

I also discovered recently that the Harry Roy Band hadn't even been that good. In her book *Talking Swing* Sheila Tracey gives him a whole chapter to himself, as she does with Joe Loss and Lew Stone: it turns out that he was regarded as a thoroughly second-rate player, even by those in his band, especially by some of those who were on the tour. Nat Temple, his saxophonist, who went on to create his own band, playing for BBC Radio's comedy *Round the Horne* and even cropping up in Frederic Raphael's fiction of Cambridge life, *The Glittering Prizes*, says, 'As a player Harry was terrible, his playing was an absolute joke.' Stanley Black, the band's pianist, claims it damaged his reputation among serious musicians to be seen playing for Harry Roy, who was regarded more as a vaudeville turn. He must have stood back from all that for he went on to a seriously successful career as conductor of the BBC Dance Orchestra. Many years afterwards, being offered hospitality at the Brighton theatre where John Osborne's *The Entertainer* was enjoying a revival, I was ushered into the company of a small, stooped man, once dapper but now frail. I couldn't resist remarking, 'Mr Black, we knew each other back in 1938. I think I sat on your knee.'

I was sad to read these revelations, disappointed

to find the players hadn't rated their own band very highly. But, then, they too are only memories, coloured, perhaps, by the rising fortunes of younger men passing judgement on the older. The Harry Roy fan club survives to this day, sending out a regular newsletter, *The Bugle Call Rag*, that keeps the discography up to date and publishes reminiscences of the band. Even, on one occasion, my own.

CHAPTER FOUR

BEING A GIRL

Intimation of what it meant to be a girl came early to me, when I was about three. My auntie Ada was to be married at Droylsden Methodist chapel with the reception held at Ryecroft Hall, Audenshaw. There was much fussing and feminine excitement about what everyone should wear, and I was swept along with it. I was to be the family showpiece. To this end, my mother designed and made for me a dress in cream silk, with a row of tiny flowers embroidered in different-coloured silks round the bottom of the skirt an inch or so from the hem, which fell to just above my chubby knees. The outfit was completed with traditional black patent shoes and white socks. I was paraded and much admired. I relished the attention.

At the wedding, naturally, the bride—in a sliver of cream satin holding a discreet fall of lilies—took over as the centre of everyone's approval and as the mood of the wedding changed from gentle cooing to more robust celebration I was able to be more spontaneously myself. My natural choice was to join my boy cousins in a rip-roaring exploration of our surroundings. In one corner of the hall there were stacks of bentwood chairs, piled high to make space for the dancing that would follow. I had found just the place to hide where I could not be found. Without hesitation I was down on my knees, scuttling within the network of chair legs: the journey seemed endless, convoluted by the twists and turns made by the jumbled furniture. Sometimes I would disturb the equilibrium and feel the shapes and shadows shifting around me. But I was exhilarated to have outwitted the boys, who had clearly forgotten about me. The forest darkened the further in I went, and excitement subsided, giving way to bewilderment, then panic.

And then there were the splinters. Many floors in public buildings remained uncarpeted, no more than bald planking, ungraced by sanding and staining. They were worn and scuffed, held on to clumps of fluff, caught up the grit—and developed splinters, which got into my knees and began to hurt.

At some point in the celebrations several events converged. Someone noticed I was missing; I noticed the game had somehow moved away and realised I was lost; and I began to cry. The cry was traced, the mountain of chairs dismantled, and I was snatched to bright lights and retribution. One thing became clear: silk dresses with embroidery round the hem were not made for playing; even worse, dresses stitched with a mother's labour and love are even more freighted with hazard. The dress was a ruin and my mother's rage, deflected in public behind a certain tense laughter, was choked back and laid in store for the reckoning to come. Reckonings to come became a feature of my mother's behaviour towards me.

Meanwhile my boy cousins were still running and chasing and having fun, whooping and shouting louder than ever. I was led away, chastened and bewildered. I minded then and I mind now. Why were girls so different from boys?

Do I really remember all this for myself? After all, I was only three. Yet certain objects remained to remind me: the dress survived, demoted from its role as my Sunday best to clothing for my dolls, whom I in turn would chastise and exhort not to get dirty. And there is the wedding photograph—just one. My aunt, in her sliver of cream satin, remains unblemished, unaware of the uproar I had caused, caught for all time in her calmness, holding the hand of a new and playful uncle.

But the story became a family legend, repeated with benign laughter and, as I grew older and more assertive, a certain impulse to put me down. Perhaps I am reading more into it now than I realised at the time. Who is to say? What matters is that this family fable somehow passed down the generations as evidence of my true nature, depending on who was making the assessment: 'an adventuring spirit' from the bold cousins, 'a cheeky little rascal' from doting aunts. For my mother it was the first indication that I would go my own way in defiance of what she felt. And I went on wondering why I was expected to behave in a different, more restrained way from boys.

*　　　*　　　*

My sister arrived when I was six. She, too, had been conceived mid-Atlantic. Clearly, for our parents, a life on the ocean waves had real meaning. I like to think they found something liberating about being at sea, a last freedom before war broke out: the immediate pleasures of the minute were to be enjoyed. Certainly, from my mother's hints and discreet remarks in later life, their sex life had sometimes been tense and inhibited. Knowing that they wanted another child must have freed them from 'being careful'—my mother's phrase for avoiding pregnancy.

I learned literally at my mother's knee how to be a mother, by mimicking her every movement. A six-year-old can be expected to resent a new sibling, and I, puffed up with the recent attentions of the South American trip, might have been difficult. In fact I adored my sister Susan. I was given my own doll and encouraged to wash and dress her in parallel with my mother's own routine for the new baby. I copied exactly everything she did—the reaching for the soap, the washing of the hair, the flannel binder, which in those days was wrapped tightly round the child's navel as though it were a bandage healing a wound. All this I did to my doll, like a session of synchronised swimming, until my mother was driven mad. I had to be asked to break the exactness of the routine, rather as an army crossing a bridge must break step or risk damage to the structure, but so thoroughly did I rehearse the same actions that I could re-create them now: the towel across the lap, the elbow test to the water in the enamel bowl, the Johnson's baby powder, the binder, the crossover vest with its tiny ribbons, the longer nightie, the gauze nappy, the heavier towelling nappy, the bootees.

Was there ever a more absolute example of mother passing to daughter the duties, expectations and skills of mothering? I sense it was what happened in most families in those days. No doubt in her childhood my mother had learned the same from hers, and back, generation by generation. Women know what women are; they pass on the knowledge like a secret rite. It transmutes over the decades as change quickens, but the rituals attendant on a new baby vary little. This most awesome of human experience, the bringing into the world of another life, was rooted deep in my psyche from then on, and rooted with all its sensual pleasure, concern, commitment, and the overwhelming love focused on the small powder-smelling, shawl-wrapped cocoon of new life. The die was cast. I knew then that I would want children of my own. I didn't know the rest.

Around this time I was told a story. My memory tells me I was in a classroom, but I don't know where. I can still feel the hard shiny surface of the green lino on which a row of small children were sitting cross-legged. A tall shadowy teacher stood above us, telling us that we must listen and then act out the tale. It concerned a matron of ancient Rome in conversation with another. One was displaying to the other her wealth of jewels; the other declared she would fetch her own jewels and retreated to the interior of the house. She returned with three small children: 'These are my jewels,' she declared. I knew this story was telling me some eternal truth about families and children. I couldn't wait to act it out, aching to take the part of the mother. Instead I had nothing more to do than stand around as one of the children. Yet the story has stayed with me ever since.

Sixty years later I tracked it down, and found out who the woman was. With the help of classically minded friends, and reference books, I discovered she was Cornelia Gracchus, who lived in the second century BC, the era of the late Roman Republic. She was certainly well connected: her father was Scipio, the Roman general who conquered Hannibal in the second Punic War; her husband was Tiberius, aristocrat and consul; and two of her surviving three children (she bore twelve), Tiberius and Caius, became famous as the Gracchi, political leaders who championed the Roman people in a time of political turbulence. Her husband, who was much older, died while her children were still young. She was then offered an equally grand match by one of the Ptolemys of Egypt, but she refused. It was from this refusal that the legend was born. Evidence that she ever described her children as jewels is absent, but she behaved as if they were, devoting her time and efforts to their education, encouraging in them a sense of civic duty and political responsibility, and shaping their future. Cornelia outlived them both, continuing influential in Roman affairs, considered wise and honourable in her old age. Two centuries after her death Plutarch celebrated her. So did Seneca. She was as powerful and highly regarded as any woman could be in ancient Rome, certainly an unlikely role model for a Stockport schoolgirl two thousand years later. And her grand life was far removed from the uncomfortable floor of a draughty classroom. But I took the immediate message to

45

heart. Children came first. The next generation were worth all we could give them.

*   *   *

There were many things my mother never taught me: many things were never said. Dodie Smith's 1935 play *Dear Octopus* provokes laughter when the little girl reveals her secret rude word: 'District Nurse'. A whole vocabulary was attached to sex and childbirth, which was never spoken or, if ever, then only in whispers. We never spoke the word 'pregnancy' or 'breast'. A woman who was 'expecting' would wear long loose garments to cover her 'condition', one might almost say 'shame', as though pregnancy was a dirty secret. I never saw my mother breast-feeding. I knew nothing about the male body at all. I did not even know there were words for its different genital arrangement. It was only around the age of twelve or so, when I was first taken to museums and galleries where there were nude sculptures, that I observed what those differences were. Of course, it was unacceptable to remark on them. My mother, had she been there, would have hustled me away.

The grip of working-class respectability was tenacious. My grandparents, held fast by Victorian morality, were all too aware that any straying from the narrow path might spell disaster. The threat was real enough, especially for girls: they could be seduced, get pregnant, end in the gutter. The threat of this ultimate horror, the impending shame and disgrace, was passed to their daughters. My mother, who by now was aspiring to middle-class values, knew there was even more at stake:

one slip and all the modest gains on the class ladder would be lost. My father probably agreed, but left such matters for her to decide. Of certain things we would not speak. Sex above all. And certain things we would never do. What did I make of such contradictions? Here was this adored sister, cherished and pampered, inspiring me with the desire to be a mother, but surrounding her were all these secrets, women whispering, just out of earshot, things they didn't want me to hear. And beyond that, there hovered clouds of disapproval, landscapes of female behaviour loaded with magical power and awesome taboos, words and deeds into which one day I would be initiated. But not yet. Meanwhile there was another confusion: I had decided I'd rather be a boy.

It was quite a simple matter. I wanted to play with boys' toys. I yearned for a Meccano set. In the 1930s Meccano was, of all toys, the most boyish. It had been created in 1901 by Frank Hornby for his young sons, a metal construction toy originally sold as Mechanics Made Easy. Then from 1907 it was known as Meccano and consistently advertised and promoted as 'The Best Boys' Toy of the Day', and 'A New Hobby for Bright Boys'. By the 1920s Meccano had its own *Magazine for Meccano Boys*, there was a Fellowship of Meccano Boys, and in 1924 the Meccano Boys Jersey was created by Jaeger (selling for nine shillings and nine pence— just less than 50p). So it was no simple yearning on my part for a few pieces of coloured metal and the nuts and bolts to hold them together: I wanted to be in the boys' world, along with the magazine, the fellowship and the jersey. My engineer father braved the taunts of relations and gave me a

Meccano set for Christmas. For his time he was a remarkably enlightened father. It was he who gave me my night-time bath, playing games and singing songs I would remember for years. He tucked me into bed at night, first into my bedroom in the mornings, an involvement with his children that was rare among his contemporaries. And if he balked at changing nappies and left matters of discipline to my mother, it was because he wanted only pleasure and fun with his children. In consequence we associated him with laughter and playfulness throughout our lives.

The Meccano was a more specific kind of bonding. I must have been about eight. Of course, he built most of it himself, but from then on, he was on my side. He would have no sons, and I, as the elder child, would carry the burden of his dreams; he sought to realise through me the unformulated hopes of success and glory he had harboured as a boy. I had now felt powerfully the impulse to be female, and the yearning to be male. Whose world would I choose? It seemed, even then, that some sort of choice might have to be made.

In the event the world changed, and the choices became more complicated.

CHAPTER FIVE

WARTIME

I was six when war broke out. I remember vividly the day it was declared. The recollection is framed

48

by my bedroom curtains, pink and floral, billowing round the upright mirrors of my dressing-table, with its displayed matching set of pink brush, comb and mirror. I was proud of this because it indicated I had the status of a girl rather than a child. I was bouncing around on the bed, inconsequentially but evidently inappropriately since I was gently reproved. I noticed why: something disturbing was going on. My grandmother—Nanna, as I called her—was sitting on the bed crying softly and my mother was standing beside her, not knowing what to do. I didn't know what to do either.

Tears sit uneasily on an old face, deepening the ravines, smudging the soft down of papery skin. I was appalled and embarrassed by my grandmother's exposure to such humiliation. My mother was distressed, too, loving and concerned at her own mother's grief. Here were two generations of women, and I growing into the third, allowing the spill of emotions to wreck the received family etiquette of the day.

In those days tears marked one of the frontiers of acceptable behaviour. Tears were for babies, children with scratched knees, station-platform partings. Even then the exhortation to 'be brave' was never far away. Emotions were concealed inner things, better kept that way. From earliest consciousness I knew that what I felt to be my feelings, passions and anger, even joy and happiness, somehow exceeded the norm. They must therefore be schooled, restrained, even denied in the interests of good behaviour. If others dared to have feelings too they didn't reveal them. Even at moments of great intimacy they were often held back.

49

Yet here, as war broke out, the two women in my life were demonstrating the opposite. War, with its separations and suffering, its hopes and losses, was to bring about a major shift in such national sensibilities. Here, as family tears were spilled, was a hint of what was to come: the war exposed emotions, put them under strain and finally released the barriers to feeling that had been erected and had survived since Edwardian times.

War is one of the most intense experiences a community can go through. For children, still learning how the world worked, it was full of contradictions. We looked around and assumed that what was happening was normal life, that somehow these disruptions, flares and bombs, stringencies, sudden rules, tears and odd behaviours were all something to grow into and adapt to. At the same time the tension and nervous alertness of the grown-ups hinted that something exceptional was happening. It was all very confusing. War made us quick on our feet and quick-witted in making sense of the irrationality around us. War moves fast but digs deep, leaving traces in memory and outlook that surface again and again.

I realised the uniqueness of war in the 1990s when I made a television series called *My Generation* and asked others who were around my age what they remembered. Many of their memories—not merely of major events but the little homely things—tallied closely with my own. Like me, David Attenborough was struck by unusual displays of emotion as his family stood round the radio listening to Chamberlain's broadcast: 'My father was visibly moved, more moved than I can ever recall. I thought he was probably swallowing tears which was an extraordinary thing for me to see. I couldn't imagine my father crying.' For Claire Tomalin, today a renowned biographer who was also my contemporary at Cambridge, the memory was of a more public occasion: 'I saw all these grown men, the teachers, with tears rolling down their cheeks, and that made a great impression on me. I don't think I'd ever seen a man cry before.'

Behind these emotions lay a stoic resolve. Children sensed that, too. It was part of the air we breathed, part of being British. We were taught it at school. The first chapter of my geography textbook, published in 1937, was called 'The Fortunate Isles', referring, of course, to Britain, and declared: 'Nature gave the British Isles wonderful advantages when she made them as she did, and set them where they are on the map of the world . . . and the geography of their Homeland has enabled [the British] to develop qualities that go to make a great race of seamen, merchant traders and empire builders . . .' who 'in less than four hundred years built up an Empire greater than that of Ancient Rome'. Such was our sense of being different and superior to all other peoples. Of course we were convinced that we would win the war.

As the war got under way something else that was strange happened: the men vanished and the women took over. Fathers, uncles and older brothers were conscripted and disappeared from our lives. Their departure was shrouded in unspoken fears: A. S. Byatt, now a Dame and a distinguished novelist but then a fearful child,

51

described to me the moment when her father left: 'I remember standing on the landing at the corner of the house, watching him go out of the front door with his kit-bags and his canvas bag and his folding camp bed and his blue air-force cap . . . and it took me probably twenty years to realise that in many ways my world ended provisionally then.' Everyone had someone in uniform; it was a matter of honour. One of my uncles was in the army, another in the air force; one of my aunts was engaged to a Canadian soldier. There was always a flurry of interest around letters, which came via the censor and were handed round the families. The most exotic came from Dehra Dun, where Uncle Arthur, now Captain Rowlands in the Royal Engineer Corps, a professional artist in civilian life, had been sent to help draw up the official map of India.

I was lucky, though, and not allowed to forget it. Families in which the husband and father had been called up would whisper maliciously and speculate about how mine had escaped. I didn't care: as far as I was concerned he could do no wrong. And there was an explanation: my father was thirty-six when the war came and he was an engineering draughtsman. His work was designated a 'reserved occupation'. Then, and for the rest of his life, he let us believe that he was excused conscription because his work involved grain silos and keeping up essential supplies of food. We accepted this: it made sense. But it wasn't so. In fact, I learned recently, he worked on tanks. Although he never told us, he had let on in a chance remark to his army brother: 'You know, Arthur, these tanks will never work.' Fifty years later my cousin John, Arthur's son, has passed the remark on to me, a minor but significant correction to family history.

Throughout the war there was a famous poster: 'Careless talk costs lives.' Perhaps my father took it literally enough not to tell even my mother about his job, and felt bound to keep the secret even to the grave. There were many times later when he and I talked of the war, sometimes over a drink, reminiscing nostalgically, but he never let go of his secret. It was his personal war effort, not available for gossip.

In December 1940 there was a major air-raid on Manchester. The Luftwaffe was aiming for the docks as well as the factories. My father was in the city that day and was not home by night-time. I remember my mounting hysteria as we realised where the bombs were falling. He arrived at midnight, having had to walk all the way. We stood together in the garden of the house in Hazel Grove and, from a distance of some fifteen miles, watched Manchester burn. The sky was red, lit up by the huge conflagration. Not the red or gold of sodium lighting or even the glow of peacetime bonfires: this was apocalyptic . . . like a vision of hell. And without a sound.

In many ways, wartime was wonderfully liberating for children. Our parents took the burden of austerity and stress upon themselves, leaving us to enjoy a greater freedom than they might otherwise have wished. They were too busy, too preoccupied with making and mending, to be always aware of what we were up to. What did a few local tumbles or being out in all weathers matter compared to the bombing? Discipline was not so much slackened—in my home at least—but simply became too difficult to impose, what with the searching for scarce food, trawling from shop to shop in the hope of a delivery of tinned fruit, regular baking days to put the flour and margarine to good use, and the endless washing and ironing, cleaning and polishing that became an almost ritual defiance of an enemy determined to disrupt our way of life.

Children were out of doors, playing on the streets. After air-raids there was shrapnel to collect, bombed houses to loot, ruined buildings, their walls tipping dangerously, to be explored. Living where we did, south of Stockport, we were never directly targeted but after the Luftwaffe had bombed Manchester and its docks, and been chased away by our defences, the planes would unload their left-over bombs as they fled south. On one occasion a German pilot came down by parachute in fields just beyond the house. When we got over there in the morning he had gone, taken into custody. But a sense of danger still surrounded the pitiful crumpled plane. Then we were on to it, grabbing at bits and pieces, carting home lumps for our own collections and for the keen swaps market. Decades later the fashion designer Mary Quant counted herself even luckier: she and her friends, who watched the Battle of Britain fought out in the skies over the South Downs, and chased on bicycles after crashing planes, found a real live German pilot lying utterly helpless: 'We rounded him up, told him he was arrested and stood around him until the army and the police arrived.' Enid Blyton couldn't have bettered that.

We knew danger, but we didn't worry about it. It came to be taken for granted. Bombs were exciting. Ken Loach, known now for his films of gritty social realism, remembers not the fear but 'the smell of damp plaster and the smell of explosives and the people running up and down the street. I knew people had been killed in the street.' Photographer Don McCullin recalls that, as a child of eight or nine, 'I'd roam through all those houses, looking at people's possessions, looking at their family albums, or displays of photographs . . . but then if the homes were really badly bombed we used to rip up the wood and sell it to old ladies for their winter fuel.'

This sense of freedom, of excitement, made us self-reliant, responsible for our own actions. It was assumed we knew how to look after ourselves. We roamed the fields and streams, climbed trees, trespassed into grand houses, collected frog spawn in jam-jars, picked wild flowers and took them home to press. It was a natural education. By 1946, in a letter to my father—who by then was travelling to Spain and Turkey on company business—I remarked that I had already collected sixty-three different kinds of flower but that day had found a further eight. Days when I wasn't at school were governed by nothing more than the need to get home in time for tea—about six o'clock in the afternoon—without tearing my clothes, getting too dirty or causing any hue and cry among the neighbours.

It led to something called The Secret Game, a private fantasy created with my special friend Ann Howard and her sister Janice, six years younger, who was Susan's best friend. Together we made up a foursome, the two younger girls ordered about by Ann and me. Our parents were friends too, and soon had important roles as intermediaries. The two families lived out this imaginary game throughout the war. As children we could dip into it at any time, explicitly when we were on our own but continuing with a meaningful wink or nudge whenever we were with the grown-ups. We grew adept at leading a double life in public, quickly acquiring the ability to listen to one conversation while holding another. We realised early that among any group of people several agendas were being addressed at the same time. It was a child's lesson in adult ways, and taught me how to follow conversations at other tables than my own in smart restaurants.

The object of the game was to win the war, no less. We were constantly open to the propaganda that told us how victory depended on the efforts of each and every one of us. We took the responsibility seriously. The Secret Game was played out around where we lived. Bakewell Road, part of a 1930s ribbon development between Stockport and Macclesfield, hadn't yet been paved, and petered out into a patchwork of fields, traversed by pathways. Beyond, through the fields, Ann lived in Rutland Road. We pursued the game across the land between us, under hedges, along footpaths, beside pools, within dens of hawthorn bushes, and secret places in sheds and outhouses.

The premise was simple: Ann and I had been specially chosen for a secret assignment, which was to identify, pursue and foil two German spies, twin women agents called Magda Hester and Hester Magda. As I typed their names sixty years later, I felt a pang of anxiety. Anxiety, and recognition of what it had been like to cower under the boughs of English trees, smelling the hay and heat of summer, while plotting to defeat two fictitious enemies in a real war.

Magda Hester and Hester Magda: the names were never to be revealed, they were never written down in the coded instructions we created for each other. They were the essence of villainy, and to write their names was to give them a potent reality. Magda Hester and Hester Magda were cunning and treacherous, and hunting them down could excuse anything—clothes torn in the dangerous chase, lateness for the prescribed meal-times. There was no risk too great. Having committed such crimes we could make no excuses to our parents, staying tight-lipped about our assignment and taking the appropriate punishment like the heroic prisoners-of-war we saw in the films. How had we alighted on the two deadly names? Thinking back, I had assumed Hester came from a swashbuckling film of the day, *The Wicked Lady*, which starred Margaret Lockwood as a ruthless and self-seeking highwaywoman. We certainly endowed our two enemies with her courage and defiance. Besides, we admired her clothes. Now I discover the film dates from 1945. But Magda was a name we believed to be German, which was enough to make it villainous in our eyes. Years later I learned that Goebbel's wife was called Magda and had died at his hand, with all of their children, to escape the humiliation of defeat. Had we, perhaps, read of this Magda and unwittingly caught her up in our game as the most infamous name we knew?

As the war progressed, the game became more complicated. We assumed numerous aliases: I became Kay Carswell, and Francesca Gascoyne, a

57

name that to me was endowed with aristocracy. The makers of the film *Kind Hearts and Coronets* would soon agree. Both Ann and I now led fictitious gangs of other girls, commanding them to search and destroy the German twins who themselves had gathered additional forces. Conspicuously, no men or boys featured in this warfare of the imagination. The fields and woods were still the setting for our exploits, but the plots and counterplots grew more convoluted. The fact that our forces were under instructions to keep cover and move stealthily without giving any indication of their presence reinforced our belief in their reality. After all, as we surveyed the horizon of hedge and cornfield, were they not doing exactly as instructed and staying out of sight?

Back in our homes we continued with the communiqués of war, sending out maps and plans of manoeuvres in the coat pockets of our parents when they were meeting in the evening. Sometimes we gave concerts, dressing up for the final tableau as the embodied spirit of the four great allies: Russia, benign Uncle Joe Stalin, then the heroic leader of the people who had withstood the siege of Stalingrad represented as a shapeless figure wrapped in my mother's rabbit fur jacket; China, the nationalist leader Chiang Kai-shek, in *Mikado* fancy dress. The United States and Great Britain were rendered more simply as Uncle Sam and Britannia, Roosevelt and Churchill being somehow subsumed into the greater image. Besides, it would have been no fun to dress up as Churchill. And we all aspired to play Britannia. The parents treated the whole enterprise with proper seriousness.

This, then, was our life: night was become day

with the fires and explosions. The men had left, and the women were in charge at home and at school. Households were disrupted: first we were all sleeping in an Anderson shelter in the garden, made of corrugated iron dug in seven feet down, full of spiders and water, then later indoors in the Morrison, a cage-like structure put up in the living room. Sometimes homes disappeared overnight. I remember going to school and being told, 'June Beresford's home was bombed last night. It doesn't exist any more.' But she was back at school within a week, housed, I suppose now, with relatives or friends and keen not to miss her schooling.

Most of the people whose childhood memories I called on remember feeling exhilarated rather than depressed by the war. But I learned a sustained and worrying apprehension about life. I think I caught it from my mother: she was under pressure from unkind neighbours who implied that my father had dodged the call-up. And in secret, I think, she, like many others, had unspoken fears: of invasion, occupation. Already close to her emotional needs and tensions, I felt it in the air. I remember throwing a desperate tantrum when my father fetched his rifle from the hall on his way to a Home Guard practice. In my imagination it was as bad as the front line. I screamed and clung to him, trying to prevent him going. I was never going to be physically courageous.

*   *   *

And then there was evacuation. The evacuee story has been often told: on film and television it carries the much-used footage of children herded at

59

railway stations, made conspicuous by the label pinned to the right-hand lapel of their coats, and the square-boxed gas-mask slung across one shoulder. Again for my series *My Generation* I collected memories. The writer Arnold Wesker, leaving from Liverpool Street station, is convinced he heard a teacher say to the mothers, 'Well, say goodbye. You may never see them again.' Others remember—with gratitude—that their parents decided that if the family was to die then it was better they all died together. Don McCullin, reminiscing in his fifties, recalled how, aged four and a half, he was sent with his three-year-old sister to Somerset where they were separated: the little girl went to the big house and Don to a council house in the same village. Such traumatic disruption affected thousands of families.

Back at home in Bakewell Road I wanted it to affect mine: I wanted to be on the receiving end. I longed for our family to take in evacuees. One midday a straggle of children—wan and listless, making no noise—was shepherded along our road. They were escorted by harassed women in some sort of uniform, and there weren't many of them. Perhaps those most favoured had been picked off earlier, as looking cleaner, better behaved, free of nits. It reminded me of those agonising moments in playground games when two team leaders take it in turns to pick their side from the class: to be the last chosen proclaims to everyone your absolute unpopularity. Those evacuees were at the end of the line, being hawked from house to house in our street. They stood huddled together on the dusty track of the un-made-up road, where the milkman's horse had deposited a steamy dollop of manure, swiftly scooped up by housewives eager to fertilise the allotments. I watched from behind the curtains, as did my mother, to see who was offering them shelter.

I longed to have a new friend, an ally, someone strange and exotic from as far away as London, but my mother set her face against the idea. I tried to persuade her: 'But we have a boxroom!' It was heaped, it was true, with boxes, a trunk or two, some old curtains. It would need to be cleared, but my mother, with two children already, wasn't in the mood for extra work. She was even happy to join the neighbourhood sniping. Two spinster ladies who lived nearby with their insipid greyhound were found wanting: 'No children of their own to look after, they could make the effort.' But no one was obliged to. In the event it was families with children who took in more, making for noisy but normal homes. Except my own.

Evelyn Waugh's *Put Out More Flags* depicts evacuees as snivelling horrors, and mocks the genteel unease of the landed classes on whom they are billeted. For me the reverse was true: I thought evacuees were glamorous, easy-going, cheeky, full of tricks and guile—the sort of child I wanted to be, but lacked the courage to become. I was attached to two in particular: twin boys, Jimmy and Billy. In memory I have them sketched with their socks round their ankles and grinning faces full of freckles in the style of *Just William*. I know they were Cockneys and proud of it. One had a shock of bright red hair, the other tousled black curls. Their strong accents had for me a lilting charm but filled my mother with dread. She had a Manchester accent but, with aspirations towards gentility, disapproved of their influence. They were not made welcome, but that didn't deter them. They would call at the front door of the house in Bakewell Road, a solecism of the first order because only visitors on Sundays used it. Friends and tradesmen were meant to call at the side of house, a few feet away, but a yawning social chasm. They would ask if I could go out to play, a question I referred to my mother even though I already knew the answer. Refused, they would linger, lolling in the doorway, keeping me talking, leaning on the door jamb, kicking stones, swapping film-magazine gossip about Betty Grable and Ray Milland and driving my mother mad. Eventually she would find some pretext—'Your tea's ready!' Or, more classily, 'Time for your piano practice,' to call me indoors. I would dawdle, defying her with relish, knowing that while she had refused point-blank to take in evacuees, she could not bring herself to be rude to them. It was a foretaste of the tension between us that surrounded all my encounters with the opposite sex. While I wanted to be a boy it seems my mother wanted me to be a nun.

*　　　*　　　*

Austerity made us frugal and resourceful. During the First World War food rationing had only existed during the final six months of hostilities. By comparison with the shambles of the earlier conflict, provision for the Second World War was remarkably well organised. This time the government had made arrangements early: plans laid long before snapped into action in the first

62

weeks of 1940, within five months of war being declared. First, sugar, butter and bacon were on the ration, then tea, margarine and cooking fat.

I grew up under a regime subject to overarching government control in which food supplies were centrally distributed for the broader public good. I couldn't but be aware that food, including sweets, was in meagre supply and it wouldn't do to complain. I took on my parents' mood of stoic resignation, and even something more: a sense that governments could make things fairer for people who had less. There was a flourishing of individual resourcefulness. People kept chickens to augment the one-egg-per-week ration. We had names for each of them and cuddled them as pets. Flowerbeds were dug up, and dull root vegetables made regular and unappetising appearances on our plates.

The government issued recipes. Dr Charles Hill, a future BBC chairman, went on radio to spell them out. Woolton Pie, named after the Minister of Food, was meat pie without meat; omelettes were made with a yellow powder, dried egg. Chip omelettes were my favourite. The tastebuds adapted and became familiar with the bland and repetitive. After the war, the sudden arrival of avocados and aubergines knocked us out, with their exotic colours, textures and flavours—like stepping from black and white movies into colour.

But there was another truth about our diet during the war: for many it was the healthiest eating they had ever known. Several of my aunts and uncles had grown up with rickets, a curvature of the limbs believed to be caused by a diet lacking vitamin D. It was common in the sunless, smoke-choked inner cities at the start of the century. The war brought recommended rations, equal for all, with free supplements of orange juice and cod-liver oil for children. My generation was measurably healthier and taller than the one that had gone before.

From our early years we learned to make a little go a long way. Many of us have remained thrifty throughout our lives. The impulse to save left-overs, hoard elastic bands and paperclips amuses our children. The habits learned as a matter of survival have stuck with us anachronistically in a world glutted with goods. Where now the economic imperative is to sustain consumer spending, we grew up believing that spending was wasteful and wrong. We learned as a generation to be satisfied with our share so that others did not go without. It shaped our left-leaning politics. We came to believe that ambitions for ourselves, the acquiring of wealth beyond that of others, the lure of fame and success were glamorous and exciting, but somehow reprehensible. The children of the war took its influence forward into their lives.

*   *   *

Images of the front line reached us primarily in the cinema. The fledgling television service had closed down in 1939 and, anyway, television sets were beyond the means of most people. But we could all afford the cinema and everyone went, from the vicar to the butcher, from school teachers to chimney sweeps. Whole communities turned out in wind and rain, travelled by bus and tram, queued in the cold, then sat on hard seats to gain a warming glimpse of the golden glow of Hollywood. It was usual for children to go on their own. An A certificate (no admission without an adult) film presented no problem: we would simply hang around the swing doors and ask a stranger to take us in with them. No one thought it was any kind of risk. From the age of eight I probably went twice a week—to the Marcliff, the Davenport, the Carlton, the Ritz, the Super, the Wellington or the Plaza. Only the art-deco Plaza, complete with its Compton cinema organ, still stands, now grade-two listed.

It is hard to convey how glittering and remote the glamour of Hollywood seemed. And how its most spectacular melodramas matched the intensity of our own experience. Even something as exaggeratedly overwrought as *Gone with the Wind* and the burning of Atlanta showed us what we knew to be true: that wars blight and destroy families and communities. It gave me a taste for cinema's heightened reality, and for the self-dramatising that overtakes me from time to time.

Then there were the newsreels. We now know that there was blanket government control of what was seen and said, and that newsreels were a highly manipulated way of giving people the facts while sustaining morale. Even Dunkirk was transformed into a triumph of the indomitable British spirit. Yet I believed them unquestioningly. We had to, or our resolve would have faltered. Then, towards the end of the war, there was something else. Something so shocking that the world-view of children who saw it was utterly changed.

The April of my twelfth birthday was a grim one in history. As the Allied armies advanced towards victory, a secret already known to some, but never revealed to the public at large, was slowly revealed. On 15 April Allied troops liberated Bergen-Belsen: on the seventeenth US troops entered Buchenwald; twelve days later they liberated Dachau, and on the next Hitler killed himself. The scale of what has since been called the Holocaust hadn't been imagined.

I saw the films as part of the newsreel: heaps of dead bodies, thin like sticks, in different piles; walking skeletons, people only just able to stand, staring blankly. The shock of those pictures is still with me. No one thought they were too horrific to put before the public. Anything that showed the utter depravity of Germany and fuelled our hatred of the Hun was to be encouraged as good wartime propaganda. Parents, rather than wanting to shield us from such bestiality, regarded it as a powerful and terrible warning. I had never encountered death in my young life and remember a strong physical reaction: my hands were clammy with cold sweat; shivering started at the back of my neck and spread down my arms. The novelist Beryl Bainbridge saw the films too, and was equally appalled: 'When you're young you think life is all going to be wonderful. Seeing those films, I thought, No, it's not. The dream is over. The world is like that . . . those pyramids of bones.'

There were relatively few images in the world around us: newsprint was rationed, magazines were few, printed in black and white, posters were bold, direct and simplistic, many of them government propaganda. Our eyes were hungry, so for us each image had an overwhelming impact. It registered, was observed, digested, held our attention, delivered the full weight of its content. We knew the cinema would glut us with pleasure, each film a feast for parched appetites, but this footage was terrifyingly different.

I remember a pall of sorrow falling across the cinema audience as we watched, and the shocked silence in which we shuffled out and walked home. The images sank deep. I have hardly been able to see them since without that same sense of hopelessness seizing me. It has never quite gone away. Rather it has crystallised into a sense of 'never again', the need to be vigilant and take a positive view of political action.

The cruelties were with us for a while yet. The war with Germany ended in May 1945, but there was still the sprawling war in the Far East and across the Pacific. Then came the atom bombs: the first fell on Hiroshima in August 1945, the second on Nagasaki three days later. We all rejoiced—of course we did. It made absolute what we had so long dreamed of: the end of the war with Japan. Within a week surrender had followed. But even then, as with the concentration camps, there was a dawning realisation that a new frontier had been crossed into a world of horrors from which there was no return.

For the time being, though, we were carried away by the euphoria of the victory celebrations. The sudden release of emotion by the adults again surprised their children. The small boy who became today's film-maker John Boorman recalls: 'I was very alarmed at the victory, by the way the adults seemed to be so out of control and getting drunk and shouting and singing. I found it very scary, much more scary than air-raids.'

On 8 June the King sent me a letter: I had glimpsed him once from the pavement as he toured the North-west, his open car speeding past, his face a mask of orange-coloured makeup. I knew he did his best, crippled by shyness and a severe stammer. He wrote:

Today as we celebrate victory, I send this personal message to you and all other boys and girls at school. For you have shared in the hardships and dangers of a total war and you have shared no less in the triumph of the Allied Nations.

I know you will always feel proud to belong to a country which was capable of such supreme effort; proud too of parents and elder brothers and sisters who by their courage, endurance and enterprise brought victory. May these qualities be yours as you grow up and join in the common effort to establish among the nations of the world unity and peace. Signed George R.I.

Sadly, it's dated 1946 . . . a year late. Perhaps the post was delayed or the bureaucracy had other things to attend to. I once mentioned on radio that I had been given such a document and received complaints from those who hadn't. Clearly there was a lot of muddle as we got back to peacetime.

*   *   *

For me and thousands like me a new day dawned with the passing of the Education Act in 1944. Its architect, R. A. Butler, Minister for Education in the wartime coalition government, piloted through Parliament a major shake-up in the way education worked in Britain. I was one of those shaken up. The Act not only raised the school-leaving age to fifteen, it introduced state-funded education for every child over eleven. In Stockport it was either the grammar school or the secondary modern. Your fate depended on the 11-plus: for the first time an entire generation of bright children, who could pass exams, was given free access to the grammar-school education that otherwise they could not have afforded. Evelyn Waugh mocked it as 'a scheme for giving education away free to the deserving poor'. It was hailed by others as a tremendous breakthrough into the old preserves of money and privilege. And so it was. We weren't aware then of how it would create divisions of its own. At the time it promised golden opportunity.

Ours was a house divided: I, the family swot, was serious-minded, with straight brown hair stretched plainly back in plaits; Susan, the family charmer, bubbled with fun and tossed her fair curls in defiance. We were different but close: Susan, the second child, much freer and easier with herself, more spontaneous, loving and fun; I, the spoiled first child, heaped with family favours but also expectations, tense and serious. Susan should have been jealous of the fuss and praise heaped on my smallest achievements, but nothing ever qualified her affection for me, and all her life I was her touchstone for approval and advice. When it came to exams I, pressurised by my parents, tried and passed. Susan resisted their pressure, idled and failed.

More good things were promised. In July 1945 a

Labour government was elected, for the first time with an overwhelming majority. We held a mock election at school and I, knowing nothing but siding sycophantically with the most popular in the class, was for the Tories. I went home to find I'd made a big mistake: 'Oh, no, we vote Labour.' Next day I was on the other side. Most of the debate focused around the need to thank Churchill for the victory by supporting his party. I felt bad about that. So did many people. A lady diner at the Savoy was said to have declared, 'They've elected a Labour government and the country will never stand for it!'

But there was an appetite among people for huge social change. Churchill, for all his great war leadership, was a Tory grandee, and now it was the turn of the common man. During the 1930s depression there had been talk in the Labour movement of how much needed to be done. Now it intensified. My father and a neighbour went regularly to Labour Party meetings, the women left behind to mind the children—paid babysitters were unknown: if family or friends couldn't stand in, you stayed at home: the question of trading money for such favours would have offended everyone. So, the men went out and talked of the country's destiny, and my father talked about it to me. Everyone waited for things to get better.

The moment could not have been more propitious. The war had bound people together in a common effort. Food rationing was fair to all, conscription had loosened class ties. Never before had a population willingly accepted such a formidable amount of government regulation. The war effort had been a socialist undertaking in disguise, and now was the time to build on that sense of purpose. The welfare state was the result.

Once the war had ended, people were released from their worries. They eased up: they smiled more, whistled as they went about and thought up new things to do. Slowly the lights had come on in shop windows and cinema foyers, sending their bright colours into the streets in a way that I'd once thought dangerous. I joined the Church youth club, went youth hostelling with school groups around the Cumbrian lakes, the Derbyshire dales and the Yorkshire moors. I played tennis, went to Hallé concerts in Manchester's Free Trade Hall and noted, with some surprise, that there were two women in the orchestra. I sang in a choir, girls' voices only, raised high in Purcell's 'Nymphs and Shepherds', and songs from Edward German's *Merrie England*. There was a lot happening.

I attended well-meaning conferences organised by the World Forum of Youth, and the Council for Education in World Citizenship sponsored by the *Daily Mail*. We had lectures about the new United Nations, and world peace. I swallowed whole the optimism and idealism. Then, in 1950, my class was called to a meeting and told by a serious-voiced geography teacher that another war had broken out, in Korea, but this time we were fighting alongside the Americans against the Chinese, who had had a Communist revolution and were now our enemies. We were confused. I looked at maps. None of us was much aware of how and why Europe had been divided up at the Yalta Conference, or understood the significance of Churchill's declaration in 1946 that an iron curtain had descended across Europe. The adults were

71

suddenly reversing all the facts they had so recently told us were true.

I was astonished that Russia, whom we had so keenly portrayed as our staunch ally in that innocent Secret Game, had changed sides and was our declared enemy. I had noticed a book called *I Chose Freedom* on my father's bookshelf, but hadn't read it or understood its significance. It was a polemic written by the Soviet defector Victor Kravchenko, denouncing Stalin and giving details of orchestrated famines, concentration camps and slave labour. George Orwell had published *Animal Farm* in 1945, but my orange Penguin edition is the 1951 reprint. I learned only slowly of the brutality of Russia's regime.

It wasn't, as the celebrations and the King's letter had led me to believe, peace for ever more. In 1946 another war was upon us, the Cold War, which would cut off entire countries, even continents, from each other. For four decades my generation would live with the mystery of 'the other side', the Communist states where things were different and terrible. Only in my adult life would I have the chance to observe them at first hand.

CHAPTER SIX

CERTAINTIES

I grew up when there was a thirst for serious academic learning. People believed in it: it would solve problems, get them better jobs. More than that, it was relished for its own sake. It was felt that

72

for generations those with power and influence had kept the secret and the riches of education locked away for themselves. And now the keys suddenly were ours. There was the excitement of going to a grammar school.

In some way this was still the running tide of enthusiasm that had followed the introduction of universal education, education for working people, at the turn of the century. In those days, miners' libraries in South Wales were stocking up on political and economic classics. Since the nineteenth century Mechanics Institutes had sprung up across Britain, charitably endowed places of learning to which working men could go for free lectures. There was even one in our village, Hazel Grove. The Workers' Education Association, founded in 1903, was dedicated to providing lectures in the evening to working people. There was a branch in Stockport. My parents, believers in self-improvement and eager to make up for lost chances, were students there, studying everything from philosophy to Beethoven. When I got to Cambridge I found that parents of my fellow students had been involved with the WEA, too. But they had been lecturers.

Girls' education had been given parity with boys' in the 1944 Education Act. Girls' grammar schools—even of the grand fee-paying kind—had only been established on any scale in the late nineteenth century. The North London Collegiate School for Girls was founded in 1850, Cheltenham Ladies' College in 1858, Roedean in 1885; the Girls' Public Day School Trust opened its first school in 1875. There is no doubt that Stockport High School for Girls, which was founded in 1894, saw itself in this tradition, with as high aspirations in terms of achievement and scholarship, equally dedicated to giving girls as fine an education as boys. What they would do with it was never asked. What they have done with it was never imagined.

There was a minor fracas in 1907 when Stockport High School applied to the local authority for financial help in providing a new building. The council objected, claiming that such funding was 'anti-social as it secures privileges for the few out of public rates and taxes'. There was a considerable fuss: a public inquiry, a conference, and finally the Board of Education overruled the objection: the school, it said, would be 'a strong influence on the intellectual life of the entire town'. And so it was. After 1944, when the school's fees were abolished, those high-minded ideals did not waver. This was a school that saw itself in the line of the finest public schools, aspiring to teach what Matthew Arnold, in his essay, 'Culture and Anarchy', had defined as 'the best that has been thought and said in the world'. And for my teachers there was the added urgency and adventure of educating women. Surely we were in the vanguard of something new and important. For a time we even adopted the Harrow School song as our own: 'Forty years on when afar and asunder / Parted are those who are singing today . . .' I little thought that forty years on from my generation, Stockport High School for Girls would have been abolished in the great push towards comprehensives. It had lasted just eighty years. I was heartbroken when I learned it had gone.

* * *

Most of my teachers were single women of a generation whose men had been slaughtered in their thousands on the battlefields of the First World War, the missing generation of the men they might have married. It gave them a curious take on education. They welcomed greater opportunities for their 'gels', but at the same time they had a rather wistful, misty-eyed view of what a woman's destiny might be. On speech days not a single prize, or scholarship, or university entrance was ever announced from the assembly-hall platform without a final aria from the headmistress, Miss Lambrick, that a woman's true calling was to be a wife and mother. 'Thanks a lot,' we would mutter, after we had worked so hard to gain these trophies. But in spite of ourselves we absorbed the message. The teachers stared blankly ahead, their young men long since dead in the trenches.

I cannot claim the unique influence of just one inspirational teacher, no one declaiming Donne, or taking me to productions of Shakespeare after hours. Instead I was overwhelmed by a body of women resolved to shape and instruct me in their shared world-view. They were a cohort of the army of self-improvement, steeped in the same entrenched, spinsterly values of learning, duty and obedience, tempered with a little laughter when exams weren't too pressing. The school motto set the high-minded tone:

Self-reverence, self-knowledge, self-control,
These three alone lead life to sovereign power.

—lines taken from an obscure poem by Tennyson,

'Oenone', which no one could pronounce. The lines were engraved on the four tall stained-glass windows along one wall of the assembly hall, and I fretted regularly about what they might mean. Self-control was obvious—everyone was always banging on about that—but I got stuck on self-reverence and sovereign power. How did you recognise the first, and who wanted the second? I still don't know.

For my teachers the school was their life, not only their calling but the institution to which they were married. A teacher who married in the real world had duplicated her role: she had to leave to look after her home and husband, a job regarded as full-time; only war brought a temporary concession, as an emergency measure. There was no debate about it. This was what happened. It was what we half expected to happen in our own lives.

Many teachers shared their homes, pairing off and staying together for years. They had met as young women, probably at teacher-training college, and stayed together into their retirement: Miss Nichols with Miss Glover, Miss Nation with Miss Hancock. All were devoted to their girls. Nowadays there would be sneering comments, but we knew neither the vocabulary nor even the concept of lesbianism. Perhaps they didn't either, although the school was awash with crushes on teachers, on senior pupils; the febrile sexuality of a single-sex establishment. We took our teachers as they were: adult lives were not our concern.

There was Miss Jones, the gym mistress, who must have been touching fifty, incongruously lithe and slender at a time when women of forty thickened around the waist and got ready to be old.

She played along to this eccentricity by dressing girlishly in a navy tunic that flared to just above her knee, a plaited yellow girdle round the waist. Beneath it, a shantung-silk blouse, with billowing sleeves, fell in voluminous folds—like a Ginger Rogers dress—as she demonstrated exercises. Below the tunic she wore impeccable grey silk stockings held up by suspenders, hidden from view by folds of silvery pink knickers, into whose elastic she tucked her handkerchief. Her hair was steely grey like the stockings, but cut in a twenties bob, probably a style decided in her youth and held to ever since. When I arrived she had already been at the school for twenty-seven years.

Miss Nichols taught maths: tall and willowy, she favoured full skirts and high heels. For us she defined glamour. She would write on the blackboard talking the while, 'The square on the hypotenuse . . .', then swing on her high heel towards us, the skirt moving with her, 'bisect the right angle,' back to the blackboard, the skirts building their momentum, 'and QED: *quod erat demonstrandum*'. She would subside into her chair, no doubt to take the strain off her heels, and hand out homework.

Miss Glover, who taught science and biology, was known as Cuddy—in the cruel way of children—because her two front teeth were disastrously prominent and we joked that she was chewing cud. She was happy among the bunsen burners and retorts, less happy with the dissection of a frog, and totally at sea explaining the reproductive system of a rabbit, when she would stare unblinkingly at the back wall of the lab, go bright red and gabble her way through the information. It was unkind of us to persist with our questions.

I have their group photograph on my desk, sent to me by Miss Hancock's surviving nephew, who saw me on television. Here is Miss Baugh who taught me to love Latin, and whose posture was so upright that she might have had a poker up her back; we said it was because she rode to hounds. Miss Atkinson walked with a wrenched back that, rumour said, was the result of a motorcycle accident. Miss Waggott, gracious and powdery, was rumoured to have had an affair with Rupert Brooke.

And then there was Miss Ashworth, whom we killed.

She gassed herself one afternoon in the house where she lived opposite the school. It was years after I'd left but I was part of the cause. Miss Ashworth—Millicent Ashworth, Millie to the girls in the upper fifth, but only when they were speaking among themselves—taught French. She got off to a bad start with the eleven-year-olds, who were required to bring a hand mirror to school so that they could distort their mouths into the correct shape to form the French sound 'oe'. What surer way was there of making children feel self-conscious and hating her for it? From then on, year after year, she was teased. Generation after generation of girls treated her mercilessly, mildly but continuously naughty so that her lessons were wrecked. We were unforgiving, enjoyed driving the blood up the wrinkled skin of her neck, which turned from red to purple as it ascended her throat, then burst into full bloom across her face as her temper erupted and we were triumphant. Yes, it was fun to tease Millie. The effects were so predictable.

Years later at a school reunion I learned what we had done. The teasing had been a light matter for us, but it had broken her. One day it had just been too much. It amounted to sustained bullying, as though the barbarian children of *Lord of the Flies* had found their home among the decorous teachers of *The Prime of Miss Jean Brodie*. We had turned on Millie, discounting her kindnesses, her enthusiasm, her devotion to us. In the sixth form I had loved her lessons. She knew all about Charles Baudelaire and Victor Hugo, Alfred de Musset and Alphonse de Lamartine. I fell rather soupily for Lamartine whose *cri de coeur* in 'Le Lac' against the passing of time chimed with my own obsession:

> *Aimons donc, aimons donc! De l'heure fugitive,*
> *Hâtons-nous, jouissons!*
> *L'homme n'a point de port, le temps n'a point de rive:*
> *Il coule, et nous passons!*
> Let's love each other then; enjoy, before
> It is too late, each fleeting day.
> Man has no harbour, time no further shore—
> Hours drift by and we fade away.
> [Translation: Harry Guest]

Time preoccupied me in those days. I was frightened by it, by the idea of its passing beyond recall. I tortured myself with the idea of 'now' becoming 'then', what Tennessee Williams somewhere calls the 'continual rush of time so violent that it appears to be screaming'. Each New Year's Eve, when its passing became actual, I

79

worked myself into a fine frenzy of panic and dread as the seconds ticked by, only to subside into a heap of relief as the chimes sounded and daily rhythm was restored. I began to collect poems about the fleeting nature of time and the inevitability of loss: Andrew Marvell's 'To His Coy Mistress':

> Had we but world enough, and time,
> This coyness, Lady, were no crime.

Sir Walter Ralegh's lines written on the eve of his execution:

> Even such is time, that takes in trust
> Our youth, our joys and all we have,
> And pays us but with age and dust.

Even Longfellow's morbid:

> The air is full of farewells to the dying
> And mourning for the dead.
> The heart of Rachel for her children crying
> Will not be comforted.

I was resolved that if life was short, I would live it to the full, take everything it offered, and not waste it on what was unimportant. I was just fifteen years old.

*　　　*　　　*

The curriculum, like the teachers' attitude, was on the cusp of change. When I arrived, embroidery and recitation were still on the syllabus. I have my school reports still, yellowing and formal: 'Joan's stitching could be smaller'; 'Joan's enunciation needs care.' The school was relentlessly competitive and selective. Even within its grammar-school framework we were streamed into A and B classes. (The As did Latin, the Bs domestic science.) The six houses were named after significant women of achievement: Brontë and Gaskell we knew as local northern writers; Austen a writer, too, but from the South; Nightingale, every girl's heroine, then Slessor, after the great Victorian explorer Mary Slessor, and Beale, Miss Beale having been a founder, with Miss Buss, of great girls' schools. The six houses competed for a silver cup awarded to 'the most deserving house', the winner arrived at by compiling exam results, with netball and tennis tournaments, house drama competitions and musical achievements. There were even awards for deportment—for anything that could be marked. We got hooked: it became a way of life—so much so that a gang of friends within the fifth form set up their own ratings system and subject schedules, marking charts, and fines. I know because I was their secretary: I kept the records and collected the money. It was a mirror image of the school system, but subverted to serve our own ends. We agreed that we intended to break school rules and we knew we'd be more benignly treated if we achieved high marks. So we resolved to do both.

The rules were remorseless, dragooning us in every particular of behaviour. Uniform even meant the same indoor shoes for every pupil; hair-ribbons had to be navy blue. The school hat had to be worn at all times to and from the school; girls caught without were in trouble. To essay a little glamour we contorted them into every kind of shape, pinched, tucked, held on to the very back of the head with hatpins. We strove to be different. Yet in the school photographs, there we all are in serried ranks, feet together, hands in laps.

The heaviest burden was the no-talking rule: no talking on the stairs, in the classroom, in the corridors, in assembly—anywhere, in fact, except the playground. We were a silent school, shuffling noiselessly from class to class, to our lunch, to the cloakroom. Each whisper in the corridor, each hint of communication on the stairs was quashed, conduct marks apportioned and lines of Cicero copied out in detention. Why? What possible purpose was served? It built up a head of steam, which intensified the talk once we were out of bounds. Perhaps that was why I made a career out of talking.

Among this welter of disapproval—conduct marks, detentions and, finally, a severe talking-to by Miss Lambrick—physical chastisement was unnecessary. We were cowed long before things became that bad. The cane in the headmistress's room was redundant. When a girl got pregnant— the worst conceivable crime—she was expelled without fuss before she could contaminate the rest of us. It happened just once in my day, and was a major scandal. He was an American, a GI soldier, and she was rumoured to have done it for nylons. She had the gall to come to sports day carrying the baby!

Home had already laid the ground rules for the regime to come. Discipline and duty were what mattered here too, and smacking imposed them. In the 1940s smacking wasn't a social issue. It was simply how most families instilled obedience. My grandmother had had a legendary temper: my uncle Bill bore the scar on his shoulder from where she had hit him with a carving knife. My mother had a habit of discharging any petty irritation with a quick clip to my head, 'a box of the ears'. This hurt, but not much. Its persistence, however, was such that I grew to expect it, even developed an involuntary flinch as I passed close by her. There was no knowing when the blow might come. It wasn't possible to calculate when something was wrong because something was always wrong. In the many decades since then smacking has become something you're either for or against, allied at one end of the spectrum with child abuse and at the other with government guidelines. For me it was part of my relationship with my mother. But the word 'relationship' wasn't used then either.

My father was kept apart from all this, sublimely, almost wilfully detached from it. My mother invoked his name as the ultimate sanction, the greatest threat: 'What would your father think if I told him?' So eager was I to retain my father's unqualified approval, to shine in his sight, that I submitted to her judgement and punishment with dumb acceptance but a rebellious heart. Between my father and me an idealised relationship of the good daughter and the benign father grew up, while between my mother and me there festered the age-old rivalry between women for the approval of their men.

The rigours of wartime had strengthened my mother's belief in discipline. In the early months of rationing our palates hadn't yet adjusted to the

83

absence of sweet things. The sugar bowl sat in its exact place beside the teapot in the middle of the table. Once my mother had popped into the kitchen next door, I licked my finger and dipped it in. The reward was immediate but transient. I knew it hadn't been worth it even as the sweetness dissolved on my tongue. Suddenly it tasted sour and bilious. When she returned she could not have missed the a gaping crater that had opened up among the sugar crystals. The bowl had not moved, but the sugar had changed its configuration.

I denied all knowledge of the crime, which merely added lying to stealing. Both were forbidden by the Ten Commandments, which I was learning off by heart at Sunday School. There was no further discussion of the matter. My mother took me upstairs, took down my knickers and smacked me with the flat of a slipper across my bottom. Even as she manhandled me across her knee I was thinking, 'this isn't doing any good'. I remember the flood of confidence as my resolve hardened. I would not allow myself to feel humiliated.

When it was my turn to be a parent, my mother gave me her advice about bringing up children. 'First you have to break their will,' she confided, hardly aware that she was speaking to quite the wrong person: by my adolescence it had been clear to her that she had failed to break mine, and this failure was unbearable to her. None the less a tacit bargain of sorts had been made. This assertive will of mine could range free in the outside world, but at home, within her sanctum, where her word must go unquestioned, I would play a role or, as she saw it, try to master what she called my 'utter selfishness'.

Early in my grammar-school days, from the age of eleven, I realised that the cloud overshadowing our lives would intensify as the years went by. My mother's melancholy was beginning to take hold. There were long periods of silence, days that crept into weeks—even months. The affairs of the household, meals, washing-up, cooking, shopping, would proceed as though it was natural for family communication to go into limbo. We tiptoed round this inner grief, bereft and often angry. There might be brief bitter exchanges: 'What's the matter? Please try to explain.' 'If you don't know then there's no point in my telling.' We didn't know, and neither did she, but she conjured blame from the air. As a consequence I lived in two worlds: the world of spontaneity, which I found at school where I could be, at least in the playground, my noisy, ebullient self, and the closed world of the inner family, which I had to negotiate with precise care, from moment to moment, treading with trepidation lest my mother's demons break out and damage us all.

My father, my sister Susan and I came together in our misery. The family dynamic shifted, went out of balance. I can see now that our intimacy only emphasised my mother's sense of isolation, and I, the elder daughter, now in my early teens and growing ever closer to my father, must have made her jealous. Even the geography changed: where once my parents had sat together by the fireside, listening to the wireless, my father now sat beside me at the dining-table ready to be called on if I needed help with my homework. My mother's deepening gloom, intensifying with the years, drove him to confide in me rather than her. By my late teens he was confiding in me about her.

Yet we would be startled sometimes by an unexpected bout of merriment on her part, which fired us with eager hope. It was as though dark clouds had suddenly given way to dazzling sunlight. Her eyes would take on their former liveliness. When something, some chemical in the brain perhaps, released her whole body from its lethargy, she was effortlessly nimble, graceful. On an instant her warmth and sense of fun would be restored as from an icy sleep. On such occasions I could see my father glimpse the bright, witty young woman who had made him so happy. At such moments his tenderness tore my heart. But then a casual incident, a remark—what its significance was, we couldn't tell—would trigger another plunge into the depths.

To say that this melancholy had my mother in its unremitting grip is not quite the whole story: there was one presiding rule that all of us had to observe, including herself. Indeed, it came from her, transmitted wordlessly as an almost unconscious act of control: the outside world was not to know; it was to have no inkling of the increasing trauma within the family; the outer show must be maintained; there must be no suspicion that we were less than the perfect family. And who could say that that outer show didn't have as much reality as the drama being lived behind closed doors? In public we talked to each other, rather stiltedly, perhaps, but we kept up the behaviour of a model family with every appearance of happiness: my father successful in business, the lovely, spotless home, the pretty, healthy daughters with promising

86

prospects, the modest selection of worldly goods. A few chosen friends were invited round, and we made visits to trusted kith and kin. It was the safe, contented dream of those seeking to better themselves.

One of those invited round was my cousin Pauline, who was Susan's age and came to stay and play with her. Years later when I wrote publicly of my mother's moods she wrote me a tender, personal letter to set the record straight. She had adored my mother, she said, describing her as 'stylish, elegant, kind', and concluding, 'She was indeed the one whose intellect and striving for success—not for material possessions but for an improvement in the quality of the mind—is what I have to thank and remember her for.' Many who knew the public woman would share that view of her. It is part of my own remembrance, too, but tempered by my knowledge of the private, tortured person who hurt us all, and none more than herself.

In her deepening unhappiness my mother sought some kind of equilibrium in her daily life. She became a perfectionist and, with no function in the wider world—her job, after all, was to run her home—she turned the perfectionism on her surroundings and on us. The house must be spotless at all times: no speck of dust was allowed to settle. Each day every room was treated to a routine of thoroughness that we now associate with spring cleaning. Dusters, furniture polish, metal polish, floor cloths; and the early domestic appliances, such as the Ewbank, an early carpet sweeper, then the first vacuum cleaner, were all brought into action. There were few miracle cleaners in those days: we used a dolly and tub and a mangle for the washing, and took a cane carpet-beater to the rugs, which were hung out on the clothes-line in the garden. The cleaning occupied the whole of every morning, but that suited my mother's need: it took time and dedicated hard work. The job required her consistent application. It defined her place in the world.

When her perfectionism turned on Susan and me, it was painful indeed. We must have perfect manners, good school reports, remain tidy about the house and maintain a reputation for good behaviour that brought credit to the family. It was easy to transgress—so much was forbidden. The petty social snobberies of suburban life imposed their own rigours: diction mattered in the world out there, the world of the grammar school and of scholarship, the world to which I aspired. I was sent to elocution classes to iron out virtually my entire speech. Of course we all had northern accents—naturally: we came from the North. My father was from Salford, my mother from Gorton; we lived on the periphery of Stockport. How else should we speak? When the posh lady with lah-di-dah manners gave the class a preliminary test, I scored the worst. It was a shock to be told that everything I said was wrong.

*   *   *

The Church was the third, and clinching, institution resolved to set its mark on my character. From an early age I had taken my problems to Jesus. It was quite a personal matter, directly between myself and Him. I knew what He looked

88

like from the picture on the wall at Sunday School, which we attended every week as routinely as we went daily to school. We would crayon in pictures of the disciples attending to various miracles: bright-coloured clothes with stripes, like they had in hot countries. We sang hymns, among them 'There's a Friend for Little Children Above the Bright Blue Sky'; although Stockport skies were often grey I reckoned He would make allowances. The picture on the wall showed a blond man in his twenties, with blue eyes, but exotic to me because he had a beard. I had never seen one in Hazel Grove. It was reddish, and his red/blond hair reached to his shoulders. Over it he wore a white cloth with striped edges that hung down over other baggy white clothes. This was how people in the Bible dressed. Jesus (I didn't think of him as the Christ—if he was to be my friend we had to be on, as it were, Christian-name terms) stood with his arms outstretched to embrace a whole range of children of every colour, little black natives with grass skirts, yellow children with kimonos, children in furs and boots, some in beribboned peasant skirts, some like me. I realise now that he was the perfect embodiment (apart from his dress) of how the British Empire saw itself: paternalistic, all-powerful, peaceful. God on our side indeed.

It was family routine that I should say my prayers every night, kneeling by my bed in the cold bedroom or, in winter, beside my mother at the living-room fire, the only source of heat in the house. This was the better arrangement because I could listen to the radio at the same time as I silently addressed the Lord. When the programme was the popular *Monday Night at Eight o'Clock* on the Home Service, my prayers grew longer. My mother hardly dared intervene. When she did, I would plead that I hadn't yet finished my conversation. But I had to remember not to laugh at the radio jokes.

Sometimes, early on, I got things spectacularly wrong. By taking things literally, as with the blue sky, I misunderstood the injunction to 'love them that persecute you, do good to them that hate you' and 'love thine enemies'. I pondered the ramifications of this long and hard, and found myself in the unhappy position of praying that Hitler would win the war. It seemed required of me that I should sacrifice everything—friends, family, the world I loved blown to smithereens—so that Hitler should feel loved. I felt bad about this, and desperately wanted my prayer not to be answered. But was even that a sin?

The word 'sacrifice' cropped up a good deal in Sunday School talks, as did 'humility' and 'sin'. I knew that home, the Church and school all talked the same language of morality with absolute certainty, and much of it was directed at me. Only the Church offered me someone with whom I could be totally frank, and I could do that because He knew what I was thinking anyway—and His love was unconditional.

As I grew into my teens church-going became my own choice. My parents hardly ever attended, and did not pressure me to go. So I went, in a tiny act of self-assertion. This was to be my place, my privacy, my arena of independent thought. Sometimes I went with friends and we did the usual things children do, flicking pellets, drawing in the prayer books, ogling the boys. But sometimes I went on my own and was serious. This was the one space I could find to think, to be, to develop some interior life. St Thomas's Church, Norbury, was low church, nothing fancy, no bowing to the altar, no incense, but I learned what it means to enter a holy place, to have a sense of the sacred. From the often wet and windy weather outside, I would pass into the quiet of the place, and into the shared quiet of the people there. I learned the hymns, ancient and modern, soon had them off by heart, didn't need to read from the book. The liturgy I soon knew too, a matter of enjoying the orotund roll of the phrases rather than grasping what it might all mean. As I got older, I grew more critical of the texts 'Cleanse the thoughts of our hearts', 'We have done those things we ought not to have done and there is no health in us.' Just how much guilt was I meant to feel? And Communion with its hint of cannibalism—'Take, eat, this is my Body'— suggested gorgeous and terrible rituals quite beyond the whitewashed walls of the trim little church. But I kept going. I needed a place to be myself. And I still do, even though now I no longer believe the Church's dogma. All my life I have felt the unresisting comfort of being in a church: the predictable layout and furnishings, the polished brass of the lectern, the neatness of the pews, the grave authority of the pulpit. Over it all there hangs something in the air, a sense that what is transacted here matters.

In practical terms, of course, the Church was armed with more dos and don'ts than my family and school. Together, the three presented a formidable array of pressure, overlapping and reinforcing the only values I knew. At my

91

confirmation, at the age of twelve, my godfather, John Williams, had written to me: 'Think before you act, and ask yourself this question: Would my mother and father approve of what I am about to do? If you can say "Yes" to this question then do it with all the power you possess. If you think, "No", shun it with all your might.' I could see that I would have to get away.

The combined fire-power of these three institutions was directed with particular keenness and unanimity at one unambiguous target: sex. Mystification set in early. Once, on holiday in North Wales—I must have been about thirteen—I had had a physically delicious sensation while galloping a horse along the sandy beach at Benllech Bay. At the time I didn't know what to make of it, or for some time to come. I was ignorant about my own body, and too shy to ask.

The shyness had already got me into trouble. At primary school I had been told a smutty playground joke. I found it impenetrable. I tried to understand but it remained stubbornly beyond analysis. I couldn't make sense of any of it, but repeated it none the less. Small hands were cupped over guilty giggles, the whisper was repeated from group to group and convulsed them all. I joined in vigorously, laughing louder, whispering more frantically, all the while thinking, I'll find out what it all means later . . . My eagerness for popularity was my undoing: word went round that I was a fund of salacious tales and other children approached, pleading for more. I demurred. Then, an early candidate for MI5 put this to me: 'Tell me another or I'll tell your mother what you've said.' My imaginative resources simply weren't up to it. I had to plead that this was my one and only dirty joke. My popularity was over. And I still hadn't understood a word.

In my early teens I had my first sight of a flesh and blood penis: a man exposed himself. Without brothers, I had had to resort to classical art to find out about the male anatomy, but here it was on display asking to be looked at. I seized the chance—we all did. I travelled to school by tram, a rattling contraption with seats that slammed to and fro, and upstairs a curved bench along the back. It was as we descended these stairs in single file at our destination that he seized the moment and opened his flies: we each saw a rather purply flap of flesh dangling between his legs. He effected this without those sitting at either side realising what was happening, although the slow pace at which we descended and the direction of our stares might have alerted them. In those days, nobody seemed to care much about such events. Miss Lambrick—virginal in her smart Gorray skirts with the box pleats and pert black hat—sometimes caught the same tram and sat downstairs. No one told her what was going on. What words would we have used?

There was one word we couldn't use. Ever. No one should. Ever. But sometimes it appeared on walls, chalked or painted in bold capital letters. Between the tram stop and school there was a long, high-walled alley, no more than ten feet across, and some two hundred yards long, a short-cut. The headmistress took it and so did we. Occasionally she would hover, in her smart suit and suede court shoes, to see if any of her gels would walk along with her. Mostly we hung back, reluctant to be seen as toadies, but also because someone had painted, in bold red, this forbidden word on the wall of the alley. Several times. The thought of her eyes, and ours, lighting on FUCK at the same time was more than we could contemplate. We would have died with a shame that wasn't our own. The embarrassment would have convulsed us. Until, that is, we got to school and could share the tale. How could a single word have such power? Obviously words were worth attending to.

By the time I was in the fifth form I had my first serious boyfriend. By then my friends and I had hung around on street corners plenty of times, while boys on bicycles circled and sometimes stopped to talk. I had been to school conferences, drama productions and dances shared with boys' grammar schools during which there had been controlled fraternising. On such occasions couples had even breached the roped-off areas that led to dark classrooms and shadowy corridors to amble around, arms entwined, not knowing quite what to do next or daring to try to find out. I had attended ballroom-dancing classes at the Osborne Bentley School of Dance, where we learned the foxtrot and the valeta to Victor Sylvester recordings. We enjoyed the frisson of bodily contact and the volcanic excitement of a mistletoe waltz or an excuse-me quickstep. Walking home in the rain, there might be a few fumbled kisses in shop doorways but we had to watch out for spies.

Then, in 1950, when I was seventeen, I won a travelling scholarship to Holland and Belgium, sponsored by the two local Kemsley newspapers. Two pupils from each of Stockport's schools, those who had done well at School Certificate, were to travel by coach on a tour of the Low Countries, staying at youth hostels and seeing the sights. We wasted no time: within a few days of departure we were smoking, drinking and pairing off. Terry was tall and gawky, with loose, easy limbs, soft brown eyes and a large soft mouth. He joshed and joked with the other boys, his big Stockport voice leading the uproar. And he chose me. Looking back I can conjure our young selves, innocent and tender, our passionate feelings tethered by the way we'd been brought up. Everyone knew that nice girls didn't do it. But nice girls could be put under pressure. Terry didn't put me under pressure. And we were happy as we were, childishly happy, giddily pleased to have discovered this new treasure, the possibility of being suddenly close to a stranger. Every move was exciting, every gesture, every breath: we explored tentatively and together things neither of us knew about. And it was enough. We would continue to be a pair—virginal but passionate—until we went to different universities.

Terry appeared three more times in my life. Once in the mid 1960s, he arrived at my London home in a red Ferrari to take me to lunch at the Ritz, demonstrating his spectacular rise from a Stockport terrace to something successful in the City. Then, in the early 1970s, I arrived at a Richmond hotel near midnight and noticed his name in the guest register. I insisted even at that late hour that he was fetched from his room. He came bounding out, clothes evidently dragged on in a hurry, feet bare, to hug and fuss over me. We drank until after 2 a.m. The person I was with—not my husband—was not very pleased. Finally, a few years later, I turned on the radio news one morning in Edinburgh, where I was reporting on the festival, to hear that a helicopter carrying four British businessmen had crashed in the sea near Nice. Terry was named among them. There were no survivors. But that was all in the future.

Our love affair was more than enough for my mother. I had taken my camera on the trip to Holland—a box Brownie. Someone, fooling around, had taken a photograph of Terry and me kissing. We were fully clothed, in full daylight, at the back of a bus. Foolishly I took the print home. Out of the blue my mother called me to her: she had the knowing patience of someone who has you in their power, and the offending photograph in her hand. She proceeded with a humiliation ritual. Slowly she took newspaper and kindling, arranged it in the hearth—it was summertime, so there was no fire burning, but I was cold with the agonising slowness of it all. She heaped on the coal, and lit the paper. Once the fire was burning briskly she took the photograph and, waving it before me, lowered it dramatically into the heart of the fire. I was limp with pain, shame and humiliation. We stood together and watched it burn. She asked for no explanation and offered me none, concluding the occasion with 'And that's the last I want to see of such behaviour. Ever!'

I didn't know what to do with the shame. I went upstairs, sat on the bed and stared out of the window for a long time. There were no tears, just shock. Then, slowly, the blood began to flow again, and I dared to let my own thoughts emerge, to savour them, to feel comfortable with myself. I could recover from this. I must. I was being forged in some bitter fire of my mother's will, and I must

96

survive the moment and emerge as myself. Suddenly I was savagely and tremblingly angry. All the judgements being passed, the controls inflicted, must be defied and defeated. I could assess as well as she what was good or bad, right or wrong. In all my childhood, that was the moment when I had a sense of growing, of my essence under pressure to change, and deciding to be myself. That was the end of innocence, not the loss of virginity or any fumbling that fell short of it. It was when I crossed into adulthood, knew my own mind and was sure of who I was.

*   *   *

I needed to be in touch with other sorts of people, people like me interested in ideas. But how and where could I look for free spirits, dissenting voices and questioning minds? I was unaware of atheist intellectuals, who defied the received wisdom. In my younger years my *Girl's Book of Heroines* celebrated Grace Darling—the daughter of a lighthouse-keeper who had rescued drowning sailors—but didn't mention Mary Wollstonecraft. As I grew into the sixth form, we were warned against George Bernard Shaw. He was dangerous, defiant, and his women were assertive and bold. That was good enough for me. How did one get to be a Bernard Shaw heroine instead of the soppy do-gooding sort? How did you meet those sort of people? The answer, I discovered, was an institution called a university. They were grand and remote, and there weren't many. In 1937 there had only been twenty-one and none of my family had ever been to one. When my teachers urged the

possibility, my mother suggested Manchester—
'Then you can live at home.' That wasn't the idea
at all. I asked around and settled on one of the
agreed best: Cambridge. I set my sights on going
there without knowing what it would entail or even
what it looked like. Friends bought me a book full
of sepia pictures, views of colleges, but without any
people. I kept it by my bed. Cambridge became my
single-minded purpose in life. I had sidestepped all
the discussion about careers, vocations and earning
money—people didn't go in for that much then
anyway, certainly not women. I simply wanted to be
with clever people, living the life of the mind. I
started to work hard.

Slowly my horizons broadened. But I had a long
way to go. I didn't know where to start because I
simply didn't know what was out there. The
scholarship trip to Holland at the age of seventeen
had been my first time abroad since I'd visited
South America at five. The war had put a stop to
all personal travel, and after the war credit
restrictions were prohibitive: each adult was
allowed a mere twenty-five pounds' worth of
foreign currency each year. When the family
holidayed in France in 1951 I wrote of 'walking the
strange streets'. Everything had been new.

My school, I realise now, wasn't much help. My
French teacher could enthuse about Baudelaire,
but made no mention of Gide or Camus. The
school library was meagre: it offered stories by
Arthur Quiller-Couch and Harrison Ainsworth,
Hugh Walpole's *Rogue Herries* and John
Galsworthy's *Forsyte Saga*, but no Evelyn Waugh or
George Orwell. I settled for Vera Brittain's
Testament of Youth. Even in the sixth form my exam

98

choices weren't my own. I yearned to study English but that idea was dismissed: I had got only a 'credit', not a 'distinction' in School Certificate, which wasn't considered good enough for me to go on to the Higher. Privately I knew that the English mistress had taken against me, and there was no challenging that. There was no challenging anything, in fact. I settled, formally, for geography, history, French and Latin.

And I embarked on my own education, simply took off on my own. The Festival of Britain helped. The Arts Council commissioned and sent out touring exhibitions of British painting and sculpture. It was my first encounter with contemporary art, then as now sneered at by the press. I didn't know what to make of it, but I knew I wanted to see more. I remember the impact, like a jolt into a new way of seeing, made by Lucian Freud's *Interior near Paddington*. In 1951 it was part of an Arts Council touring show, which also included work by Francis Bacon, Ivon Hitchens and Victor Pasmore. At the Festival itself, on the South Bank, I escaped my family and made for the international sculpture in Battersea Park: Moore, Hepworth, Giacometti, Epstein. This was more like it, new and daring, what the current generation of creative people was up to.

Shakespeare, too, came into focus. I had learned the School Certificate set text—*Julius Caesar*—by heart. I played Hermia in the school's production of *A Midsummer Night's Dream*, joined the Garrick Society's junior wing and started acting there too: *Much Ado About Nothing*. I sought out Olivier's film of *Hamlet* and noted, self-righteously, 'Too much camera'. Books were not available in such abundance as they are now. Wartime restrictions had limited the amount of paper available to publishers and domestically there wasn't money to spare, so it was a rare treat to find a copy of *King John* in a second-hand-book shop. Relatives and friends didn't have much on their shelves either: our family had *Pears Cyclopaedia*, Bulwer Lytton and Samuel Butler in glass-fronted bookcases. And stacks of *National Geographic* magazines, which, like other children, I raided to see pictures of native women with bare breasts. I put it around that I would like all my Christmas and birthday presents to be books, and then at last they started to flow in, the standard classics—Dickens, the Brontës, Mrs Gaskell, Scott, Trollope, *The Oxford Book of English Verse*. The Brontës and Mrs Gaskell in particular were not only women but locals, writing about landscapes and cityscapes I knew. I lapped them up, acquiring as I went a dangerous, if predictable, infatuation with Mr Rochester and Heathcliff.

But it was drama that became my chief love. Here I was lucky: by the late forties cinema was the main popular entertainment, yet the repertory theatre system was still going strong throughout the country, with resident companies in even such small suburbs of Stockport as Bramhall and Wilmslow. An entire community went weekly— bunched under umbrellas through the regular rain—to see players they knew taking on different roles in plays that ranged from Robertson Hare comedies to, daringly, Noël Coward. In the bigger houses—Manchester's Palace Theatre and Opera House—Shaw was in the ascendant: his ideas were daring and outspoken, something to get your teeth into—*Pygmalion*, *The Apple Cart*, *The Doctor's Dilemma*. The fact that his ideas struck home more than his characters or wit is evidenced by my own attempt at writing a play. It was to be called 'These Things Will Be' and dealt with 'the struggle of the individual within the needs of democracy'. I worked on it excitedly for a week, night and day, then recognised its shortcomings and threw it away. But I was, in passing, cavalierly scathing about Shaw: 'One day he will be seen as a brilliant antique: Shakespeare will always be modern.'

This was a time when culture was flowering: Benjamin Britten's *Peter Grimes* at Sadler's Wells in June 1945 signalled the debut of the post-war revival. The Edinburgh Festival was founded in 1947, the Aldeburgh and Bath Festivals in 1948. People like us didn't go to such things, of course, but we knew about them because in September 1946 the BBC launched the Third Programme. It is hard to comprehend these days—now that broadcasts flow like water out of a tap, with lots of taps and different coloured waters—just how sensational the impact of radio, and especially the Third Programme, was for my generation. Like water, yes, but water brought to those parched in an endless desert. Here were concerts, talks, dramas, discussions of the highest intellectual standing, music I had not heard before, plays and talks about plays, reviews of art and exhibitions, news of the latest books. It was a cornucopia of riches—and people of my age clung to it, listening, learning the contours of criticism, arguing with friends about what we had heard, and even speculating about what golden creatures, blessed by knowledge and opportunity, must work for the BBC.

*   *   *

By January 1951 I had won a place at Newnham College, Cambridge. It was a dizzying moment. My headmistress set about organising for me a gap-year visit to France, but it was speedily vetoed. The burned photograph had spoiled my chances. Instead I stayed on in the sixth form, becoming head girl and head of house. I would have to wait a while to be free.

CHAPTER SEVEN

CAMBRIDGE DAYS

My arrival from the narrow, self-contained world of my home and school into the Cambridge of the 1950s was the single most significant event of my life, moving me for ever from the values and outlook of my limited horizons forward into whatever future I wanted to shape for myself. It was the biggest culture shock I have ever known. Jetting in later years from affluent metropolitan London into the poverty of Bombay, crossing Checkpoint Charlie from gaudy West Berlin to the austere, Stasi-ridden East, flying into James Bay to join the Inuit on an Arctic wild-goose hunt—none of these had such an impact on me.

For many of my contemporaries it wasn't like that. They arrived, effortlessly it seemed to me, the boys either directly from their public schools or officer-rank national service, the girls from such schools as Roedean, Cheltenham Ladies' College and St Paul's, into the next predictable stage of their education. Yet even they, unsurprised, were delighted with what they found. The recent war, still buzzing in our heads, had threatened our future. Now peace stretched to infinity. Here was certainty, beauty, freedom, opportunity, excitement and learning. We had all worked hard and here we were. As the trunks were deposited at our doors by college servants we smiled shyly, knowing we had entered paradise.

How much more so for me, stepping into the unpopulated sepia photographs of my Cambridge guidebook to find that I had, for the first time, a room of my own (alas, Mrs Woolf, no income of £500 a year), a hem-length black academic gown and a schedule of lectures to attend as only I would decide. The gown was obligatory wear for all lectures and for being out of college at night. As we rode our bicycles the voluminous sleeves flapped behind us, transforming us into a flock of giant dishevelled crows. I had a college scarf, too: grey and royal blue with an orange band running down the centre. Scarves were much in evidence among the newly arrived, a matter of pride, and a fast way to identify who was at which college. At Newnham I quickly made a nest of friends in Peile Hall, close girlfriends, whose temperament, regardless of background, somehow fitted well with mine. They gave me my core security from which to venture into the wider university. We all had bicycles, each with its owner's college name and number splashed in white paint on the rear mudguard. We would leave them unlocked at all times as a kind of common property and if one went missing, which was rare, we could be pretty sure it would turn up soon in the police cycle pound. No one had a car. There was little concern about security: we never locked our rooms and regarded it as a matter of friendship if someone popped in to borrow a glass or some biscuits. Books and coal were different: coal because we hoarded our weekly allowance so we could toast crumpets over the glowing embers of an open fire when we invited a favoured man to tea. The only security was the 'sported oak' in the older colleges, a heavy outer door that when shut meant the occupant was not to be disturbed, either studying hard or making love.

A good sprinkling of us had arrived courtesy of the 1944 Education Act and we were expecting to work hard. As a college scout put it to Jonathan Miller: 'Once they were all gentlemen on this staircase. Now there are more of them "up on their brains".' I was 'up on my brains' and believed myself to be in the vanguard of many more such students from modest backgrounds who would surely pour in after me. Although I knew we were privileged to be there, I thought we had earned it and also that the so-called elite—the 'gentlemen on the staircase'—was breaking up. Decades later I am amazed and disappointed that public schools still command so many places at Oxford and Cambridge.

Looking back I can see that I was indeed part of an elite, a chosen group to whom much was given and from whom much was expected. The fifties generation took those expectations seriously. Frederic Raphael, with whom I played tennis on long, sunny Cambridge afternoons, would call them

The Glittering Prizes. Many of those who became my friends were destined to write—biography, fiction and poetry—research, edit serious magazines, hold chairs in universities, engage in committed journalism, work at the BBC and even transform the post-war British theatre. But all that was still to come. No one mentioned getting rich or famous. If it happened, so be it, but what mattered was the work and our sense of purpose.

*   *   *

Because I was the first of the family and the second from my school to get to Cambridge I arrived loaded with armfuls of generous goodwill that probably hadn't propelled those whose family had come for generations from Eton. The vicar had written his good wishes. So had the editor of the local paper—the one that had sponsored the travelling scholarship. My godparents, the neighbours, teachers, of course, but also friends of my parents, my father's employer all sent me on my way as though I were an explorer heading for uncharted territory. My parents were tremendously proud. But it didn't do to be showy with emotions: my father beamed with delight; my mother hinted that there would be risks ahead.

And the Manchester aunties had been busy. They seemed to think that what I would need most were rayon tablecloths edged with heavy cotton crochet and embroidered with multi-coloured silks. These were lovingly subscribed, together with a medley of knitted jumpers and cardigans that didn't quite match, jam-pots, cake-stands, serviette rings and a cretonne bedspread. I tucked them guiltily out of sight at the bottom of the wooden chest in my room, known as a coffin, and brought them out only when my parents came visiting.

At Newnham I was living with girls whose clothes had come from shops, and who knew what cashmere was. Most of my things were the result of home dress-making, help from a lady in the village who ran things up, and the occasional prized item purchased for a special occasion. Even though I was eighteen my mother still chose my clothes: my own stunted taste ranged exotically in style from Betty Grable to Katharine Hepburn. Such fantasies had to be held in check, and my mother held the cheques. There was no youth culture as yet, no teenage market or younger generation. We dressed, for the most part, like our mothers.

In today's cultural jamboree, it's easy to dress outlandishly but hard to be noticed. In drab 1950s Cambridge even a modest flurry of display could make a splash. With the restraints of home and, for the men, two years of National Service completed, there was a good deal of sartorial flamboyance, some of it the theatrical camp of silk cravats and velvet smoking jackets, some the languor of Brideshead reflected in coloured waistcoats, garish bow-ties. Men's hair, which had been short-back-and-sides, was beginning to grow. It was regarded as racy to have it touching your collar. These were the arties—with whom I chose to mix—as opposed to the hearties, men in flat caps and twill trousers with red, county faces who gathered at the Pitt Club. And it was all irredeemably male. I bought myself a red coat: it was the least I could do. I little imagined that by my third year I would be lending my frocks to gay friends for their unconventional parties.

It wasn't only my clothes that weren't right. Neither was my accent—at elocution tests I had always scored badly. Living in Stockport, I hadn't got the hang of what supposedly correct speech sounded like. At Cambridge I could hear at once that some of the grander girls spoke in braying, honking tones that indicated class and money. Perhaps I should copy them, I thought. I made the switch instantly—and disastrously—affecting a sound locked somewhere at the back of my throat that emerged through tightened lips in a parody of speech that was in itself an affectation. I hadn't the confidence to be myself. That came slowly, and by then I was lumbered with a hybrid accent that no one could identify. Useful for a broadcaster, though.

*   *   *

I had won my place on the strength of the history entrance examinations, and for reasons now beyond recall had decided to embark on a degree in economics. My decision might have owed something to the fact that the new economics—of Beveridge and Keynes—underpinned the exciting new welfare state and the government's commitment to intervene in the interests of full employment, a stable economy and the redistribution of income. All this chimed with my burgeoning Labour Party politics and my belief that you could improve the world by rational means and thus be effective in making it a better place. And it was all tantalisingly nearby. Keynes had been at King's and was only recently dead. What was more, his example—as a member of the Bloomsbury set, founder of the Arts Council and of the Arts Theatre, Cambridge—demonstrated that economics needn't be a isolated discipline but could relate to the finer things in life. Joan Robinson, one of the greatest economists of the century, was currently working in Cambridge, the aged Professor Pigou, author of the magisterial *The Economics of Welfare*, still sat in his deckchair on a sunny corner of King's lawn, his rug and misshapen hat in place.

I was left entirely free to decide how hard I should work. It was truly alarming to have no one to tell me what to do. I didn't know how to function. I was issued with a reading list, and a chart of lectures. But all that was required of me was to deliver an essay a week, to be read aloud at an hour-long supervision shared with one other student, and which was then rigorously examined and analysed before we were sent forth with the next subject for the following week's session. In an eight-week term this meant eight essays. It sounds modest enough, but the hinterland of those essays was vast, covering, in my case, the whole range of economic organisation, the laws of international finance, statistics, trade, taxation, production, employment and investment. I was impressed, eager to please.

My supervisor was Ruth Cohen, one in a line of formidable women who demonstrated what I had already come to believe, that ideas were exciting in themselves, and that the life of the mind was an exhilarating prospect. Such women—and Newnham had plenty of them—slowly taught me how to concentrate, to bring all my resources to bear on the matter in hand, and to take pleasure in where my thinking would lead. This was learning for its own sake. No one spoke of careers, job prospects or earning potential.

Ruth Cohen received us—my friend Gillian Comins, who was my supervision partner, and I—in her Newnham rooms, full of colour, books and big lamps giving golden light. She would sit on the floor before a blazing fire, legs stretched wide apart before her, a packet of cigarettes and a lighter lying on the carpet between. She smoked continually, a dribble of ash trickling into the thick wool of her voluminous sweaters. Her hair, yellowed by cigarette smoke, was greying and dishevelled. I thought she was wonderful in her disregard for appearances. When in 1954 she was elected principal of Newnham, she took herself off, lost a couple of stone in weight, acquired a new wardrobe of smart suits and fine jewellery, styled her hair and took some notice of cosmetics. It was a transformation. She knew what was appropriate.

I proved no match for the study of statistics, and in my second year changed to history for Part 2 of my tripos. Eric Hobsbawm, then a lecturer at King's, was my tutor in economic history. He had arrived as an undergraduate in the 1930s, the first of his family ever to go to university, to find himself 'a stranger who knew nobody while, it seemed to me, everybody else knew somebody'. But this was the man who would become one of the great historians of the twentieth century, his autobiography *Interesting Times* providing a unique record of the European Left throughout his lifetime. In the early fifties, he was in his mid-thirties, lanky and eager, living the life of a single don. He had beautiful rooms in Gibbs Buildings, where we discussed my social life as well as the early history of trade unionism. He was also a Marxist and a member of the Communist Party. I wasn't shocked: there had been two Communist MPs in Attlee's post-war government after all. With the Korean war and the 1950 defection of the Cambridge spies Communist academics found it hard to get jobs. But Eric's academic reputation was already high, and he was made a fellow of King's in 1949. We would chart together the growth of early trade unionism.

My supervisor in European history was Betty Behrens, a woman of ferocious intelligence who had served in Whitehall during the war. She was ferocious in manner, too, impatient with those who weren't fluent in several languages. My Stockport teachers seemed pallid and dull by comparison. She had a thin, rangy elegance, striding the room waving a cigarette as she dissected every sentence with pitiless precision. She had money of her own, and lived in style and comfort. Her Newnham room had a brittle glamour, bright, acid-green silks, ashtrays and flowers. I loved being there, enjoying the boldness of its rarefied surroundings but living in fear of her exacting standards. 'What evidence do you have for saying that?' 'What makes you think that is true?' She was merciless. On occasion I fled in tears back to my room, clutching a demolished essay. But it was an excellent training for a journalist.

In my first term I flung myself into every kind of activity. I couldn't believe the freedom. When I explain to young women today how far women have come in just my lifetime, they gasp in shock at how rigidly controlled we all were. It is hard to convey that, in comparison with the values and world of the 1940s, the 1950s was a time of challenging new ideas.

One was existentialism, which then held sway in France under the reign of Sartre and de Beauvoir. It filtered through to Cambridge in film, theatre and even dress. I wasn't sure what it meant but it seemed to be a philosophy that sought freedom of action, that helped liberate the individual from the shackles of the past. The fable went that in an attempt to demonstrate the *'acte gratuit'*—the independent purposeless act—someone had, on an impulse, stabbed another with a lighted cigarette. I wasn't sure I relished freedom on that scale but it was certainly different from home.

To us there was glamour in all things French. Juliette Greco was then the existential *femme fatale*, singing her throaty songs in Left Bank *boîtes*. From my meagre pocket money I bought clothes that mimicked her style: tight black trousers, flat black pumps and black polo-neck sweaters. And I flaunted a long black cigarette holder. In those days black was not the universal choice it is today: if you wore black it was assumed you were in mourning. You were an object of sympathy and social tendernesses. So, in its tiny way, black was an assertion of difference.

We were passionate about the films of Jean Cocteau, *La Belle et La Bête*, and in particular *Les Enfants Terribles*, with its action—the passionate intensity of incest—set to the urgent sound of Bach. We took our cue from there. In an undergraduate production of Gabriel Marcel's *Ariadne* I, playing the lesbian Clarissa Beaulieu, was directed to make my entrance on the second phrase of Bach's Double Violin Concerto: a deliberate crib, but it carried just the degree of Gallic sophistication we were looking for. Ever since, whenever the music reaches that particular cadence, some tiny muscle in my mind gets ready to make my entrance on stage.

During my first term the freedom went to my head. I went to parties and got drunk. At home I had been allowed the occasional gin-and-It—Italian vermouth. One only. On the scholarship trip to Holland I had drunk beer and smoked. But now, let off the leash, I went out of control. I didn't realise the lethal effects of sherry, then the favoured party drink. Sometimes I passed out and had to be delivered home by friends who sobered me up before depositing me, just about able to walk, at Newnham's Lodge by ten o'clock at night. I wasn't the only one. As the route to Peile Hall is down one of the longest corridors in existence, I was often among several figures in the obligatory gowns weaving their way unsteadily towards their rooms. The hangovers were terrible.

Within my first weeks I had joined the Mummers Dramatic Society, the Heretics, the Labour Club, the English Club, the Marshall Society and the Film Club. I made friends in each of their different circles—almost too many friends, but I wanted to feast on everything, do everything, meet everyone, study hard, go to parties and, above all, to be perpetually in love. Women were in short supply and it was easy to be popular. I might have been intimidated by the women from posh schools, but not by the old Etonians or other ex-public-school boys, who were clumsy in their wooing and had no

112

more familiarity with sex than I had. I was as gauche as they, but much more anxious. There was no pill and I wasn't about to risk my hard-won freedom by sleeping with anyone. I went to their rooms for afternoon tea with cream cakes from Fitzbillies or the—inevitable—sherry . . . and disappointed their hopes. Meanwhile I lived in a state of high sexual frustration. And the partying became more frantic.

It couldn't go on. By the sixth week, I scarcely knew who I was. I recall leaning my forehead on a chill white-tiled surface somewhere and thinking, Stop this. Stop this. It isn't what you want. So I did stop it. Sudden freedom from the rigidity of school, the discipline of my mother's punitive depressions, had swept me too far, too fast. It was time to make choices.

*   *   *

In my second term the King died. I was attending a lecture in the Arts School lecture rooms where banks of seats rose steeply before the podium. As usual the lecturer entered, full-length gown flowing, disposed his papers on the lectern and began to intone a lecture he had obviously given many times. It allowed no room for exchange with students, no questions, scarcely even recognition that we were there. Scholarly, and absorbed in his scholarship, thumbs tucked into his gown, he paced, declaimed, walked up and down. Quietly, but visible to all, a college servant entered. In those days they had a particular style, almost but not quite servile, on the one hand aligning themselves with the dons rather than the students, on the other eager to be in cahoots with whichever of the 'young gentlemen' they thought might matter. This servant had a more purposeful air, clearly aware that he was the messenger of Destiny. The lecturer and servant whispered together briefly, then the servant left, looking neither to right nor left, on the next leg of his historic mission. The don turned to us. 'Ladies and gentlemen, I regret it is my duty to inform you that His Majesty King George the Sixth has died peacefully in his sleep.' There was a sharp but discreet intake of breath. No one had known he was dying—we knew little about royalty in those days. Our lecturer continued slowly and with dignity, as though the next statement was just as important: 'As a matter of respect this lecture will not be completed and you may leave.' He gathered up his papers and left. And so did we.

The same had happened in other lectures. Soon the streets were thronged with students not knowing what to do. The thing was to find friends, to have coffee, even a drink. I made for the Copper Kettle, a favourite rendezvous on King's Parade. None of my friends was there. Then I began to walk the streets without direction, wondering whether this was an historic moment and what would now be different. Gradually I became aware of a universal sense of bereavement—not sadness or weeping, that would have been too personal, too intimate, just a general sense of loss, austere and somehow loaded with significance, although we weren't quite sure what: the loss of a monarch.

George VI had been a shadowy figure in our lives. Not many people had television, and radio didn't help him as he had a terrible stammer. We had listened in reverent silence each Christmas

Day as he struggled to get out the phrases. No one, not even the youngest child, was permitted to giggle. We depended on black-and-white newspaper photographs to know what he looked like: rather slight and unremarkable. At school I had cut out a photograph of his daughter Elizabeth's wedding dress. I found it utterly glamorous and remote, and her husband, Philip, had just a hint of Snow White's prince. Now she would be queen, a woman on the throne, and one not much older than ourselves. There was a sense of lightheartedness about that: it felt, well, sort of contemporary, the turn of our generation.

Next day the Queen was proclaimed from the steps of the university's Senate House. I recall figures in red speaking rather pompous phrases in loud voices, and thinking that this was how it had always been, and would always be. 'The King is dead: long live the Queen': the quiet certainty of historical absolutes. But it counted for no more than a mention in my diary, alongside another of the day's events: 'Trinity party with Karl Miller, Thom Gunn, John Coleman, etc.' I wonder about the 'etc.'

In the months after the funeral the press filled its pages with a good deal of fanciful rhetoric. There was much talk of the New Elizabethans, a generation that would match in achievement that of the first Elizabeth. We were prompted to see ourselves in those terms, but we were not beguiled. When the Oxford Union held the Coronation debate 'That this House welcomes the New Elizabethan Age', Anthony Howard, then a student at Christchurch, spoke against what he called 'this maypole nonsense' and the motion was defeated.

For the Coronation, on 2 June 1953, Newnham, like many other colleges and households across the country, had acquired its first television set. But my own circle had other preoccupations: I was in the cast of a new play that was to open at the ADC Theatre the following night, and this was its dress rehearsal. We had no problem deciding our priorities. We rehearsed heartily all day long throughout the Coronation ceremony, then went across from King's to the Eagle to enjoy the extended licensing hours. We took it no more seriously than that.

*   *   *

The major choice I made in my second year was to become more involved in the theatre, to offer myself as an actress. To use the term 'amateur dramatics' would be to dishonour the high degree of self-regard and, indeed, national status that was then afforded to productions put on by students at Oxford and Cambridge. Many such performances were reviewed in the national press, which usually sent their leading critic to anything offered by the ADC or the Marlowe Society. Theatre blossomed in Cambridge at that time: virtually every college had its own drama society. Through the keening wind of Cambridge winters we would huddle into the welcoming warmth of dimmed lights in college chapels given over to their own productions. On luscious May nights we would sit among the powerful drift of scented flowers in Fellows Gardens along the Backs, and as the stars came out count ourselves blessed to be hearing Shakespeare in such a setting.

116

T. S. Eliot was then the establishment's darling. His anti-Semitism, now examined and condemned, went unremarked. The publication in 1944 of *Four Quartets* had struck a chord with the public at large. Post-war angst was about to creep up on us. What had all that struggle and effort, sacrifice and rhetoric been for? And what were we to make of our lives now the imperatives of conscription, austerity and patriotism had been removed? I had seen his play *The Cocktail Party* at Manchester's Palace Theatre in April 1951 and had somehow identified with its heroine, a sophisticated woman in the spoiled world of wealth and success who gives it all up to serve the natives in the poor world and meets a tragic and gruesome death in martyrdom. What sort of schoolgirl masochistic fantasy was that? Today it reads as merely silly. In 1949 it was the box-office hit of the Edinburgh Festival. Since the sixth form I had long felt Matthew Arnold's 'melancholy long withdrawing roar', of 'Dover Beach', as my own Christian faith receded. It simply ebbed away. Eliot's high-flown Anglicanism held it a moment longer: the beauty of his poetry told me I could love the liturgy and the ritual, the beautiful expression of Christian ideas, without accepting the doctrine. I still do.

I found myself in a production of *Murder in the Cathedral*. Its director was an American postgraduate student called Robert Gottlieb, who has since become a celebrated editor of the *New Yorker* and a publishing mogul. He arrived already married, with wife and baby in tow, and set up home in a house nicknamed Sibling Rivalry, where he presided over a court of adoring intimates, mostly women, of whom I was not one. He was tall, thin and hyperactive, with a mop of unruly hair falling over his face, goofy glasses and an implacable sense of what he wanted. Rehearsal periods were gruelling: we had to speak in unison and with the right expressionless delivery. The production was staged in Pembroke College chapel, and the boisterous clash of armour as the four knights broke in through the door and raced up the aisle to slaughter Thomas à Becket on the steps of the actual altar thrilled me every night. It was so flagrantly in defiance of how to behave in church.

Performances were given in the weeks of February 1953, when vast areas of East Anglia were under the worst floods the area had ever known. Sea defences from Lincolnshire to Kent had collapsed: 280 drowned, 13,000 were evacuated; people hung in trees and sat on roofs awaiting rescue. It was a real calamity to which we responded by joining Flood Relief—the habits of the war effort had not been forgotten. Gangs of us abandoned study and spent the daylight hours sorting and distributing clothes and goods for the homeless, then returned to Cambridge each evening to appear in the play. No work was done. We weren't so cut off in our ivory tower that we didn't know where our civic duty lay. Just as well I had another year before my finals.

Plays came from all cultures and in all languages. There was a production of Gogol's *Inspector General* in Russian. (Michael Frayn, as an inn servant, jammed the door on his exit, seeding, perhaps, an idea for his play *Noises Off.*) There was a production of *The Agamemnon* of Aeschylus in the original classical Greek, and a production by

118

John Barton of Shakespeare's *Julius Caesar* in what he claimed was the original pronunciation. This owed a good deal to Shakespeare's local Warwickshire, with a rolling Devon lilt and a component of my family's native Lancashire thrown in. We had no idea how John knew all this but we didn't doubt him. He was a rising star, already a postgraduate at King's, and soon to meet up with Peter Hall for their partnership career in the theatre beyond Cambridge.

My own share in this was modest enough, but for me, still loaded with my Stockport inhibitions, it represented a step into the searing limelight. I joined the Mummers rather than the more professional ADC so that I wouldn't be overawed by the apparently prodigious talent then on show. I needn't have bothered with my own petty anxieties. People were far too absorbed in developing their own personas to have time to sneer at others. I played the young girl Vera Alexandrovna in Turgenev's *A Month in the Country*, and Cecily in Wilde's *The Importance of Being Earnest*. In both cases the reviews noticed rather than praised me. Any tiny hope at the back of my mind that I might be destined for the stage received no encouragement.

Then I had a letter from Peter Hall, addressed, in the formality of the day, to Miss Rowlands and inviting me to audition. He had left things late at Cambridge: with serious ambitions such as his, he had wasted two years as an actor in not very big parts in other people's productions. In this, his third year, he would stage his first undergraduate production. He stepped fully fledged into the task, as though he'd been born knowing what to do. He never hesitated, worked minimally but precisely with his actors, deployed lighting and stagecraft with an accuracy that impressed us all. He recognised his calling at once: he directed four more productions that year, and left Cambridge to move directly to the Arts Theatre in London, which he proceeded to transform. There was to be no swifter or more purposeful rise of talent within our generation. But he was not alone. Round him coalesced a group of talents he would take with him to the top: Michael Birkett, who was president of the ADC and became Peter's deputy director at the National Theatre in 1975; John Barton, a lecturer at King's, who left academic life in 1960 to become Peter's assistant director at the Royal Shakespeare Company, and remained there as associate director, then director until 1991.

Point of Departure, by Jean Anouilh, starred Tony White, the one truly outstanding actor of our generation. Having won the minor part of First Girl I was on the stage with serious talent. It was like being close to a brazier of glowing coals. Tony had a natural easy grace, an animal beauty that put him in a class of his own. He swept through Cambridge theatre playing all the leading roles: Gaveston in *Edward II*, Mark Antony in *Julius Caesar*, Petruchio, Romeo and Cyrano. He went on to a career at the Old Vic where he was spoken of as the new Richard Burton. But the shallowness and inauthenticity of theatre troubled him and he gave it all up to become first a lamp-lighter, then to live in the remote West of Ireland. He has something of the 'Beat' spirit about him, anticipating hippie drop-outs by some ten years. I found it hard to understand the idea of dropping out when I was so eager to drop in. Tragically, he died in his mid forties, after an embolism following a football accident.

The play was a retelling of the Orpheus myth in modern dress—Cocteau's film *Orphée*, in which death is represented by leather-clad motorcyclists, seemed the most avant-garde chic at the time. My role required me to stride about the stage in very high heels, behaving like a trollop. I can't have done it very well. Karl Miller, already practising the critical wit that would see him through a lifetime of literary eminence, described me as 'playing a tart like the Virgin Mary'. Karl had been a friend from when we arrived in Cambridge—we went for coffee together after an early meeting of the English Club. He would invite me to Downing for tea served in white mugs round whose rims he had painted the names of his favourite poets. I recall Shelley and Dylan Thomas. So I forgave the comment, and reckoned it might well have been true. Of others in the cast Michael Mayne, who played the pimp, went on to be Dean of Westminster Abbey and Tony Church to be Director of Drama at London's Guildhall School. Michael Bakewell became BBC Television's Head of Plays and, in 1955, my husband.

*   *   *

Yet amid all the bliss that was happening, I found myself excluded from much of the fun. You will read nothing here of my excursions into the Cambridge Footlights or their legendary Smoker Evenings—private club performances for members and male guests. The freedom to smoke implied

121

the exclusion of women, who weren't allowed to join. My laughter was not among that greeting Jonathan Miller, newly arrived from St Paul's and famed for his Danny Kaye impressions. Instead, I knew Jonathan as someone intensely focused on ideas: I recall him on one occasion cycling past me, braking abruptly and dismounting to regale me with his latest insights into Wittgenstein. Nor was I witness to the early efforts of Frederic Raphael or Leslie Bricusse in Footlight sketches and songs. I knew them personally, but had to accept that there were many arenas to which women had no access. I didn't feel affronted: the world was like that. Women had to make do with invitations to the May Week revue, rather like Ladies' Night at a Masonic Lodge. Men might lust after us and buy us corsages of roses to wear on our ballgowns, but we were marginal to the real business of things. It was not until 1957 that women first appeared in a Footlights May Week Revue. Dorothy Mulcahy and Ann Jones were there at the insistence of the show's authors, Michael Frayn and John Edwards, but in the teeth of considerable opposition. Then Bamber Gascoigne, ignorant of the rule that kept women from Footlights Smokers, wrote a part in one of his sketches for Eleanor Bron. She was allowed to play it, but the rules weren't changed.

Other exclusions existed too. Women were not allowed in the Cambridge Union so we had no chance to gain debating skills. It was assumed we wouldn't need them. I joined the Labour Club and attended meetings addressed by John Strachey, Hugh Dalton and James Callaghan, but I hadn't the confidence to debate there. Instead, I sheepishly requested Clement Attlee's autograph at a Labour Club dinner. My role was a passive one, as listener and payer of my dues, only seeing any action when recruited to the dogsbody task of canvassing for the 1951 election, which Labour lost.

There were many things women couldn't do, but there were also many things forbidden to us all. Theatre itself was hedged around with ludicrous censorship. I have a letter from the Lord Chamberlain's office, sent to the Mummers when we submitted the script of Gabriel Marcel's *Ariadne*. Marcel was the heavyweight French intellectual who had actually coined the term 'existentialism'. None the less, we were required to cut the following exchange:

> 'Nine times out of ten these professional invalids are perverts.'
> 'Lesbians, as a rule! Oh! They don't always know it, of course.'

Quite what damage to our youthful psyches these words were meant to do, I can only guess at. I was, after all, at a single-sex college where such dalliance was not unknown. All of us knew that the adult world was full of constraints on our behaviour. We objected, complained and writhed in irritation, but in the event accepted the strictures of authority, we had no option. But we knew that the generation to which we belonged would get round to changing things in due course.

*   *   *

Already, in my first year, I had been caught up in a highly enjoyable row about blasphemy. Mark Boxer was a Cambridge star, handsome, witty, stylish. His sights were set on London society where he would lavish his talent on the then new world of glossy magazines, and scatter his witty drawings—signed 'Marc'—across the British press. In a May edition of *Granta* he published a poem 'Aubade' by Anthony de Hoghton, which denounced the deity in rather crude rhyming terms as 'a lazy old sod'. The proctors—who enforced the laws of the university, stalking the streets after dark for students who were without the obligatory gown—decided, on advice from the police, that the poem was blasphemous. In those days blasphemy counted for something, and plenty of people took offence. With my collapsing faith, I found it cheeky and bold that my friends on *Granta* went ahead with publication. Mark was rusticated—sent down from Cambridge until the end of term. *Granta* was suppressed for the rest of the calendar year. Nicholas Tomalin, *Granta*'s editor-in-waiting, took this particularly hard, and there was a great university fuss. I loved the sense of crisis, of scandal. Even E. M. Forster forsook the privacy of his life in King's College to join the protest, writing, with timid circumspection, that 'The proctors had a problem and were obliged to take some disciplinary action over the *Granta* poem', but calling on the prohibition of the magazine to be rescinded because 'It suggests that discipline has degenerated into the desire to punish.'

What makes the whole episode seem now such a period piece was the style of Mark's exit from Cambridge: a Victorian funeral hearse, complete with plumed horses and swathes of black crêpe, collected him from the front of King's, where Hugh

Thomas, at that time president of the union, later ennobled by Margaret Thatcher, delivered a funeral oration. Then the procession of students left for the station, Mark sitting aloft in black topper with crêpe ribbons. Like many others, I wore black for the occasion.

Mark, who already had links with London publishing, later invited me to pose with bare breasts for *Lilliput*, a fifties magazine that interleaved short stories with discreet sepia-toned photographs of draped nudes, offering tasteful excitement appropriate to the times. Mark planned an edition of 'Cambridge lovelies', promised me forty pounds and a young photographer called Antony Armstrong-Jones. My family kept me desperate for cash and I needed the money. But at the last moment I lost my nerve. The ghost of the burned photograph hovered in my mind. Such exposure wasn't worth the risk, even for the satisfaction of defying my mother. Instead I confided in my father about the proposed deal. On the quiet he gave me the forty pounds from his own pocket even though he must have known that I wouldn't have had the nerve to go through with it. But by now he was doing well in his job and enjoyed sharing his money.

We liked our crises laced with theatricality, and we liked our studies that way too. I didn't only attend the often arid lectures on my degree subjects: I couldn't resist going to hear those of high-performing dons and lecturers. Noel Annan, soon to be a relatively young provost of King's, delivered his lecture on Leslie Stephens with all the panache of Henry Irving. His domed head held high, his immaculate suit and bow-tie, the gorgeously sonorous voice, the pleasing vanity of his self-regard made him a star.

F. R. Leavis was a star of quite another kind: his attitudes of high moral judgement dominated the thinking of many of those then reading English. It seemed you were for Leavis or against him, and he certainly saw it like that. The war was on between Leavis at Downing College, with the magazine he edited, *Scrutiny*, and the English faculty, entrenched at Kings' College. Leavis put morality at the heart of all his judgements, an attitude that infected an entire generation. Unhappily his judgements involved insulting those he didn't admire, and often his lectures were spiked with malice—students responded to that too. I heard him lecture on Auden, taking a poem I admire, 'Musée des Beaux Arts', and destroying it line by line, persistently and repetitively spitting with contempt the name 'Mr Auden'. Many friends spoke of Leavis's brilliance, and his courage in crusading for writers he regarded as the central canon of English literature—D. H. Lawrence, George Eliot—but I couldn't bear the hurt and jealousy of rejection that fuelled his vituperation. I caught from it, perhaps, a whiff of frustrated energy gone sour that I recognised from home.

Nikolaus Pevsner was different again. His lectures attracted hundreds newly dedicated to appreciating the wealth of architecture we have in Britain. The war hadn't long gone, and it was strange to find a German—albeit a Jewish refugee—taking it upon himself to chart with such meticulous scholarship the architectural wealth of Britain that German bombs had recently done so much to demolish. Published from 1951, the

Pevsner Guides were an instant hit and remained so. Years later, for a BBC television programme, I took my original edition of *Derbyshire* and explored again the places he described across the county. Some wheel had come full circle.

E. M. Forster didn't lecture but we all knew he lived at the top of staircase A of King's College, which had been his permanent home since 1946. He seemed to reserve himself largely for his college, but on one occasion I was invited to a party he hosted, as I recall, for the English Club. I went in awe to meet the legendary figure and was soon neatly hooked on a nice piece of Bloomsbury condescension. I had travelled recently in Italy for the first time and was eager—too eager—to share my enthusiasms with him. He was kindly disposed as I praised the Donatellos and Della Robbias, listened with patience to my extolling of Orvieto and Urbino, even joined in with a reminiscence or two of his own before allowing me to run on unguardedly about Leonardo's *Last Supper* in Milan, 'and the cathedral,' I rattled on, offering myself unthinkingly as bait, 'those soaring Gothic pinnacles, the stained glass, what an amazing place'. He smiled his agreement. 'Yes, yes,' he replied. 'It is all quite hideous, isn't it?' I recoiled as if hit across the face. Such a condescending rebuff, and from the man who had made the phrase 'only connect' the motto of his morality. Later I reflected on what another Bloomsbury figure, Virginia Woolf, had said of James Joyce: 'A self-taught working man and we all know how distressing they are, how egotistic, insistent, raw, striking and ultimately nauseating.' Yes, I thought, and I know whose side I'm on.

*   *   *

In the early 1950s there were two colleges exclusively for women, Newnham and Girton, home to some thousand students, and fourteen for men, housing some nine thousand students. No one had begun to consider that they should be integrated; no one would do so for another twenty years. Many of us—both men and women—had arrived from a life already spent largely in single-sex institutions. The boys had been to prep then public schools, followed by two years' national service, an unquestioned obligation left over from the war that was only abolished in 1960. While still at school I had written plaintively in my diary: 'This conscription is terrible. The boys leave home at 17 and go in the army . . . life for girls at home is wretched. There is much letter writing. Feminine society is depressing.'

We all arrived at Cambridge eager to make up for lost time. But the two sexes were strangers to each other. Many of us were virgins, full of the passionate lusts of youth, but awkward and nervous in our early encounters. I was interested in the whole person, as keen to talk as to kiss. But that wasn't what many men had in mind. There were to be brutish and bruising moments in my first terms when I, having accepted coffee or drinks by way of, I thought, proffered friendship, would find myself fighting off forced attention, crying, 'No! No!' and meaning it.

Newnham knew the risks and had in place rather muddled rules supposedly to keep us safe. Men were not allowed in our rooms after ten o'clock at night, and each woman leaving college for the evening had to sign out and then be signed back in by eleven. No problem there. In my first year I had a room on the ground floor with large sash windows opening on to the gravel path. It was around midnight that the tapping would start and girls, dishevelled from climbing the wrought-iron gates or the college's encircling fence, would use my room as a route to their own. It was all rather larky, reminiscent of the antics in girls' boarding-school fiction I'd once envied. By the third year we had become more adept, not signing out at all, leaving a rolled blanket to masquerade as our sleeping selves and passing the night in the men's colleges. Discovery would have meant immediate expulsion. Even then, these weren't occasions of unbridled debauchery. We frowned on promiscuity, believing in our solemn way in love and loyalty, and tentative sex. And later, but not much later, marriage.

I had met Michael as a fellow actor in *Point of Departure*. I had first noticed him passing in the street, and wondered who it was with such a strikingly handsome head, always so intently engrossed in conversation. Gradually we found ourselves drawn into overlapping circles of friends, Michael being particularly close to the poet Harry Guest who was then, with Ronald Hayman, busy founding and editing small poetry magazines. Michael had done his national service in the air force where, at his interview for consideration as an officer, he had boldly stated that he believed Taiwan should be handed over forthwith to Communist China. The interview and his prospects of promotion had ended there. Undeterred, he resolved to use his time to good effect, deciding to read a book a day for each of his days in uniform. He arrived at Cambridge prodigiously knowledgeable about the literatures of several cultures. I was impressed, by his defiance of conventional ambition and his single-minded sense of what mattered to him.

Michael was a good actor. He had a soft mellifluous voice and a proper understanding of how poetry should be read aloud. He was reading English at King's College, and was something of a favourite with his tutor Dadie Rylands who would in our third year cast him as the Fool in his virtually static but brilliantly spoken *King Lear*. Michael loved theatre and literature and music and art with a kind of intensity I came to share. Long before we were lovers—several terms before—we became closer and closer as friends, finding each other's company easy, sympathetic. We always would.

Before I knew Michael I'd been on a merry-go-round of love affairs: some fleeting, some flirtatious, some briefly heart-wrenching. Some were rather more boisterous: Snow White being hunted by wolves. With my Stockport shyness and sexual ignorance I must have come across as a bit of a tease. When Karl Miller spoke of a mutual friend as 'sexually fluent' I nearly fainted at the sophistication of it all. The only way to avoid being called 'sexually clumsy' was to say no. But Michael and I came from similar backgrounds, modest lower-middle-class parents living conventional lives and pinning their pride on the achievements of talented children. With Michael there was plenty I didn't have to explain.

In the summer of 1953, I had my mother's permission to travel with my Peile Hall friend Angela Linger to Rome. Angela, who was studying modern languages, had arranged for us to stay with a family. But things didn't happen like that. In defiance of the plans drawn up and agreed at home, I stopped off in Paris to meet up with Michael, who was doing a summer course at the Sorbonne. After a week together we travelled on to Rome where we found Angela already happily involved with an Italian called Giorgio. Michael and I, pausing only to hear Martinelli sing in the Terme di Caracalle, took off for Florence where we rapidly and thoroughly fell in love.

Two things must strike the modern young woman about this: first, the enormous palaver that was needed to escape my mother's dictates—why didn't I simply ignore her and push off? Second, the innocence that then surrounded the concept of falling in love. The two were not unconnected. Despite our problems my mother was still one of the people I loved most in the world. That love, crystallised in so many snatches of memory—being lifted before the firelight into my parents' arms, the laughter of a young woman on the deck of a transatlantic liner, the person leaning tenderly over my sister and teaching me motherhood—was something I couldn't abandon. Better to hold on in hope. But Milan Kundera, who writes so wryly of such things, calls love 'the glorification of the present'. Falling in love brought that kind of intensity. It didn't obliterate what had gone before so much as transcend it. I had found a new way of relating. I felt as if my life was lightened. I walked on air. Soon Michael and I were talking about

131

spending the rest of our lives together. That could only mean one thing.

But we weren't interested in the stale, old-fashioned model of marriage we saw in older people. We knew that to be full of hypocrisy, boredom and disappointment. We knew that divorce would be a wretched admission of our failure. But we would have a new relationship, direct, equal, passionate. We had read our D. H. Lawrence and we were fearless. Not for me the ignorance and anxiety that had so repressed my mother's generation: there would be no more burning of photographs.

Rodin's sculpture *The Kiss* reflects just such idealised passion. In 1955 the Tate Gallery was mounting a campaign to raise funds to buy it. Whenever Michael and I went there, we contributed whatever our purses could afford. It was a sort of pledge between us. Today the statue looks both chaste and tender, the cold white marble of the two naked bodies, hardly meeting, their mouths scarcely touching. The couple are ageless, without character or identity. Their tenderness is poignant but stops far short of sexual abandon. It has taken Cornelia Parker, who bound the statue in string, to bring them into more passionate contact. Yet for me it always conveyed the passion I had repressed for so long.

*   *   *

Given the monastic nature of much schooling at the time, it isn't surprising homosexuality was widespread, but the easy way it was accepted at Cambridge astonished me. King's College was renowned as its citadel. Bonds between teacher and taught had long been the tradition of the public schools. Teachers and dons would take parties of young boys climbing in the Alps, reading poetry on the Rhine. It was the legacy of the culture of Housman and Lytton Strachey, J. T. Sheppard and A. C. Pigou, the classical ideal re-created in the lyrical beauty of Cambridge. No one spelled it out: it wouldn't have been wise. There was both a civilised acceptance of such relationships, and at the same time a sharp awareness that in the wider world disclosure, certainly any element of flamboyance, could bring down the law.

That was exactly what was happening. In 1951 the British diplomats Guy Burgess and Donald Maclean, who had met at Cambridge in the 1930s, defected to Russia for whom they'd been spying. Burgess was a colourful homosexual and the idea was gaining ground that homosexuality, and the secrecy it entailed, implied subversion. Police seized the chance to crack down, especially on the indiscretions of public figures. In the summer of 1953 Lord Montagu was jailed for a year for indecent assault; that autumn the newly knighted John Gielgud was arrested for soliciting in a public lavatory. Once again, as with censorship, there were civilised values and there was the law. They didn't coincide.

This was true of publishing too. D. H. Lawrence—along with Evelyn Waugh, but for different reasons—was hugely popular at the time. His concept of the sacramental marriage of the flesh, his explorations of the sexuality of men and women were just what we needed. It chimed both

133

with our tentative experiments and high-minded moral judgements. *Sons and Lovers* and *Women in Love* made me catch my breath with recognition. These were real people—or, at least, real in my head. And here was someone whose books, in orange Penguin paperbacks, were selling like hot cakes, who was lauded by Leavis and others, yet whose most daring book, *Lady Chatterley's Lover*, was banned as obscene. Nor could we read Genet or Henry Miller. We couldn't wait for the law to catch up. We bought copies in Paris during the holidays and smuggled them home.

The prevailing ethic was not to get caught. The same injunction applied to sex. There was no pill and, as far as I was concerned, total innocence of birth control. One or two girls had liberated mothers who marched them off to the doctor and had them fitted with contraceptive caps—those mothers tended to be divorced, which went with the racy lifestyle I so admired—but my own mother couldn't help there. She herself didn't know the facts. Eventually I explained birth control to her. Later, when I was married, she admitted, rather shyly, 'I wish I'd known all this when I was young.' But it was too late for her, for me, and for our relationship. At Cambridge, I had to go it alone. Even then I was defeated. In my third year I went up to London to see a doctor, wearing a putative engagement ring. He was large, florid and Irish and didn't know who I was. I was curtly dismissed with 'A young woman like you should want lots of babies.' I returned to Cambridge in tears and took my chances.

My friend Elizabeth Palmer was less lucky. She found herself pregnant and didn't know what to do.

So she did nothing, and went on doing nothing about it, attending lectures, studying for exams and keeping her secret. Eventually the sight of her cycling full tilt along the Backs, coat flying open, left no one in any doubt. But still we didn't speak. There was a kind of moral paralysis, a panic, a sense of leaving it to her. In the end she was called in to see her tutor, who was concerned and sympathetic but insisted she must inform the principal, Dame Myra Curtis, who was less generous, insisting she pack her bags and leave Cambridge at once. Her boyfriend, Nigel Calder, at Sidney Sussex College, stayed and took his degree but was rusticated. Lizzie never took hers. They were married at Hampstead register office when she was six months' pregnant. In the afternoon they defied their banishment and returned to Cambridge for a party at a friend's rooms in Jesus. The invitation was a defiantly witty version of *The Waste Land*:

Elizabeth and Nigel, six hours wed,
Forget the cost of living and the rustication
And the better or worse,
     A current in KP
Tells their tale in whispers. As they change their station
They pass the stages of their age and youth
Entering the whirlpool.
     Gentile and Jew,
O you who drink the cup and take your Tripos
Pause for party, and exult it fall not upon you.

After the party they took a bus to Huntingdon for a one-night honeymoon. In 2004 they will

135

celebrate their golden wedding anniversary.

*   *   *

Into all this sunlight and shadow would descend my mother and father, usually once a term. Their were strange visitations. Within a single weekend I would revisit the entire evolution of my life with them.

On their arrival there was no question that my mother was delighted to see me, proud, bewildered, without bearings in the social ferment of student life. Nervous too—that I might not perform well in the play they had come to see. My father, my ally, exuded pride. At first my mother's excitement set the tone: she loved learning new things, being told about art and music, theatre and books. It was fun to kindle her interest. She would enjoy gossip (carefully screened) of friends and acquaintances. And I, putting aside recent hurts, would respond, hoping to snatch something from the wreckage. Having discovered such a wonderful life in Cambridge, I could afford to be generous towards her. And so I would begin, loving, eager to please, trusting. But soon old patterns rose up to defeat us: her failure to curb my will, her obsessive anxiety that I might do something—anything—to disgrace a family that had fought so hard to improve its place in the world. My father was helpless to reassure her. All the while she was alert and watchful, prowling my life for clues. And there was always something. On one occasion a friend had left his jacket in my room, forgotten, unremarked. But it was obviously a man's jacket. It was as though she had found us naked together.

136

The nausea of the burned photograph came instantly over me, rising in my gorge with the stickiness of a black crime as I stuttered some explanation. The sparkle had gone. Willing as I was, eager even, I came to realise I would never share the joy of my life with her. Somewhere there was too much damage.

*   *   *

By the beginning of 1954 I was looking at Cambridge through the eyes of a departing lover. There was all the tension of the final degree examinations to distract me, and then the usual flurry of parties, plays and May balls that followed. But beyond that the prospect loomed of leaving somewhere I had been so completely happy. The beauty of the place was almost painful: it would continue, of course, but no longer be mine. The friendships, the secure ones, would continue, too; there would be work and opportunities in the world outside. London—a strange and mysterious place where serious business was conducted—would be the next stage for me, and I was enthusiastic to embrace it. But Cambridge had beguiled me. I was in thrall to its beauty. In those last weeks I walked its streets in raptures, gazed at its doorways, arches, cornices, its towers and spires, gateways and alleys. I sat in silence in its chapels, glided in punts along the Backs, dawdled in its gardens, gazed at the shifting green shadows of its river, and walked and walked. I drank it in, deep nourishing draughts to sustain in me for ever a belief in learning and purpose. And the knowledge of friendship, love and happiness.

Then I packed my trunks and headed for London.

CHAPTER EIGHT

THE BIG WIDE WORLD

London was in many ways a continuation of Cambridge by other means, an undergraduate life writ large. The world was ours for the having. In the mid-1950s there was little unemployment, plenty of the kind of work we were qualified to do. Money was not an issue: the country had embarked on the post-war boom, inflation was low, and a couple could live well enough on the income of one. So what were we to make of the world that lay before us?

With no burden of student debt, we could afford to coast. In the corners where I moved, we had been auditioning for our futures in the places where we were also having fun: acting in and producing plays and musical shows, writing and editing *Varsity* and *Granta*, writing poetry and founding poetry magazines, running the English Club, the Labour Club, the Film Club. These were the arenas in which many of us would find jobs. Others were following their training as doctors, architects and scientists. There were paths to take, routines to follow, but no one felt under pressure either to earn or achieve. If we were any good these things would come, but mostly we were simply interested in what we did.

The overwhelming mood of optimism that had

swept the country at the end of the war had by the early fifties been seriously tempered by disappointment. Austerity had intensified after the victory and rationing got harder: bread, which had remained unrationed throughout the war, was suddenly in short supply. When I went up to Cambridge, cheese had been rationed to an ounce per week, and we were given a small portion of butter and sugar too. There was no central heating and each girl was allowed two buckets of coal per week for the open fire in her room. When word got round that so-and-so had lit a fire, we would all crowd into her room and huddle round it for warmth and cocoa. We were perpetually cold: the brisk winds across the icy flat expanses of Cambridge numbed our limbs and reddened our faces. Now, heading for London and jobs with our own incomes, we were ready for things to get better.

And things were getting better, though at an intolerably slow rate. Rationing only came to an end in 1954, almost ten years after the war had ended, and national service had another six years to run. I wonder now how we all put up with it, but we had been schooled by wartime disciplines to obey, and to accept the direction of our lives by the state. The older generation were too exhausted by what they'd been through to have the energy for the sort of popular pressure that would be brought to bear today. There was grumbling and complaining. People muttered about what winning the war had been for. In 1951 they voted out the Labour government but greeted the return of the ageing Churchill with little enthusiasm. His moment of greatness had passed. Fourteen years later I would take my six-year-old daughter to watch his funeral. A kindly policeman at the edge of the pavement held her hand as the gun-carriage went by. I wanted her to see history happening: Churchill had been part of mine.

By the mid 1950s a mighty tide of change was on the way. A new popular culture was in the making. Records were beginning to matter. I'd always collected a few—heavy black shellac recordings with paper sleeves, Pee Wee Hunt's 'Twelfth Street Rag', and Joe Loss's 'In the Mood', swing music for couples dancing together, but now vinyl was coming in, and the new craze for heart-throbs and fans was getting out of control. In 1954, my sister, still a schoolgirl back in Hazel Grove, went silly at the sound of Johnny Ray's 'Such a Night'. Then, in 1955, Bill Haley's 'Rock Around the Clock' hit the country: on a return visit to Cambridge I heard it played at all the parties. The dancing was suddenly uninhibited, too. By 1956, when Haley toured Britain, young people were rioting in cinemas, tearing up seats, screaming and shouting, defying the police. It was both shocking and exciting. As far as we knew, nothing like it had ever happened before. Looking back, I can see that this was when the idea of 'the teenager' took off. In my adolescence, whenever we had come together in groups we were seen as shadows mimicking the style and behaviour of our parents' generation: the junior tennis club, the Junior Garrick Society, the junior choir. Suddenly the term 'junior' was defunct. Now my sister's friends were choosing this new music. Soon all she and I had in common was Sinatra's *Songs for Swinging Lovers*. Pop music began to define and divide generations.

How do people make choices? How was I to decide what to make of my life? I didn't have a career plan or any specific ambition. In the spring of 1954 I had cycled out of Cambridge to a large house set in leafy grounds, off the Trumpington Road, that constituted the University Appointments Board. The section that dealt with Newnham was run by Kay Baxter, herself a Newnham graduate. I had given the idea of a job virtually no thought until I deposited my bicycle against the fence and went inside to listen. I don't think I can have listened very carefully, for I don't remember any mention of business or banking, corporate companies or management institutions. I don't think we were particularly interested in such things. It might be that an inner censor put them beyond my hearing, or a cultural snobbery awarded them the status that 'trade' had once held among the aristocracy. The fact was that companies and banking were about money, and money didn't rank high among my values.

Getting rich was not the main objective. I saw money as a superfluous part of the equation. What I wanted was a fulfilled life. It seemed to me that it was better to examine what the components of that 'fulfilled life' might be and move directly towards them, rather than to suppose that having plenty of money would allow you to buy them.

As far as I was concerned, the components stacked up quite simply: interesting and meaningful work where I enjoyed the freedom to exercise my own choices, an engagement in some way with the world of ideas, a matrix of strong relationships, with both family and friends, at the heart of which would be the intimacy of a good marriage and the rich satisfaction of bringing up children who themselves would be happy and fulfilled. I had made a start: Michael Bakewell and I had decided to spend our lives together. That mattered more than anything else.

I have written it down as I conceived of it then. In today's terms it sounds both high-minded and platitudinous. Indeed, at the time I *was*—many of us were—high-minded. In her diary of 1957, Sylvia Plath, who arrived at Newnham the year after I left, described for herself and Ted Hughes 'the life we believe in living: never becoming slaves to routine, secure jobs, money; but writing constantly, walking the world with every pore open and living with love and faith'. 'Writing constantly' was not on my horizon but otherwise I shared her vision of freedom and exhilaration. As for 'platitudinous', it is of course easier to write a broad and gushing expectation of life than to live it. The thing is to keep the target in your sights.

In the house off the Trumpington Road, I learned my options: the Civil Service—I wasn't clever enough for the higher echelons and didn't fancy the rest; teaching, a more prestigious and authoritative career than it is now, and many friends chose it, several returning to the public-school system from which they'd come; publishing, which lured many English graduates, especially women who combined being readers with caring for children and becoming writers themselves; and then there was the BBC.

My application form says I was interested to

work in 'programme production in either Sound or Television'. In the 1950s radio was still what people meant by the BBC. It sat at the heart of London in the handsome, liner-like Broadcasting House in Langham Place; somewhere out in West London a doughnut of a building was going up to house television studios. But the essence of the BBC resided in the complex of radio studios that were to be found behind the marble entrance hall of Broadcasting House with its lofty inscription approved by Lord Reith, which probably a good percentage of its employees could translate from the Latin.

It was the autumn of 1954 and I was applying to be a studio manager: 'Miss Rowlands is a communicant member of her parish church and is a young woman of high moral character. She has a pleasant manner, speaks well and is of good appearance. Her family is of good standing and her home background is a cultured one.' So said one of my two referees. With my moderate degree, and some boasting about my exploits in Cambridge theatre, it was enough to get me an interview in which I was asked, by way of testing my general knowledge, what characterised the architecture of Cheshire manor houses. 'Half-timbered, black and white,' I said, and I was in, a signed-up member of the BBC staff. That was all it took.

Other Cambridge friends had already come this way. The year before, Eve Burgess had travelled straight from Girton to become Auntie Eve in the legendary *Children's Hour*. But in 1954 Claire Delavenay, later Tomalin, who had a first-class English degree, was rebuffed: 'It is not the policy of the BBC to consider women for the general trainee

143

scheme.' There were other blanket bans, too: 'People do not like momentous events such as war and disaster to be read by a female voice,' ran a 1951 announcement declaring that from now on news would be read by eight selected males, none with a 'dialect voice'. It wasn't merely discouraging: it said to me and thousands of other women that in the post-war world the heights of public life were to be largely a male preserve, conducting affairs in standard English.

After a mysterious excursion into the world of secrecy, Michael had arrived straight from university as a fully fledged BBC radio drama producer. The excursion concerned a recommendation from his tutor that he turn up for an interview at Hyde Park Gate where all would be explained. It wasn't. In fact, the circumlocution of the interview was so obtuse that it was only half-way through that he realised he was being recruited as a spy. He wasn't called back.

Drama producer suited him much better: he had been a fine actor and director at Cambridge, president of the prestigious Marlowe Society. All that theatre at Cambridge was proving fruitful. My job at the BBC was on the other side of the tracks: I was to be a studio manager—it was a way in, from which I hoped to make it across to the creative production side, but it turned out to be a bad move: I took the training course twice and proved to have no aptitude for it at all. I couldn't handle the technology, modest as it then was. I didn't understand electricity, sound waves, decibels, frequencies, any of it. I was simply a non-starter, a no-hoper. But I wasn't discouraged: my sights were stubbornly set on the Drama Department, where

144

Michael was having some success. And the BBC persisted with me—they didn't sack people for incompetence in those days: I enjoyed a brief attachment to Drama.

In the 1950s it was customary for each major radio drama to employ three studio managers and rehearsals would last anything up to a week. It was normal for a ninety-minute play to have five days to rehearse and record, rather than the two and a half they get now. The grander producers in the Features Department—Douglas Cleverdon, who cajoled Dylan Thomas into writing *Under Milk Wood*, and Louis MacNeice, who was a law unto himself—could even rehearse for up to eight days. There was no sense of stress and usually, after fairly low-level huffing and puffing, nothing was denied them.

As well as employing freelance actors, producers also drew on the resources of the BBC Repertory Company, which, like any regional rep, included actors who could cover the whole range of typical parts. Its members were in and around the Broadcasting House studios every day; they became familiar figures, friends. The canteen would be full of programme-makers—actors, producers, studio managers—a community of colleagues dedicated for the time being to a single creative enterprise. It was my first experience of one of the strong but fleeting rewards of making programmes, and one of the reasons I continue to do so after four decades.

Of the three studio managers working on a drama production the most senior would control things from the gallery, presiding over the panel of knobs—sound-pots, we called them, which brought together the entire sound output of the programme—actors, music, sound effects; the second would work in the studio among the actors, making the noises, stirring teacups, slamming doors, clattering coconuts as horses' hoofs, even squeaking bedsprings to indicate sex, or slicing cabbages in half to sound like the guillotine in action; the third would preside over a bank of gramophones in the gallery where heavy old 78 rpm records furnished other sounds—music, seagulls, crashing cars—called for in the play. The technique for getting this recorded moment right was extremely crude. A large yellow crayon was sharpened to a fine point, then jammed into the record groove at the spot just before the sound arrived. The record was then wound backwards by hand and the machine switched off. When the actors reached the cue, you switched it on and swung the record into play by hand, hoping it would find the right speed as you turned up the volume. The idea was to bring forth the sound with inspired timing and seamless plausibility, without catching too much of the hiss created by the bits of crushed crayon.

In 1954 the status of the BBC had never been higher. It enjoyed an unrivalled reputation from the war: unrivalled because it was the sole voice to tell people at home what was happening, and to keep their morale up with innocent comedy shows from which jokes about religion, sex and politics were banned. But by the mid-1950s this, too, was changing.

Two forces were now in play, which have continued in tension ever since. As studio managers we worked, ate and drank with producers

146

who were struggling to innovate and change. Michael was one of those fighting the old guard of the Drama Department, then headed by Val Gielgud, brother of John in whose shadow he stood. The crisis seems to have crystallised round a departmental meeting on 3 November 1955 to discuss experimental productions. 'Heaven defend us from an outbreak of *Godot*-scripts where the tricks only just hide an almost complete lack of anything to say,' declared the old guard. Barbara Bray, then a leading young script editor, spoke up for change: 'Third Programme planners will have to be prepared not only to be daring initially, but also to persist in the face of possible audience resistance long enough for public taste to accommodate itself.' And so it happened. The progressives carried the day. Within a couple of years a whole generation of British writers—John Arden, Harold Pinter, John Osborne, Arnold Wesker among them—were being given their first opportunities on BBC radio. The new post-war generation of British playwrights was learning its craft.

The other tension just dawning in the broadcasting world was that of competition and the ratings race. We gathered in huddled groups in the basement canteen to hear the latest reports from the world of television, how there would soon be another channel outside the BBC, and lots of jobs to be filled. Gossip and rumour fuelled our excitement. But how to get trained? And how to do so quickly?

In September 1955 Independent Television arrived, breaking the BBC monopoly. Within a year 60 per cent of the television audience had swung to

ITV. The BBC responded in panic: 300 key programme makers were offered big rises if they'd promise to stay. A memo sent to the director general in 1956 from Richard D'Arcy Marriott, who had been invited to think the unthinkable and imagine commercial radio, has a nice touch of period condescension:

> The programme policy I advocate implies the rejection of an attitude that many of us have grown up with, of having a mission to educate, to up-lift, to lead people on to better things, to give them what we think they ought to want rather than what they do want ... We ought to remember that about half the population consists of very simple people, with not very much education who look to radio for their entertainment and relaxation—and who shall say that they are wrong?

If the BBC programme culture was primarily determined by well-educated, high-minded, self-confident men, the social culture, or at least what I encountered personally, was a sort of raffish Bohemia, deploying itself across the many pubs around Broadcasting House, most memorably the Stag and the George.

This wasn't a question of anything as simple as meeting up for a drink. It represented an almost Dublinesque commitment to the pub as a cultural institution, the background to good, even inspirational talk, the setting in which to exchange and develop ideas, commission programmes, cast plays, transact business, pursue love affairs, avoid involvement in the bureaucracies that were even then shaping up inside the BBC. These were meeting places for writers, actors, translators, transient foreigners, Communists, petty criminals, debt-dodgers, folk-singers, poets, editors of small magazines, cadgers, cricketing enthusiasts and racing tipsters, some of whom might also be working as or for BBC producers.

Within such groups, the style of dress was invariably untidy, even shabby, with the occasional bid for elegance. Mostly people wore tweed jackets—for they were mostly men—sometimes with leather patches, and there was always a smattering of the sort of dark shirts worn by George Orwell, himself a former BBC producer, in the photographs on the cover of his orange Penguins. There were exceptions. Most notably Julian Maclaren-Ross, an itinerant writer with an unfocused life, who would sport suede shoes, dark glasses and a rather crumpled camel coat and always carry a gold-topped malacca cane. Anthony Powell would depict him as X. Trapnel in *A Dance to the Music of Time*. I recall him as always being on the look-out for favours, either money or a commission. He frequently got both. The mood of the times was one of benign friendship.

The pubs were dingy. People stood around. Comfort was not the point: the point was male bonhomie fuelled by drink and ideas. The smoke was thick—cigars and cigarette holders on display above ashtrays brimming with the debris of wizened Craven A and Players' Senior Service. There was Guinness and whisky, beer from the barrel. I seemed the only one to drink lager but, then, I was one of only a few women to stand around listening to the men. This was where Dylan

149

Thomas had drunk, and where Louis MacNeice still did. He once listed 'standing in pubs' as one of his likes. Louis, who had a big laugh and large yellow teeth, seemed to me to have a complicated private life for one so old—he must have been in his forties. I recall his passionate love affair with the actress Mary Wimbush. Many years later she played Julia Pargetter in *The Archers*, but in her prime she had a dark, exotic beauty and richly curvaceous shape. No wonder he was smitten.

Here, too, was R. D. Smith—Reggie—an ebullient drama producer married to the novelist Olivia Manning, who depicted him as Guy Pringle, the disorganised cultural representative in her trilogy of Balkan novels. Reggie was a member of the Communist Party.

Sometimes the talk was about politics, never more so than over the turbulent events of autumn 1956: Suez and Hungary. These were days when we seized on the newspapers each morning, followed it from bulletin to bulletin. Suez was one of the last exploits of a dying empire. Britain, led by Prime Minister Anthony Eden, plotted with France to invade Egypt, whose President Nasser had nationalised the Suez Canal. Everyone we knew was outraged at Britain's duplicity: the attack was reckless and the whole country was up in arms about it. Michael and I joined thousands at the huge protest in Trafalgar Square. Everyone was resolved that the government action must stop, and protest was the way to do it. We really believed we could be effective. And perhaps, in a small way, we were. Events moved quickly: the UN intervened and Britain handed over its control of the Canal zone.

The Russian invasion of Hungary—where a popular uprising against occupation was enjoying some success—had come merely days before the Suez debacle. We were equally outraged about that. Only recently Khrushchev had publicly denounced Stalin's crimes, and Soviet Communism was rocked to the core. The George was aflame with argument: should British Communists resign from the Party or not? This was the moment when many intellectuals quit. Reggie Smith was one of them. And it was in the George that Reggie came up with one of those casual suggestions that change people's lives. I had been complaining of my recent technical incompetencies when he suddenly said, 'Why don't you try television?'

'But if I can't do radio, I'll never do that!'

'No, no, no. I mean in front of the camera.'

There had been talk of television, of course, but this idea was new. It planted the seed.

But I was to try other things first. My job in Broadcasting House—the first and only time I was ever on the BBC staff—lasted little more than a year. My BBC staff file shows that after I had been defined as 'Married to Drama Producer Michael Bakewell' I was leaving 'for personal reasons'. The two were not unconnected: the BBC had a policy that husbands and wives should not work in the same department. Once married, my drama aspirations—eventually to produce, to direct—were out of the question. I conceded without a fuss, but was not prepared to hang around being unhappy with my lot.

If I felt less than aching regret at not yet having found my place in the world, it was because there *was* no great regret. Getting to Cambridge and

151

savouring all it had to offer had been the summit so far. What came next might equal but never better that experience. But something else softened those disappointments. There emerged in the post-war years an attitude of mind quite different from that which had sustained the war effort, giving women the chance to serve in the armed forces, in the armament factories, take jobs vacated by men gone to fight. We came to believe that, whatever job we might find, marrying and having a family was the best thing to do with our lives. It came to seem that my spinster teachers had been right all along. We expected that work would have its place in our lives, and it was for this we were qualified by our education. But it would not eclipse the deep satisfactions we would find in our families. And in the pursuit of these ideal families many of us became addicted to what Betty Friedan would later call the Feminine Mystique.

I had been born a mere five years after women finally got the vote; I had gone up to Cambridge only five years after women had been allowed to take degrees there. Yet here I was, one of the fortunate few, rushing into marriage and having children in my early twenties. What had happened to the heroic hopes, the energy and drive that had made these gains for women? What about the impact of post-war educational reforms that had sent many of us to the grammar schools and universities our parents could only dream of? Why were many of those who enjoyed the first fruits now opting for the choice that, when my headmistress had praised it, had earned nothing but my contempt? Married at twenty-two, I was conceding readily to the priority of my husband's career, happy to be dependent on his earnings and reading up in women's magazines and books on child development about how to create the perfect family.

A post-war era is always a time when society beds down, quite literally. The men come home from fighting, wartime infidelities are tidied up with a flurry of divorces and then the birth-rate starts to rise. 'The values for which we fought'—not just the country but the home and hearth—come to occupy the public's consciousness. Men trenched in mud or swept by the sands of deserts had dreamed of this moment. Women, their homes smashed and children scattered, could imagine nothing better than settling round the fire or pottering in the garden, free to exercise modest choices about what to eat, wear and enjoy.

It seemed then a huge gain, a transformation from the intolerable to the blissful, from threat to fulfilment. The family was central to the dream and the dream was central to social policy. As far back as 1942, the Beveridge Report—the supposedly progressive driving force for so much social change and improvement—had declared, 'In the next thirty years, housewives as mothers have vital work to do in ensuring the adequate continuance of the British race and of British ideals in the world.' My generation might have exercised a fleeting defiance as students, but we were still part of a world that didn't find such statements ludicrous.

The culture played along. This was the era of advertising's ideal family: Mother in her pinny in the kitchen, Dad putting up shelves, the gleaming children playing in tidy homes with immaculate toys. It was the era of books in which Janet learned cooking with Mother while John helped Dad tinker with the car. New goods were making the home an exciting place to be: washing-machines replaced the old tub and dolly; fridges offered the novelty of food that stayed fresh and ended the prospect of milk souring in jugs topped by beaded lace mats. These were new toys to play with, not yet the means of escape from drudgery. And there was no compulsion to escape, no compelling need for that second income. Somewhere there were educated women with nannies, training to be surgeons or lawyers, but they were exotic creatures, following the rarefied traditions of privileged families. It was not where most of us belonged. Not where I belonged.

*   *   *

In our third year in Cambridge Michael and I had been a couple: we lived in each other's thoughts and lives, studying together, sharing friends, food and Michael's bed. But when we moved to London there was no question of our living together. I had moved from my mother's shadow full tilt into the emotional embrace of my boyfriend, but I couldn't defy the conventions. There were practical problems: no landlady would rent a flat, no hotel would let a room to a couple who hadn't evidence of marriage. Searching hard, we discovered one, tucked away in seamy streets behind Russell Square, but it was in such a state of down-at-heel decay, its carpets frayed and stained, its sheets grey and torn, that we could hardly bear to touch the walls and the furniture, let alone each other.

As our jobs at the BBC brought in modest funds,

we rented separate rooms in houses close to each other in London's Swiss Cottage, then still a stronghold of German émigrés, whose matriarchs, faultlessly coiffed and jewelled, met for Viennese pâtisserie in local cafés. Both rooms were small, and Michael's had been constructed by the division of tall Victorian rooms with numerous partitions. All the residents could hear the movements of the others. I learned to identify the different breathing coming from each slit of a room. You could almost hear hands touching. If we were going to have a regular and unrestrained sex life we would have to be married.

My parents took to the idea of our marriage with equanimity. Michael came from a similar background, a similar semi-detached house in an aspiring suburb. My mother decided he was the clever one, and from then on referred to him all of the questions she might have asked of me: 'Is Picasso really any good?'; 'Are foreign films really as good as ours?' He was thoughtful and charming. She couldn't have wished for a better son-in-law.

Within twenty-four hours, having walked down the aisle in a white dress with a huge bouquet of roses, my life was transformed. Michael and I belonged to each other and to no one else. We had been admitted to the adult world where permissions were finally our own, decisions didn't have to be referred, and we could live by our own rules, defining them as we liked. Nevertheless, my parents still thought of us as children, so we weren't too surprised when they came on our honeymoon. It wasn't intended, but became inevitable. Neither Michael nor I could drive, so we had planned to travel by train to our honeymoon in

Cornwall. Suddenly there was a rail strike. My parents saw it as their duty to solve our problem, which they did by driving us as far south as possible in what remained of the wedding day. We all stayed overnight in a hotel in Southsea. Next morning Michael and I took the ferry for the Isle of Wight. Alone together. At last I was away from my mother's control. Instead I had plunged into all the old entanglements of a traditional marriage. I had never known what it was to be on my own.

*   *   *

Out of the BBC, it was time to try something else. It was time to go back to the leafy enclave off the Trumpington Road. On this occasion they suggested teaching. I had no qualification, but there was a desperate need for supply teachers in inner London. I signed on locally and turned up at a sequence of forlorn, run-down, inner-city junior schools. I didn't know what was expected of me: and my insecurities were confirmed when I walked into one classroom to find two words written in capital letters on the blackboard: BLOOD and GUILT. I enquired what the last lesson had been, and was told, 'RE.' It was a Catholic School.

Although I knew I was out of my depth, I thought this brief stint would give me an inkling of what to expect. It did more than that: it declared in letters four feet high for all to see: 'You are no good at this.' I couldn't control a classroom, couldn't impose any kind of discipline. Thoughtful colleagues would sidle up to me at break and enquire, 'Are you all right? I heard rather a lot of noise.' I murmured thanks and battled on, but I was already buckling at the knees and longing for the four o'clock release.

There was just one sustaining moment. It was when I flung myself on the mercy of a class of ten-year-olds and pleaded: 'What would it take to keep you quiet?' Together we settled for my telling them a really good story. I abandoned all idea of inculcating knowledge and instead embarked on a riotous adventure of men and maidens, intrigues at midnight, hoofs rattling across cobbles, gunfire from curtained windows, velvets and lace concealing betrayal and treachery. It not only held them, it caught my fancy too. The story became a project: they delivered spirited drawings, acted out plausible scenes, even embarked on the tricky skill of looking up facts about highwaymen and the conditions of roads in the eighteenth century. I felt the lines of stress and my clenched jaw relax. Children could be collaborative, after all. But it was a stop-gap remedy. Teaching was not for me. Ever since I have had an unqualified respect for both teachers and the power of narrative.

Back I went along the leafy drive off the Trumpington Road where they came up with advertising. I had no idea what it involved, but there was a vacancy for a copywriter at McCann Erickson. I went along to a first-floor office overlooking Waterloo Bridge and sat the exam. I was required to create three advertisements each for a brand of chocolate, a safety razor and a brand of jam. I dashed off plausible pastiches of advertisements currently in the magazines and, having submitted them rather sheepishly, was surprised to hear them greeted with cries of astonishment and delight. I was embraced as a shiny bright new recruit—in rather the same tone that would greet a shiny bright new car. If this was all that was required, advertising was clearly going to be a doddle.

I had reckoned without a crack-pot copy director, who had learned to write in a prisoner-of-war camp where he had done a deal with a fellow prisoner, a journalist. In return for being taught how to write, Eric Webster offered to do this man's chores, although what these were never figured in the oft-telling of the tale. Eric retained something of the prison camp in how he ran the department: each morning at nine thirty exactly he would be glowering behind his desk, on which sat, in lonely but conspicuous isolation, his large watch. As each of us arrived, two, five or even eight minutes late, we would meet a barrage of abuse and invective, which did nothing to make us earlier the following day and soon convinced us that the man was seething under the burden of having no power whatsoever.

These were the days when confident young graduates were writing novels about the absurdity of the world in which they found themselves. In 1953 John Wain had written *Hurry on Down*; a year later Kingsley Amis had published *Lucky Jim*. At McCann Erickson copywriter Roger Longrigg was even then conspiring to make Eric a central figure in a novel, *A High-pitched Buzz*, which would mock his employers in advertising. At the time it seemed highly subversive and the press was quick and glib enough to bunch them all together under the label 'Angry Young Men'. Kingsley Amis later explained that they weren't angry at all, merely having a good time at the expense of their elders and the obvious venality of the system.

The advertising world struck me as febrile and shallow. I worked on the Esso account, 'Put a Tiger in your Tank'; the Wrigley's account, 'Chew Wrigley's!'; the Nabisco account, 'Eat Shredded Wheat!'; and the Tampax account, small print only. In none of the first three did I come up with the headline idea, but simply found myself typing it out innumerable times for different formats and advertising spaces, but in the fourth I made an odd personal contribution. Menstruation was then a whispered subject, known among women as 'the curse' and never spoken of by men at all. Husbands and lovers made their own arrangements, often communicating with curious euphemisms, coy signs and portents. Consequently no self-respecting model would pose for a Tampax advertisement, which was why the agency had always limited the advertisements to drawings of women.

Now they planned a bold new initiative in which real women would appear. This was to be a breakthrough for realism, an advertising version of the social realism then emerging in films and novels. But there was a problem: no model could be found who was willing to do the job. Women themselves found the functioning of their bodies too embarrassing to refer to in public, too intimate to be referred to in even the most unadorned and practical prose (written by me). Impatient with such prudery, I volunteered to do the job myself, thus making my first public appearance in the media and before a camera. It took half a day, I wore a white dress and earned six guineas. I was the Tampax woman.

Advertising was full of bright young people of

talent and wit who, I thought, were wasting their energies on trivia. Worse, advertising seemed to me positively dangerous: that I should spend my time conspiring to persuade people by every trick of psychology and visual skill to buy things they couldn't afford and didn't really need struck me as downright pernicious. I could imagine it leading to much unsatisfied greed, an insatiable lust for goods and a neglect of things that really mattered. And who was to say I was wrong? I was good at it, but I was unhappy. And I wouldn't settle for that.

CHAPTER NINE

THE PARTY

Sometime in the summer of 1960 Michael and I went to a party. He was going because he knew the composer Humphrey Searle, whose party it was. They had met through Michael's work as a drama producer in BBC radio. I was going as Michael's wife, just that. The fact I had once worked in radio was known to some of Michael's colleagues, but to most of the people there I was his wife. Nothing more. It was a role I accepted, even embraced. I was proud of Michael's place at the hub of what was then a vividly creative BBC department, which was encouraging new and interesting writers, like John Mortimer, N. F. Simpson, Shelagh Delaney— and Harold Pinter.

Michael and I were leading a charmed life together. We had found a flat overlooking Primrose Hill, and if our meagre finances meant it was sparsely furnished, at least we had one great curving Arne Jacobsen chair from Heals, and curtains by Lucienne Day, chosen together at the Design Centre in the Haymarket. We had two budgerigars named Beauregard and Cherie after characters played by Marilyn Monroe and Don Murray in the film *Bus Stop*. They swooped around the flat making pretty noises and lots of mess. I can't have been houseproud. But I was learning to cook—and not the meat and two veg of my mother's tradition. The age of Elizabeth David had arrived and giving dinner parties was the thing. Her *Italian Food*, first published in 1954, was a favourite cookbook. I could recapture the exotic Italian dishes we'd had on holiday: lasagne and minestrone, things like that. I used her recipes to discover what to do with such exotic foods as avocados and aubergines, and bought kitchen utensils with French names like mouli, and *petit pots* from her shop in Greek Street, Soho.

We were culturally omnivorous, browsing London for all it had to offer, queuing in the rain at the National Film Theatre to see *Nosferatu* and *Cabiria*, hurrying to the Academy Cinema in Oxford Street to see the latest Godard or Truffaut movie, catching up with the Maxim Gorky trilogy and Jean Vigo's *L'Atalante* at the Everyman in Hampstead. Sometimes we would set the alarm for 5.30 a.m. so that by six Michael could join the Covent Garden queue for seats on the hard benches in the gods to see Callas in *La Traviata*, and Ulanova dance in *Romeo and Juliet*. In 1956, we had rushed to see *Look Back in Anger* when word spread that it spoke for our generation. We were keen to see all the new plays.

Then, in 1958, I became deliberately and joyfully pregnant. Of course it was a private matter, something you disclosed only to close friends, and you dressed carefully to avoid any evidence of a bump, but by then it was rumoured that there were new ways to give birth. Michael and I read up about them. The National Childbirth Trust was a relatively recent thing and its inspiration, Sheila Kitzinger, had only recently begun her campaign to demystify the whole process. We wanted to be in the vanguard of what was new, so Michael came along with me to classes, a little sheepishly, and even agreed to be at the birth. My parents found this thoroughly distasteful, so we didn't speak of it. We thought we were modern, but not by today's standard. Childbirth hadn't become the highly specialised matter it is today with its own recommended regimes and diets. I smoked some forty cigarettes a day through two pregnancies, ate all manner of soft cheese and pâtés and drank what alcohol I liked.

It was for personal reasons that we got caught up in the Campaign for Nuclear Disarmament. In the late 1950s America had the hydrogen bomb and China had a nuclear bomb. In the race for power, these bombs were being tested above ground, pouring contamination into the atmosphere. In 1957 there were forty-two above-ground nuclear tests around the globe. Soon strontium 90 was in the milk we were giving children. Nearer home, in 1957 there had been a major nuclear accident at Windscale, which released radioactive material into the atmosphere of Cumberland. The discharge of pollution went on for five days, driving radioactivity up to ten times the normal level. Windscale was later renamed Sellafield in the hope that people would forget.

The Easter I was pregnant with Harriet we joined the Aldermaston marchers as they came into Trafalgar Square. Our near neighbour, the American poet W. S. Merwin, had walked all the way. His plimsolls were frayed and his feet blistered, but his wife, Dido, offered us supper that night with another young couple who'd recently moved into the area, Ted Hughes and Sylvia Plath. They'd recently come down from Cambridge and Ted, whose first book of poems, *The Hawk in the Rain*, had been widely acclaimed, was keen to write for radio as a source of income that wouldn't compromise his talent. Michael and he had plenty to talk about quietly together. Sylvia was altogether more flamboyant. Assertive, showy, she had the nervous energy of a thoroughbred racehorse, virtually quivering with tension. She talked with Dido of their plans to spend the summer together at the Merwins' home in France. Talk was of herbs, and exotic cooking, baking your own bread and living close to the soil. She had that extravagant American dominance I'd admired in Katharine Hepburn, who had turned it to such glamorous effect in films like *Adam's Rib*. I felt totally intimidated, fell silent and stroked my bump.

In the event the baby was a breech birth. An attempt was made to turn it round in my tummy (there were no scans then by which you might find out the sex so 'it' was how it was known). I was left on a tilted bed, head down for two hours, then pummelled vigorously by the doctor. To no avail: the baby came into the world bottom first. Still, we knew right away she was a girl: Harriet. The pain

163

had been the biggest shock. Somehow I'd thought all the new-fangled preparations would make it less, but they didn't seem to work. Somewhere half-way into the delivery I simply gave up on the exercises, reached for the gas and air and begged for pethidine. Nothing had prepared me for such agony. The next three months followed in a miasma of tiredness. But I was overwhelmed by the love I had for this child. I pledged myself to be the best of mothers. I bought Benjamin Spock's book, *Baby and Child Care*, and came to depend on it. It recommended a more relaxed approach to child-rearing. It wouldn't be judged relaxed by today's mothers. I still used a playpen and walking reins.

By 1960, Michael and I were back in the swing of things so it wasn't surprising that in the same week in April 1960 we should attend both Ionesco's *Rhinoceros* at the Royal Court Theatre and, at the Arts Theatre, the opening night of a new play called *The Caretaker*. As the latter performance ended, the theatre erupted in cheers and applause. We were sitting at the rear of the stalls and I recall a voice shouting, 'This is the man you want,' and being aware that the author, in the front row of the dress circle and out of my line of vision, was standing to acknowledge the adulation of the audience. Minutes later we all disgorged into the bar where Michael drew my attention to a shadowy figure in the distance, the author himself. I didn't register his features. With him, being rather gallantly escorted by him, was a slender woman in very high heels with a lavishly glamorous dress, layered with rustling taffeta skirts, the author's wife. Her manner was that of self-contained and proprietorial pride. I didn't then know she was an

164

actress, but I might have guessed.

There was another role for me at Humphrey Searle's party than simply that of wife: the role of pretty woman. It was one I was used to and played to. I had time and vanity to care about my appearance. It absorbed quite a lot of the energy I had to spare from looking after a small baby. And it was my way of not being overlooked. On that occasion I had made the usual effort. I wore a dress of dull velvet, olive green. It was curtain velvet and I had made it myself for my sister's twenty-first birthday the previous January. I had learned in the days of austerity that furnishing fabrics often had more weight, more texture, more striking effect. This particular dress had long narrow sleeves, and was high at the neck but with a plunging back that showed off my summer-tanned skin. It had been tricky to make, involving much fiddling with pins, tacking stitches, buckram, pinking shears, interlining, stiffening, patient attention to cuffs, zips and fastenings. It was something I could do, and making my own clothes helped our money go further. I was proud of it. It gave me confidence. I felt and looked good.

Certain memories of that evening are vivid, but not all. Where was the party exactly? It seems to have been at a mews house in St John's Wood, but facing the road, with a steep roof and white front. I recall there being a paved area for a car or two, but also some fencing running along the pavement, upright slats of raw timber that snagged your stockings. Not the kind to lean against. Yet when I've been to look for it I have found nothing that quite corresponds. And another mystery. At first I recall it as being high summer and someone's birthday party. Humphrey Searle's birthday is on 26 August. But my diary records that I was somewhere else then—on holiday in Italy, in fact. We had taken a house at Bocca di Magra, then an obscure little village in the Cinque Terre. What am I to make of that? Certainly the dress was real. And what I remember as having happened was real enough too. I was to have a witness.

The people at the party were the usual crowd: producers, actors, writers, cronies, assorted womenfolk, a poet or two, almost certainly musicians. We talked seriously in those days, hunched over cigarettes and glasses of whisky. The air would be thick with smoke, blue smoke, ashtrays filling with dog-ends, a table of bottles from which you helped yourself. No one expected food. I was by the table when someone came up to speak to me, no one I recognised, a stranger. Someone I knew nothing about who knew nothing about me. But we stood together talking.

It was smoky and close inside, so we went outside together to get some fresh air. We lit cigarettes. Other people were taking the air, too. A quiet summer dusk was gathering. I remember Patrick Magee being around, a marvellous actor with deeply furrowed brow and gravelly voice. He seemed to growl as he talked. He was a favourite with Samuel Beckett and at the time was in many of the Beckett pieces then being produced on radio. That was why he was there. He was one of the crowd. They exchanged a greeting, a knowing male greeting, as between two men who know each other well but who are each with a woman unknown to the other. From that moment I realised who I was with: Harold Pinter. I hadn't

166

remembered him as the author that night at *The Caretaker*. Then Harold moved me out of earshot and began to speak. I had heard nothing like it. A torrent of talk—brilliant, intense, witty—the sort of rapturous speech you sometimes hear in a play. And indeed I would hear an echo of it many years later.

*   *   *

Sometime in 1978—eighteen years after the party—I was at home, alone. It was the same house Michael and I had bought together back in 1963, but we had divorced in 1972, and to minimise disruption for the children, I had stayed on in the family home with them. Now I was married for a second time but my new husband was away on theatre business of some kind in Canada. It was winter, and already dark early when a parcel was delivered by hand. I hadn't expected anything. I was neither excited nor engaged. Mildly curious, perhaps. It's hard to recall in the light of what was to come. I opened the parcel to find the script of a new play by Harold Pinter. An exciting moment. But nothing unusual. Harold always sent me a copy of a new play. He had done so ever since . . . well, ever since. I was in no hurry to read it. Relishing the chance to give it time and space, I decided to leave it until I went to bed. I would be in bed alone and would read it there.

*   *   *

The play is called *Betrayal*. In nine scenes it unfolds the story of the relationships between three people

167

who love each other. Emma loves her husband Robert, but none the less sustains a seven-year love affair with his close friend Jerry, who had been best man at their wedding. Robert, the husband, comes to know about the affair almost from the start but, rather than confront Jerry, keeps silent about it. When, years later, Jerry discovers this to be the case, he is deeply distressed, feeling betrayed by both of them.

*   *   *

Just nine years earlier, in 1969, Harold and I had met in melancholy mood to end an intense affair that had lasted over seven years, but which had by then foundered in distress and confusion. Better to end it as friends. So much had happened. There had been so much joy and so much misery. The time had come to part. There was no harshness, no recrimination, no need for any. In future, I thought, we can meet for a drink, catch up on each other's careers, sustain a concern about each other's lives.

*   *   *

Just such a scene opens *Betrayal*: two ex-lovers meeting in a pub. From that point the play moves forward describing events largely in reverse order arriving in scene nine at the moment when the affair begins, the moment on which hang all the subsequent betrayals and deceits. This final scene takes place at a party given by Robert and Emma. Jerry contrives to confront Emma alone and delivers a passionate speech declaring his love for

168

her. She accuses him of being drunk. Nevertheless he persists. He describes looking at her, how what is happening is unique, has never happened before, never been said before. By the end of the scene Emma has stopped resisting.

Between the first and last scenes, between that final encounter and the first meeting, lay a large slice of my own life. It was why the copy of *Betrayal* had been sent round for me to read.

*   *   *

By the time I had reached that final climactic scene, I was in a state of shock. It had come upon me gradually as, page by page, I began to recognise certain events. Some things seemed familiar; other things not: in a patchwork way I began to realise the plot echoed events in my own life. I sat and stared at the copy in my hand, my head empty of thought, just an appalled sense that my life was being raked over. The pain started up again.

Intellectually I knew it was a play, a work of fiction, a work of art. I knew there were nuances and ideas, points of plot and character that transcended the detail of events of which I'd been part. I was aware that writers use their own lives, take possession of what has happened to them and transform it. But even knowing all this, and telling myself it was so, I still felt hurt, hurt with an almost anaesthetised pain, the kind that comes with shock. I felt paralysed, numb. At first I took no attitude to the matter one way or the other. I was simply mute, unable to sort out any coherent thoughts or point of view. The morning after I had read the play I phoned Harold. We arranged to meet later that

169

day.

And my memory was drawn back to all that had happened. When we had met at the party in the summer of 1960 Harold's career had recently taken off with the success of *The Caretaker*. He was thirty years old. He had begun as an actor, assuming the stage name David Baron. 'What a name to call yourself,' the radio drama producer Reggie Smith wrote to him. 'I suppose you must feel there's some reason.' (This was Reggie, the same producer who—prolific with advice—had first suggested I try for a job in television.) But when it came to writing, the name had always been Harold Pinter.

His first play, a one-acter called *The Room*, was commissioned in 1956 and directed by his Hackney Downs Grammar School friend Henry Woolf, for the Bristol University Drama Department. It was from that play that Harold would later draw the name he used for me when we were exchanging secret letters: he would address the envelope to Miss Kidd. Even more oddly the part of Mr Kidd had been played by Henry Woolf who was, as we grew closer, to provide us with what we needed, which was the room. The play *The Room* found its way to the BBC's drama script unit where, in 1958, it was to Michael that Harold first pitched an entirely different idea. Michael liked it. So, too, did senior voices in the department, Barbara Bray and Donald McWhinnie. Together the three championed this new script against the forces of reaction—including both the then controller of the Third Programme and the head of radio drama. The issue went higher. Finally the assistant director of Sound Broadcasting ruled that the risk could be taken. The play was finally commissioned and broadcast a year later, its title *A Slight Ache*.

Pinter's first London stage play was also having a tough time. A production of *The Birthday Party* opened with high hopes at the Lyric, Hammersmith, in May 1958 but closed after just one week. Harold Hobson's euphoric review for the *Sunday Times* came too late: the play had closed the night before. At the time of the party I knew none of this. And I was naturally curious to find out more about this person, so quietly mannered and spoken, yet so sure of himself and what he was saying. I had been chatted up many times before. The unnatural imbalance between the sexes at Cambridge had meant that plenty of clever young men had said their pieces. I was used to flattery, extravagance, the lewd, the fanciful, the offer direct, the offer devious. I was quite experienced in the sexual game-play, and quite fluent in the timely refusal or more pressing put-down. But this was different. Here were two people standing together, sometimes talking, sometimes silent. Looking. And never touching.

And here was the distant memory of that moment, on the typed page before me.

In the days that followed my reading *Betrayal*, there were positive efforts to make me feel better about it. Years later, asked by his biographer whether cannibalising his own life and that of others ever gave him pause, Harold had replied that such questions only arose when you sent the play to the person involved. Well, that moment had arrived. Harold and I met in the Café Royal and I learned that a production of *Betrayal* was already planned at the National Theatre. I learned, too, that Beckett had admired it, commenting that

171

'from "all over" to "everything in store" wrings the heart.' I had a kind letter from Antonia Fraser, expressing her view that Emma is the stronger character giving love and commitment to the men, and that Harold had in fact written a feminist play. Slowly I developed a sense of the play as an entity with an independent life of its own. None the less I made two requests of Harold: I asked him to change the title from the single word *Betrayal* because I felt myself judged and condemned by it. I also asked him to send a copy to Michael Bakewell. He agreed to do only the latter. He had briefly considered calling the play *Torcello*—for reasons within the text—but *Betrayal* it would be. So again I went over all that had happened, ransacking the past for where the blame lay.

*   *   *

After Humphrey Searle's party nothing more happened. No exchange of phone numbers, no calls, no contact. Nothing.

I was happily caught up in being a mother to my year-old daughter Harriet. All in all, my generation was beginning to take parenting seriously to a degree that hadn't happened before. As well we might. There was no maternity leave from jobs: no jobs were held open. You simply left employment. There was no maternity pay: you stopped earning. By the late 1950s John Bowlby's work on what he called the attachment theory was becoming known. In a series of papers he examined the intense attachment of children to the mother figure and their dramatic response to separation. Reading about this, we accepted what he said and, although

172

his researches dealt with abnormal children in special circumstances, we applied his ideas to ourselves, seeing it as our duty to stay close to our babies' development. Many of us did. It became central to our lives and brooked no argument about careers and part-time work. This work was special and we were pledged to it.

But I was becoming restless. After eighteen months of being stuck at home with my baby daughter, attentive at all hours to her needs and her play, my mind was turning to porridge. This wasn't how it was meant to be. The baby books had painted a far too rosy picture. On Michael's return from work each evening I would grill him remorselessly about the world 'out there', his work, his productions, the people he'd met, the things they'd said. I was desperate to be part of that world, any world. The horizons of a pretty child and her sweet ways simply weren't enough. I didn't know it then but thousands of women graduates across the world who'd bought into the post-war fantasy of the idyllic home and family were restless, too.

I began to attend Michael's production rehearsals, and Michael began to produce a number of Harold Pinter's sketches for the Third Programme. Harold and his wife Vivien Merchant were both in the casts, sometimes together, sometimes singly.

During one afternoon of rehearsal Harold, not required by the producer, invited me to go for coffee. But we didn't go for coffee. As we left the Langham studio we turned and walked towards Regent's Park at the top of Portland Place. It was a bright, cold day, shocking blue sky—in my memory it feels like spring, neither so cold that we were huddled against the wind nor so sunny that we blossomed in the sun—just a London day. But for me it wasn't. Something was happening in my head. My mind began racing, registering things in ever greater detail, as though I'd taken drugs: the muffled sound of Harold's tread, the clack of my heels on the pavement, the dried wood of the park bench where we sat, the flaking texture of its surface. We sat casually, talking of important things in fleeting phrases cast adrift into the air. There were plenty of pauses: 'I'm happily married'; 'So am I'; 'Then what's happening?' I felt by turns elated, troubled, panicky, then as suddenly serenely peaceful. Finally Harold reached for my hand and held it within his. It was the first time we had touched.

*   *   *

This wasn't the only event to crash into my life. My mother had been touchingly pleased to be a grandmother and her quiet delight reflected something else in her life: she was already suffering, although she didn't know it, from the leukaemia that would kill her. Her spirit was muted, the old melancholy wrapped in some more profound resignation. And I, knowing why, was sad it had happened that way.

When the specialists had told my father their diagnosis they had indicated she might have only years to live; they didn't specify how many. But there were meaningful looks rather than explicit medical information. In those days matters of health were treated with as much secrecy as sex.

174

The C-word referred to cancer: it was a word that must never be spoken in full, certainly not within the hearing of anyone who was suffering from it.

Throughout the early years of my marriage I had spent every other weekend with my mother, submitting to the needs of her depression, accepting the strictures of her disapproval while struggling to lighten her days, to alleviate the punishing routines in which we were all trapped. What appalled me was that the progress of her illness diminished her strength: she hadn't even the energy it took to be depressed—and I knew that in losing the depression I was losing her. It was a terrible equation.

I recall lying beside her on her bed, slowly brushing the thin grey hair with as much tenderness as I could because too great a pressure hurt the naked pink scalp. I remember thinking, I can do this brushing ever more perfectly, I can bring to the act of brushing all the gentleness that is in me, I can do it so that she is beyond complaining, so that she finds in it some shred of sensual pleasure, some caress of what she yearns for, some consolation for whatever hurts have burdened her with such sadness. And I brushed and brushed. And she said nothing. It was a kind of content.

And now she was dead.

It was my first encounter with death. The death of someone I loved. My grandmother's death had belonged to my mother. Hers had been the central grief, respected by all. We whispered in her presence. Summoned to Surrey by a phone call at the dusty end of a summer day, I spent the evening train journey chipping the bright red polish off my nails for fear my mother might think it was not seemly to be so gaudy in my attendance on her grief.

Now I know she wouldn't have noticed, wouldn't have cared. Grief, when you are central to it, sees nothing of the surroundings, people or places. And that was where I was. Central and weeping. Weeping into the bedclothes. The phone call from the hospital, taken by my father, came at six in the morning. Weeping over breakfast . . . weeping on and on, for the past unmended, for the hurts not cured, now beyond reach for ever. But even then nothing was said except the platitudes: 'Blessed relief'; 'Better this way'. We stalked the house like ghosts, passing each other without noticing. Where should we put the grief? It was so weighty, it heaved with each second that passed. Would time ever pass normally again?

Somehow we reached the funeral. I was seized by a sense of the dramatic. It might be her rite of passage but it was my curtain call. I dressed with care. Black, head to toe. No hat. A deliberate act of defiance. Instead I found a piece of black chiffon several feet long. I wrapped it round my head and left great lengths of it flying over my shoulders in the wind. It was a sunny day with a brisk breeze. The scarves swung and cavorted behind me like kites over the funeral procession. I wore heavy dark glasses. I was mindful of recent Italian films, with Monica Vitti, the statuesque beauty, under the direction of Antonioni. The funeral was as unreal as a film. It was happening out of time, the colours bleached from the landscape, a black and white film. And my grief was the star.

My father seemed to have shrunk several inches. He could hardly walk. I supported him as we stood together by the dug earth and threw the handful of soil on to the coffin lid, a moment to make mourners gasp, that thump, insulting and final. Only the first handful makes that full, sullen noise. After that, soil falls on soil, not hitting the wood, less deafening. It falls to us, as chief mourners, the privilege of the first throw, summoning up the sound of doom. It was done, and we shuffled on to let others add their clutch of soil.

In the months that followed I was tearful much of the time. I cried on the bus each morning when I went to my new morning-only job, copy-writing for a small advertising agency, where I'd been made welcome by a former colleague, Don Paterson from McCann Erickson. I'd taken the work for the sake of the money, but it paid me less per week than we paid the au pair. So there must have been another reason. I needed to be out there doing something, in contact with the world of people and talk, coming and going. Each day I went from the terminus at Chalk Farm, having my choice of seats on the empty bus, and huddled towards the window where no one could see my streaming eyes. Such awful grief.

*   *   *

Gradually our circle of friends came to include Harold and Vivien, not the close circle of intimate friends, but the amiable acquaintance of those who came and went to each other's dinner parties, took an interest in each other's work and families. Our daughter Harriet was the same age as their son Daniel. They went to each other's birthday parties.

And I started meeting Harold.

177

Betrayal has a recurring image of happiness: it crops up within the first few pages of the text, and is referred to a second time in scene one, then again in scene six. It is a memory that Jerry refers to first, then Emma. It is a memory they share. They remind each other of the occasion when their two families were together and Jerry picked up Emma's three-year-old daughter Charlotte, threw her into the air, and caught her. There was laughter. It was in his kitchen, Jerry says, in scene one. By scene six he recalls it as happening in her kitchen. Emma corrects him. The memory is hard to pin down.

*　　*　　*

I remember it happening in the kitchen of Harold and Vivien's flat in Kew, and it was Daniel's birthday. Harold tossed my three-year-old daughter Harriet into the air and made her laugh. I remembered it years later, as I lay in bed reading the newly arrived script. But would I have remembered it if the play had not been written, and if this hadn't been what Michael Billington calls in his biography 'an episode of almost Proustian power in its ability to unlock the past'? Nine years after our affair ended Harold was setting a version of my memories before the public, crystallising events in a way I might not otherwise have chosen to remember them. And unlocking the past.

*　　　*　　　*

I could see that Vivien held a very powerful place in his life. He treated her with immaculate courtesy, surrounding her with small attentions, as though she were in some way frail, vulnerable. Her real name was Ada Thomson, she came from Manchester and had been to school at Bury convent. I recognised in her something of the strength of northern women, the sort of women I knew in my family, forthright, loyal, tenacious, unimpressed by what she saw as the world's pretensions, suspicious of the suavity of southerners. Over this layer of northern good sense she deployed the acquired attributes of an actress, a cultivated, slightly mannered elegance, an easy grace—she was an excellent dancer—and a nuanced speaking voice that barely hinted at its Lancashire origins. She had adopted the name Vivien Merchant for the stage. She was already the star of the repertory theatre when she married David Baron, an actor eighteen months her junior whom she had met on tour in Bournemouth. She always called him David: that was who he was for her. Harold Pinter was someone else, to whom she found herself married whenever they went out into the world together.

They shared to an extraordinary degree an understanding of their common craft—that of the stage and the life that went with it. They knew about landladies and digs, prompt corners and lighting changes, stage sets smelling of size, costumes and makeup, exits and entrances. They knew of 'the half' and first-night telegrams, of phrases it was bad luck to use backstage, of how to

179

take a curtain call, how to recover from a missed cue. But more than all this they knew the real business of theatre, how the encounter between individuals within a stage space can be made to yield all manner of experiences for the audience. They knew how to do it, and they refined their skills living alongside each other, highly tuned to each other's sensibilities. Throughout the sixties Harold was to write play after play, and Vivien was implicitly a part of each of them: Stella in *The Collection*, Sarah in *The Lover*, Ruth in *The Homecoming*, Wendy in *Tea Party*, and Anna in *Old Times*. Pinter denies they were written for her: 'At the time they were produced they seemed to have been written for her, but while I was writing the plays I never thought of her.' That isn't the issue. The truth is that what Harold wrote Vivien intuitively knew and understood how to play. Their concepts of what it was to be a man and to be a woman were very similar. Isn't that so in most marriages? And this was a strong one. Impregnable, I believed, like my own: the rock of certainty from which I could venture out and explore other possibilities.

The sixties was a good time to have an affair. Love was in the air. The mood of the times was relaxed, sunny. More and more good things were happening. Foreign holidays were still quite daring. More people were owning cars. I got my first in 1961 inheriting my mother's grey Morris Minor with its yellow indicator that flipped in and out at the driver's shoulder. People's demeanour was relaxed. It seemed more natural to smile at strangers than avert your eyes and hurry by. London traffic was leisurely, there were few jams and no parking restrictions. It was possible to drive across town, meet briefly, say for half an hour, and be back just as nursery school was ending. And all without any stress. There were no mobile phones, phone bills weren't itemised and there was no ring-back facility, all of which ambush today's lovers, so arrangements could be made without trace. Besides, couples didn't feel a compulsive need to be in touch all the time: they had their independent lives, he at work, she at home with the children.

Harold and I began to meet, not often but regularly. We prowled London together, walking its pavements, strolling its parks, eating in tube-station cafés and run-down, out-of-the-way pubs. The dilemma was whether to meet in obvious places so that were we to be spotted we could legitimately claim to have bumped into each other, or obscure places that would leave no one in any doubt as to what was going on. And who were we fooling anyway? We walked in the rain by the river at Hammersmith, we dined at Bloom's restaurant in Whitechapel where Harold introduced me to the delights of kosher food; we drank at the Wheatsheaf in Rathbone Place, risky because it was frequented by Fitzrovia characters known to us both; we met in the residents' lounge of the Victoria Hotel; we found ourselves adopted by the Little Akropolis Restaurant in Charlotte Street, where the proprietor always greeted us tenderly and gave us a regular table at the back. We even met at Haywards Heath, arriving by train from different directions to meander for half an hour round its suburban villas before each heading back the way we had come. On one occasion we were to meet by the lake in Regent's Park and I was late.

181

While he waited Harold wrote a poem, which he gave me:

Always where you are
In what I do
Turning you hold your arms.

My touch lies where you turn
Your look is in my eyes

Turning to clasp your arms
You hold my touch in you

Touching to clasp in you
The one shape of our look
I hold your face to me

Always where you are
My touch to love you looks into your eyes.

The intensity of the poem matched with its chasteness is an exact reflection of where we were at the time. We were meeting in public places hardly ever alone, simply to be together talking, and not talking. Eventually it wasn't enough.

Henry Woolf came to our rescue. He was one of a close-knit group of friends who'd been at Hackney Downs Grammar School together, united by what Michael Billington calls 'a love of intellectual adventure and a shared ironic sense of humour'. For this gang, loyalty—the loyalty between men—was of paramount importance. It was to sustain lifelong friendships between them all and it was this loyalty that Harold called on now. Henry was an actor and lived in a ground-floor back room in Burghley Road, Kentish Town. In *Betrayal*, the couple meet in Kilburn. By the time the play was written, in late 1977, Kentish Town was coming up in the world and wouldn't have offered the strong contrast between the couple's affluent middle-class lives and the untidy bedsit where the lovers meet. Besides, *Betrayal* is a work of fiction, isn't it?

Early in 1962 Kentish Town was seedy. The house was owned by Geoff and Maggie, who had divided it into single bedsits rented out to a motley crew of tenants who looked to Henry for advice. Henry, being an actor, kept wayward hours and—he was a generous spirit—helped them all out. There was much coming and going and no one noticed or cared when two new figures began to turn up in the middle of the day. The curse of celebrity had not yet arrived in either of our lives. We were simply friends of Henry. Henry, I learned years later, had carried loyalty to extremes and even when he wasn't rehearsing, as he'd led us to suppose, vacated the premises and took long lonely bus rides around London to give us space.

Harold once described the room in Burghley Road as like the set for *The Caretaker*. And it was creatively shambolic, a disarray of objects that signalled an untidy but intense life. But there was a system there too, designated areas having their proper function. In one corner, the bedroom corner, the narrow bed, in the kitchen corner two gas rings and a butler's sink. The window along the back wall of the house had been almost completely filled in, rendering the room perpetually dim. Against it, constituting the study, was a handsome desk and bookcase spilling Henry's papers and

183

books in no kind of order. There was a Victorian fireplace with coloured tiles and a black grate, but rarely a fire. It was always cold. And here we were happy.

*   *   *

In the summer of 1962 Michael and I took our holiday in Venice. We stayed, as we usually did, at a small, family-run hotel on the waterfront of the Lido facing the lagoon with, in the distance, a glimpse of the tower of San Giorgio on its island and the outline of the Doge's Palace. From our balcony on the first floor we could watch the sun setting, the silhouette of Venice black against the darkening sky. It was distinctly not a tourist hotel, nothing more than a few rooms above a noisy café where the crews from the boats serving the Lido came in to greet the *padrone* and enjoy his wines. Only Italians stopped here and we were the only English to stay. We liked it for that reason, setting ourselves apart from the tourist hordes who descended from the boats each morning and swarmed purposefully down the main street to where, at the other side of the island, great stretches of holiday beaches awaited them.

We had been before and knew the routine. In the mornings we, too, opted for the hired beach hut on the raked sand. In the afternoons we would see the sights. In particular we loved to take the boat to Torcello, an idyllic, virtually deserted island in the lagoon where there was no traffic and grasses lapped at the mighty doors of its seventh-century basilica. It is one of the most serene and calming places in the world.

184

More often we would cross to the city of Venice and enjoy its great art treasures, its shops and its cafés. One day I arranged things with a slight difference. I'd previously noticed a handbag in a shop window, priced it but not bought. Now, on the pretext of going to buy it, I left Michael with Harriet on the Lido, crossed to Venice on my own and made for the American Express offices behind St Mark's Square. This was the first time, so I didn't know the way or the routine for collecting letters at the *poste restante*. It wasn't all I didn't know.

There were crowds pushing and shoving, students and young people impatient for news of home, all shouting their names at the harassed officials. I joined the bustle and offered my passport as identification: Bakewell. Yes, there was indeed a letter for that name. I seized it greedily, thrust it guiltily into my pocket, and headed for a table in Florian's, the café in St Mark's Square where, having ordered coffee, I tore open the precious, flimsy airmail envelope.

The writing was cramped and tight, with a rather baroque elegance; it spidered its way in closely packed lines across the page. The expressions of affection were fulsome enough, but almost at once something began to go wrong. There were references I didn't follow and matters that were strange. I had never had a letter from Harold before, so I had had no idea what to expect, but there was something odd about this. I read on faster and faster down the densely inky pages trying to find somewhere to root my recognition of its writer and what he meant to me. But it was all disconnected and jumbled. My heart raced. I could

185

feel the sweat, the panic. Was it a hallucination, a forgery, a trap, a mistake? What?

The explanation was simple. This was a letter to Michael from a woman I didn't know. In my haste I had not seen that the address said M. Bakewell Esq. It was signed with her name. Suddenly it was all too obvious what had happened. They, enjoying their own affair, had agreed on American Express as a means of remaining in touch, just as we had. I was caught out at my own game but, then, so were they. I had the explanation, but the panic was now about something else.

I had the sense to laugh; I think I laughed out loud, startling the pigeons in the Square. I laughed because it was no laughing matter. But it was funny, I could see that. Then I ordered myself a strong drink. Harold has a phrase in *The Dwarfs*: 'Thinking got me into this, and thinking's going to have to get me out.' So I sat and thought. Then, having reached certain decisions, I bought a bottle of whisky and returned to the Lido to hand Michael his letter. Oh, and I bought the handbag.

*   *   *

Scene five of *Betrayal*, its central and crucial scene, takes place in a hotel in Venice where Emma and Robert are on holiday. It begins with their looking forward to going again to Torcello, as they have done on previous visits. It is a favourite of theirs. Then Robert drops into the conversation that, just the day before, he went to American Express to cash some traveller's cheques. The people there, noting his name, had asked whether he was a relation of Emma for whom they had a letter. They offered to hand it over. But Robert refused, recognising the handwriting as Jerry's. Gradually Emma confesses to the truth: she and Jerry are having an affair; they have been having an affair for as long as five years and, under Robert's questioning, she admits they have a flat together. The final line is Robert's. He refers again to their plans to go to Torcello.

*   *   *

Michael and I talked.

Crises in marriage can either be lived through and survived well enough for the marriage to continue, albeit now in a different form, or they can finally sink what was already a leaky vessel. Michael and I were not a leaky vessel. We were a trim little ship taking a buffeting in the open seas of an exciting life. This absurd metaphor sounds like some perky self-help homily used to disguise the fact that in reality we were deluding ourselves. The truth was otherwise. We were not deluded.

We were extremely realistic about where we were. We had a close and clear-sighted understanding of each other. It wasn't flashy or demonstrative, but it underpinned our happy marriage. And because we had both behaved in a similar way it was harder for us to trade recriminations and blame. Instead we both wanted understanding and sympathy. And we each provided it.

But we didn't go into details. There was no unburdening, no confessing all. I didn't tell him about Burghley Road, nor did he offer equivalent explanations. Dates, times, arrangements: we didn't go over any of it. That wasn't the point. Instead we discussed how it was possible, given our undoubted love for each other, to find other people powerfully attractive. The answer was obvious: because the world in which we moved was full of interesting and exciting people with whom we wished to engage. Did we want to retreat into the closed-off world of conventional marriage that had so bored our parents? We did not. Surely it must be possible for men and women to have friendships outside marriage. And here we did something remarkable: intuitively and with implicit mutual agreement we simply stopped short of sexual confessions or jealousies. By an act of will we kept the green-eyed monster at bay.

We returned to London knowing that we had each had a secret from the other, now a half-shared secret. We would keep it like that, concealing what we were up to, but not letting it hurt the other or threaten our marriage. In the end it would—but that was some seven years away and by then many things were different.

*   *   *

I returned to London and to Burghley Road, babbling of the beauties of Venice and Torcello. Within days of the holiday Michael and I attended a party given by Harold and Vivien at their flat in Kew. Both remarked, 'Hey, you're brown, where've you been?' One already knew the answer.

In the early years of the 1960s Harold wrote both *The Collection* and *The Lover*, the first about possible sexual betrayal and tension between couples who know or do not know more about each

188

other than they're telling; the second about a sexual game of changed identities played within a marriage by the husband and wife. Of these and other 1960s plays Pinter's biographer asked, 'Is he subconsciously exploring his own marital tension in drama?' If he was I knew nothing of it. Nothing of our personal lives beyond our two selves was ever discussed. It was tacitly understood that our marriages were our private concern, they were assumed to be happy, and there was nothing further to be said. As if to prove the point, in January 1963, while Harold was working in New York, I conceived my second child. I was delighted.

*   *   *

In scene eight of *Betrayal*, it is summer 1971. Emma and Jerry are at their flat. Jerry has been in America on business. He tells her that his wife Judith has an admirer, a doctor with whom she goes for drinks. But there's nothing in it. He doesn't believe she's been unfaithful. Nor has he, he says, ever been unfaithful—to Emma. It's then that Emma tells him she is pregnant. It happened while he was away in America, she explains, and the child's father is her husband.

*   *   *

In 1963 domestic arrangements were changing, homes of various kinds needing attention. Harold and Vivien moved to a beautiful Regency house in Worthing where Michael and I visited them. From being wretchedly hard up they were now enjoying considerable wealth and Vivien loved creating

189

lavish décor in her home. I remember floor-length curtains in Prussian blue shot silk the full length of the drawing room, and fine antiques on pale carpets. I was very impressed, especially as Michael and I had that same year moved into a big house near Primrose Hill where we couldn't afford to carpet the stairs.

There were changes at Burghley Road, too. In 1964 Maggie and Geoff were reorganising the house and needed Henry's room. But a new opportunity opened up. Built on to the back of their house was a large extension with huge windows on two sides, plus a tiny kitchen space and an adjacent toilet, a complete flat, and a wonderfully light and pleasing space. Harold and I took it. We furnished it. And we visited. It had our stamp on it. Walls, curtains and carpets were oatmeal, the only splash of colour a huge yellow Casa Pupo rug thrown across the double bed. It was here I cooked meals, and kept house.

*   *   *

Scene six of *Betrayal* is of the domestic life of Emma and Jerry in their Kilburn flat. She has returned from Venice with a gift, a tablecloth, an emblem of domesticity. (By contrast I had returned from Venice with an hourglass, emblem of time passing.) Harold portrays her as drawn towards a domestic life with Jerry, even hinting in one line that she would wish things other than they were, that she even dared to look forward to when their lives might change and, implicitly, change together. In the play she begins to behave like a wife, even a housewife. She makes a stew, wears an apron, and at one treacherous moment dares to ask, 'Tell me . . . have you ever thought . . . of changing your life?' I, in no way, shared that outlook. I never considered for a moment the idea of our coming together. The nearest trace of such a thought is in a letter from Harold in which he thanked me for explaining about the children. I never allowed myself even to imagine some moment in the future when all might become known, sorted and rearranged. That was never even hinted at between us.

But our behaviour grew bolder. So although we were never in Venice together, we were in Paris. For just one day. In the mid-sixties I was making a series for BBC Schools television about bridges. These were neat, matter-of-fact little programmes, scripted by someone else, with me hired to tell the relevant tale on screen. Each programme needed a day's filming, starting out from London early and returning after seven at night. On each occasion I left the children in the care of the au pair, who delivered them at playgroup and primary school and fed them tea to follow. I was home by bedtime to read their story.

This time the subject was to be the famous pioneering industrial bridge at Ironbridge, in Staffordshire. Up early again, as was the routine, but the taxi took me not to the appropriate railway station, but to Heathrow where I had already booked a return ticket to Paris. The Ironbridge programme was a fiction.

By half past eleven I had descended from the airport bus in the centre of Paris and was strolling towards Notre Dame and the prearranged meeting with Harold who was in Paris attending rehearsals.

191

I saw him grinning as he walked slowly towards me. There was no hurry: we had a whole day to spend together, so much more than the snatched half-hours in cafés, the brief afternoons at Burleigh Road. We scarcely noticed the newspaper boards that proclaimed '*grève* . . .'. Even had we noticed, our French wasn't proficient enough: '. . . *des transports publics*', well, that was obvious enough. But what did '*grève*' mean? We were too self-absorbed to care.

There is something magical about being for the first time in a new and foreign place with someone you love. The strangeness isolates the two of you together. It also sets you aslant each other, as though each had turned from within a familiar beam of light to be caught at an angle in another shaft altogether. The turn of a head, the cast of a brow look somehow different, new, ready to be learned all over again. For lovers it means a special pleasure. We walked the Paris streets, strolled past the *bouquinistes*, kicked up the white dust in the Tuileries gardens in a daze of strange familiarity, alien intimacy. The spell was shattered soon enough when on leaving Harold's hotel—a small smart place near the Ronde Pointe—the receptionist explained that '*grève*'—the word by now in even heavier lettering on the newspaper boards—meant 'strike' and there were, as of that afternoon, no buses or Métro trains running in Paris, and Air France planes had been grounded. We thanked her for the news.

The taxi driver drove a hard bargain. Indeed, there was no bargaining to be done. Harold poured notes into his hands, reckless of their value, then more, pausing for him to say it was 'enough'.

'Enough' came when he couldn't hold any more in his grasp. But I was at least in a taxi on my way to the airport, together with thousands of other travellers equally marooned. I wondered how many were in as tight a spot as I was. In the end I missed my planned flight, caught another, and was back for the children's bathtime, and the bedtime story. I even had supper in the oven when Michael arrived home later. 'Busy day at work, dear?' Well, yes, you could say that. I didn't ask where he had been.

It had been a close call. More revelations would have wrecked the delicate balance of our marriage. But rather than frighten me out of my recklessness, it convinced me I could get away with anything. I felt exhilarated rather than ashamed or panicked. Harold and I were somehow blessed, smiled on by a benign destiny. One day planning would begin for the next enterprise: this was to be three weeks in New York. But that was years ahead, and would bring the carefully cultivated network of secrecy and deception tottering towards disaster.

CHAPTER TEN

LATE NIGHTS

By the middle of 1962 something else had happened in my life: I had started to work in television. It is the question I am most often asked by strangers: how did you get into television? Certainly women were rare on the screen in the 1960s, although there had been one or two announcers when the television service began, glamorously gowned in cocktail dresses and with cut-glass accents. Briefly in 1960 Nan Winton had been the first woman newsreader.

I wasn't of that kind at all. I wanted something else entirely. I wasn't even looking for a career. Indeed, I have never thought of myself as having 'a career' as such: a career in the sense of a steadily rising series of appointments, promotions and achievements, usually with a sequence of different companies, involving increasing power and responsibility along the way and rising to something widely agreed to be at or near the top. This I have never sought and never wanted.

I began as a broadcaster, writing scripts, presenting ideas, interviewing people, reporting different stories from different places, and chairing discussions. It is what I learned to do in the 1960s and am still doing today. It's what's called being a freelance broadcaster. It combines the best opportunities of interesting work with the maximum freedom to control your own life. And in that, I am at one with thousands of other broadcasters, journalists, reviewers, writers, performers, artists, wandering troubadours and social ragamuffins—free spirits who come as close to deciding their own destiny as is possible in this over-managed, over-structured world.

But why television? Why do the parameters of the job fit so exactly with what I want from life? I remember, early on, recalling Fritz Lang's 1926 film, *Metropolis*, a futuristic vision, incidentally set in the year 2000, of a mechanised slave society of faceless individuals driven by routines and behaviours they were helpless to control. I recalled

194

too T. S. Eliot's vision: 'a crowd flowed over London Bridge, so many/I had not thought death had undone so many'. These pictures haunted me with their message of monotony and conformity. And I resolved one thing: I wanted work that was not predictable. I did not—and do not—have the temperament for rigid routines.

Television is not only varied, it is a physical activity. You actually have to make it. You are deskbound for as long as research and scripting take, then you're off on a journey to places known as locations, where with all the camera paraphernalia, you work with others to put images together on to pieces of film or tape. Later in the journey you move to the editing and dubbing suites. It is an episodic life: every day holds surprises. Often when standing with a camera crew in a howling gale on some remote hilltop for a not very clear reason, I have asked, as they battled the rain and cold, 'Yes, but would you rather be at a desk?' It's a rhetorical question.

Not only is it variable in itself, but you can decide how much of it you want to do. This was certainly the case when I began. Today things are more pressured, more career-driven. But I remembered from my days in radio how guests would arrive with a script already written, be ushered into the studio to rehearse and record their piece, then depart the building clutching a cheque for three guineas. That's a way of life, I thought then, that would fit in with raising a family. And so it did.

Above all, there is the work itself. Television offers a magpie life for the mind, a chance to have a brief acquaintance with many subjects, ideas and opinions. And to research and debate them with experts. Finally, of course, television is a public performance. It isn't acting, but it isn't just being yourself. It's being yourself as a communicator. Here was something to gratify the show-off in me, the little girl waving from the liner to the crowds on the quay, the Cambridge student who had briefly fancied being an actress. All these considerations came into focus, and coalesced around the idea of my being a broadcaster. And it was the right choice.

So, how did I begin? By ingenuity and persistence. Reggie Smith had planted the idea years before. I'd a mere one year of experience as an inept radio studio manager to my credit. Nothing more. I would have to make a big effort. I wrote sheaves of letters. I scoured the *Radio Times* for the names of producers and wrote to them. I applied for auditions. In the mid-sixties television was hungry for new faces, so I did audition after audition, picking up tips as I went along. I hunted down stories in local newspapers and the specialised press and offered to report them on screen. Sometimes I pleaded: 'If you are ever considering—even occasionally—using a woman interviewer . . .' And I didn't give up. Letters of refusal were set aside, to be revisited three months later.

Eventually, having gained a regular two-minute slot on an ABC Television teatime programme called *Sunday Break*—religion for teenagers—I landed my first BBC appearance. It was a programme called *Table Talk*: seven guests and a chairman gathered for lunch together to discuss the news items of the day—and that was it. It began at the lunch, a three-course meal with hot food served by waiters at a linen- and crystal-laid table in the centre of the studio and under blazing lights. It went out live for forty-five minutes, from the moment we reached the cheese.

The first day I was a guest was the third week of October 1962, the week of the Cuba crisis: the time when the world held its breath expecting an imminent nuclear attack. I offered President Kennedy the advice that he should act with extreme caution. But he didn't take it. Instead he was bold and defiant and won the day. He challenged the Russian leader Khrushchev who had installed nuclear missiles in Cuba, threatening to attack at once unless they were withdrawn. For several days people lived in raw terror, expecting the flash in the sky at any minute. We tended our children with extra care, looked thoughtfully into each other's eyes. After several days Khrushchev conceded. It was as close as the world has ever come to all-out nuclear war. A month later *That Was the Week That Was* opened on BBC television and launched a new era of disrespect. The world was getting both more serious and more frivolous at the same time.

In the early sixties I was beginning to put together a jigsaw of commitments, not too many as I was still struggling to balance work and family. *Home at Four Thirty* was a thrice-weekly programme made by Southern Television. I would travel to Southampton by train and make the three programmes in one day. Mostly it was women's chat, homes, childcare, cooking, but one afternoon it fell to me to interview an eager young doctor with a shock of unruly black hair, a gaunt restless body and brown eyes of commanding intensity. In three minutes on air he outlined his theory that a dysfunctional family might be a prime cause of schizophrenia. It was a new theory and no one in the medical world was as yet taking much interest in it. But his sense of his own rightness, his conviction that he had discovered a profound insight about the human psyche made him compelling to listen to.

This was Ronnie Laing. We returned on the train to London together and he continued to elaborate his theory, thrilled to have in me a captive audience, and at that stage in his career already convinced his theory would revolutionise the treatment of the mentally ill. In fact the books he would one day publish as R. D. Laing— particularly *The Divided Self*—would become the acclaimed texts for the examination of identity and interrelationships that would dominate a whole school of psychiatric thinking in the 1960s. More than that, they would change how we all thought about ourselves and each other. And encourage us to do so, facing up to our motives, responses, emotional needs.

Another writer was doing that, too, around this time, and making an even more direct and personal impact on me. In 1963 I bought the paperback of Betty Friedan's *The Feminine Mystique*, and it changed my life. She was American and had worked on glossy women's magazines whose persistent message was that women found happiness not in emulating men but in accepting their own nature, which can find fulfilment only in sexual passivity, male domination and nurturing maternal love. It was strongly expressed and I recognised exactly what she meant. Hadn't D. H. Lawrence preached the same gospel?

But something had gone badly wrong and Friedan piled up the evidence. In America more and more women were complaining to their doctors of fatigue, having nervous breakdowns, using tranquillisers. Marriages were stressed as women sought fulfilment through their husbands rather than with them. The post-war consensus that women must be fluffy and feminine, catch and keep their man by the deployment of feminine skills was breaking down.

Friedan's analysis of how this had come about rang all too true. Out of the depression and war, she suggested, had come the need for the reward of easier times and the chance for happy families. With the arrival of household gadgetry came the free time for mothers to nurture their ideal children. According to Friedan, both Freud and the anthropologist Margaret Mead must bear a good deal of blame, as they would in later feminist polemics. But so, too, should the world of advertising, the cosy world of smiling Mother in her apron, Dad tinkering with the car. The whole thing began to look like a massive conspiracy to boost the sale of consumer goods as a way of sustaining the peace-time economy.

I thought of my own mother and her private misery, driven inward towards depression. Now here, decades later, young women had from choice been complicit with the same old mystique. I had been complicit myself. I had bought the notion of fulfilment through the family; I had swallowed the D. H. Lawrence myth; I had read and accepted Bowlby's theories of the child needing an ever-present mother. I had fallen for the largely male construct of the society in which I lived. In the twentieth century most women experienced at some time a moment of epiphany when the truths of feminism touched their own lives. Reading *The Feminine Mystique* was such a moment for me. From now on I was alert to the snares and delusions of male values; I was eager to see change and improvement for women. And I began to forgive my own mother. I looked back over what her expectations had been, and how they had been disappointed, even crushed. I began to see her depression not as a medical condition at all, but as an intelligent response to the trap in which she was caught. Now it was too late to tell her I understood.

*   *   *

In 1964 the BBC's programme planners woke up to the fact that women might expect more from afternoon programmes than talk about homes and children. The newly launched BBC2 embarked on a bold six-part series called *The Second Sex*. Taking its title from Simone de Beauvoir's famous book of 1949, it was produced by women and each of its discussion programmes featured a panel exclusively of women. I chaired two episodes: 'Men as Husbands', and 'Men as Equals'. It was obvious at once that there was no shortage of women with vigorous opinions and the style and confidence to express them fluently. The tacit assumption that women weren't as good broadcasters as men was quietly laid aside. Here were the novelists Elizabeth Jane Howard and Brigid Brophy, Edna O'Brien and Maureen Duffy, even the ex-Gaiety

200

girl Ruby Miller, talking in forthright and unbigoted terms of the benefits of divorce, the pleasures of promiscuity, the reasonable possibility of wives earning more than husbands, the nuances of jealousy provoked by platonic as well as physical infidelity. Such discussions are still around in the media today, a little tired by now, a little jaded from exhaustive repetition, but then they were relatively shocking. And women, who still deferred so often to men, were coming together among themselves not only to share ideas but to enjoy each other's company. It felt good to be one of them.

And then in 1965 I got my Big Break. I was invited to join the nightly programme *Late Night Line Up*. From 1965 until 1972 I would be one of its four presenters: the others were Dennis Tuohy, a gentle-mannered Irishman; Michael Dean, a New Zealander given to the meaningful pause during which many an interviewee, made fearful by the silence, would plunge in with a comment more revealing than they had intended; and Tony Bilbow, with a background in script-writing and a habit of corpsing on air so infectious that we could all get dangerously caught up in it. Later we were joined by Sheridan Morley, large of stature and personality, steeped in the theatrical traditions of his father Robert Morley and his grandmother Gladys Cooper.

Late Night Line Up, which began with the opening of BBC2 in 1964, took as its brief the whole of television. We would criticise, challenge, mock, debate and celebrate the programmes and programme-makers, their writers, directors, actors, planners and controllers. There was no programme like it, and never would be again. It hit the screen at the peak of television's impact and popularity as the preferred entertainment for the whole country, and its three thousand editions were seminal in shaping the future of television. Yet because it went out live it spent its energies on the airwaves and left little recorded trace. The memories, however, are vivid.

I was recruited by its editor Rowan Ayers who, on a tip-off from Humphrey Burton, had seen me on the afternoon programmes I was doing for Southern Television. He called me in for a drink in the BBC bar, and decided to try me out. I was thirty-one years old. Rowan Ayers was the overarching spirit who shaped, governed and permitted what his programme teams got up to. What mattered about Rowan, who was by now in his early forties, was that he had been in the navy and carried a naval outlook forward into all he did. He was clearly of officer class, and bore responsibility lightly. Tall, long-legged, loose-limbed, with a rather raffish air, he had a lank fall of soft sandy hair and broken veins on his cheeks that gave him a cheerful joviality. He wore blazers and grey flannels, the dress of an officer at leisure. He liked good company, drinking, women and sailing. Especially sailing. (I nearly wrote 'women' but sailing probably had the edge.) He was no intellectual but had a flair for off-beat programme ideas and an instinctive knack of leadership. He was gregarious, full of fun, and took his place at the helm with an easy authority. He treated his teams as unruly children whom it was his task to liberate into creativity, and defend whenever things went wrong. It is only now, examining the yellowing papers of the BBC's archives, that I realise how diligently and often he did that. He never indicated to us just what battles he was continually having to fight to keep us on the air.

The programme took its tone from him. After all, we were his appointees. But unlike other editors who unconsciously choose a team that reflect in the broadest terms not their opinions but their own world-view, and thus achieve a homogeneity that gives a programme its character, Rowan chose wildly differing personalities from widely different backgrounds. Some were keen on sport, on rowing and sailing, some on poetry and literature, others on jazz, pop music, comedy, some on politics. I would always pitch for items about art, drama or books. And as long as we found some connection with television's output, Rowan encouraged us to follow our instincts and make the programmes that interested us. Quality control and performance targets were not relevant. A great range of ideas and arguments reached the screen, often with the very sketchiest research and scripting. We hadn't time for more. And he tended to appoint people who were more radical than himself—whether in politics, musical taste, moral perspective, whatever. This was the yachtsman who preferred the prospect of an approaching gale to the safety of a stiff breeze. Certainly there was no shared mind-set.

They must have put something in the water in the 1960s. There was certainly an air of playfulness around. The painter Bridget Riley says it was really the after-the-war party that had taken a while to get going. I knew where that spirit came from: at the Cambridge May Week revues I had seen the lyrical wistfulness of Julian Slade give way to the acerbic and hilarious sketches of *Beyond the Fringe*. Jonathan Miller, one of the *Fringe* foursome that included Alan Bennett, Dudley Moore and Peter Cook, was not only a neighbour of mine but a doctor at University College Hospital when my daughter was born. He would come tiptoeing in at odd hours for a snatched chat by my bedside. Now I heard of plans to take *Beyond the Fringe* to London, to Broadway. In 1960, *Private Eye* came along. Then in 1962 *That Was the Week That Was*. I recall going backstage after a West End play to congratulate actor Barry Foster and meeting him already dashing from the stage door: 'Must rush—have to be home in Wimbeldon for *TW3*.' There were no video-recorders then.

This was the climate in which I joined *Late Night Line Up*. I hadn't gone after the job—in many ways it was a bigger challenge than I was seeking. In that on-going balancing act between being a good mother and having fulfilling work, I had seriously to address the pros and cons. But there were decided advantages in a programme that went out live very late at night. I would be able to organise things to be at home in the afternoons when my children needed me, share their tea, put them to bed, read the good-night story, then set out for work.

Late Night Line Up had had an odd start in life. When BBC2 was launched in 1964 it promoted itself by having a ten-minute *Line Up* at seven o'clock each night when the channel went on air. As it turned out, the opening night was a total calamity: it was wiped out entirely, overtaken by the worst power failure central London had ever

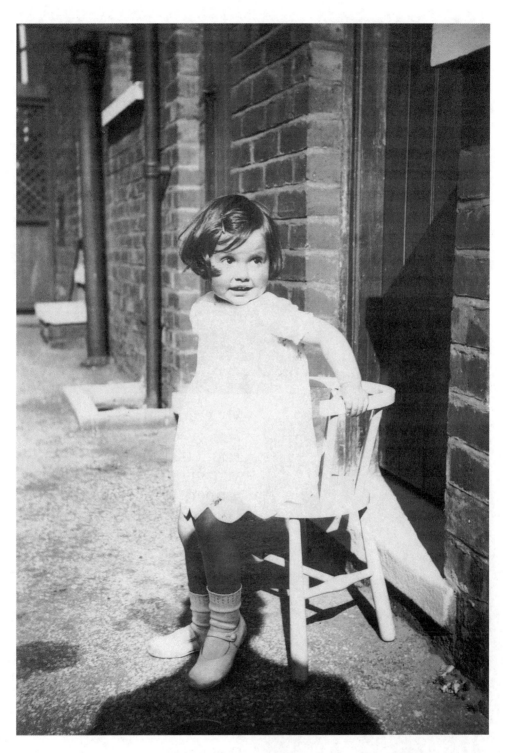

Joan Rowlands, aged five, at 11 Bakewell Road.

My grandparents.

Top left: Bill Bland proudly wearing the working clothes of a cooper.

Top right: Bill Bland of Wolverhampton married Charlotte—Lotte—Dawson in 1899. My mother, Rose, was the third of their eight children.

Left: John Morgan Rowlands of Aberystwyth married Emily Waters in 1903. My father was the first of their five children. One child in each family died in infancy.

Facing page
My parents: happy and carefree young people. They married at S George's Church, Gorton in 192

Exotic adventure: the 1938 visit to Argentina.

Top left: My mother wears a dead fox.
Top right: My first encounte with someone black.
Left: With my father on the transatlantic liner.

Facing page
My sister Susan arrives.

Top left: The only child.
Top right: Susan aged five, n aged eleven.

Bottom left: My father returns from business in Spain—Susan gets a doll, I get a new dress.

Bottom right: 'Such Devoted Sisters'—Susan even bought me the Rosemary Clooney recording.

We won the war. The foursome who had acted as secret agents against the Germans: Ann and Janice Howard, with Susan and me.

The teachers: the staff of Stockport High School for Girls, in the late 1940s. Front row furthest right, Miss Jones; second furthest right, Miss Nichols; seated centre, Miss Waggot; second row far left (standing), Miss Ashworth; fourth along (standing), Miss Glover.

The taught: the sixth form of Stockport High School, in 1950. We came together to celebrate the school's centenary in 1994 even though the school had been closed down in 1974.

At Cambridge, 1951.

Michael and I get our
degrees, 1954.

We marry in May 1955.

Family Life

Harriet, born 1959.

Matthew, born 1963.

BBC2's *Late Night Line Up*.
It ran from 1954 to 1972.

"They're fifteen denier, actually. But to get back to your views on early Byzantine wood-carving . . ."

Right: The TMC!

FIRST WOMAN INTERVIEWER
TO BE SEEN ON COLOUR TV

1968—with Allen Ginsberg.

"Yes, things are a bit quiet tonight, they're all on late-night line up."

1967—with Václav Havel, then a young playwright politically involved with what became the Prague spring of '68.

1969—with French writer Georges Simenon.

R2

"I WONDER WHAT IT IS THAT MAKES JOAN BAKEWELL'S LATE NIGHT CONVERSATION SO MUCH MORE INTERESTING THAN MINE!"

1969—with Harold Pinter.

1974—with artist Joseph Beuys at the Edinburgh Festival.

The doldrum years. Work at the BBC grew rare, but there were happy times at Scottish TV and Granada.

"DADDY, WHO WAS JOAN BAKEWELL?"
"PUNCH MAGAZINE"

Right: Rituals of the Krajny Dinner, with Clarke Tait, 1979.
Below: *Reports Action*, 1978, with Bob Greaves.

With my father in his
retirement.

With my second husband,
Jack Emery, 1979.

Above: Matthew and I in
Israel, 1979.
Right: Harriet and I, 1976.

News breaks while I am filming in Edinburgh, August 1987, that I've been dropped by the BBC.

Heart of the Matter, 1989. With Editor Olga Edridge (centre) and PA Emma Brooke. The Berlin Wall is about to come down. The bewildered East German guard in the background allows us to break off chunks as souvenirs.

1991, reporting from Quebec with an aching heart: as I film in the St James Bay wilderness, I know that back home, my father is dying.

The CBE, 1999. For services to the arts and television.

Taboo, 2001. How far have I travelled – from a narrow, conventional background to reporting today's frankness about nudity and sex.

My Generation, 1999. I look back with my contemporaries at the values and events that shaped our lives.

1990: My son Matthew's wedding. My father with his two daughters.

2002: The family today. Matthew and Sally, Harriet and Andy, and six grandchildren—Thomas, Katie, Louis, Charlie, Max and Maisie.

seen. The second night—and I was watching at home to see whether BBC2 would finally make it—*Line Up*'s presenter, Dennis Tuohy, arrived on screen bearing a lit candle. It was a cheeky but not entirely inauspicious beginning.

A year later *Late Night Line Up* came live from Battersea Power Station, an anniversary tribute to the force that had let us down. By now I was one of the team and there were other changes. *Late Night Line Up* had left its early slot and its early brief. It had become, in its own right, a regular late-night programme of substantial length. But because we were tucked snugly away within the Presentation Department, other BBC departments hadn't yet noticed us. They soon would.

Meanwhile this significant broadcasting initiative had been decided between three people: Michael Peacock, controller of BBC2, Rex Moorfoot, the head of Presentation, and Rowan Ayres. There was no more to it than that: no strategy papers, audience research, no difficult cost implications, no broader consultation. We had arrived without any fuss. In the years to come there would be plenty.

Our louche approach to what we were doing probably made it all possible. Otherwise how could we have delivered 364 programmes a year, for eight and a half years? The programme had no summer breaks, no weekends, no bank holidays. Only the news output matched that amount of exposure. Yet our programmes, coming before the nightly close-down of the channel, were always open-ended. They were of any length we chose to make them. Some might be ten or fifteen minutes, some, if the discussion was heated or the guest relaxed and interesting, went on for an hour. There was no

221

scheduled close-down hour, no union agreements. Only later, as union negotiators moved in, were we required to be off air by midnight. Otherwise we had a free hand, a small crew of mixed talents making forays from the shelter of the Presentation Department to report, promote and criticise the entire range of television's output. How on earth did it work?

Early on the routine was a killer. Each producer would have five days of preparation, Monday to Friday, then, starting the very next Saturday, seven consecutive days of programmes to get on air, then a full working week off. Michael Fentiman, one of *Line Up*'s longest-serving producers, never once seen without his leather jacket, recalls, 'By the end you were a zombie: it wasn't just the programme, it was the drink afterwards, home by 3 a.m., back in the office by 10 a.m. Crazy: we were working eighty-four hours a week. But we all wanted those nine days off!' As the years passed things got more civilised: by the 1970s there were four teams of three people, responsible for making on average three programmes a fortnight. *Line Up* had already spawned *The Old Grey Whistle Test* and *Film Night*, which had their own dedicated teams. Even so, the pace was hectic.

My first interview was a disaster. I can't remember who it was with but someone had been primed to give me an easy ride. It fell as flat as a pancake and I rushed away in shame and humiliation. But that was no use. I needed to toughen up: this programme was on every night of the year. There was no time for recriminations and long post-mortems. The thing was to get on and do it. If it flopped, there'd be another chance

222

tomorrow. And again and again. If after three months I was hopeless I'd be out. But it didn't happen, and slowly, as every three months my contract was renewed, I began to feel at home, to relax, to enjoy myself.

In the mid-sixties I was signed up for a minimum of twelve programmes every four weeks, the dates never specified in advance. I could be called in at twenty-four hours' notice. I would go in to *Line Up*'s offices in Television Centre for the ten-thirty morning editorial meeting, then, when that was through, gather up my research, make a few phone calls, possibly call in at the BBC bar for a drink or two, and head for home. Here I would settle into some concentrated research, write the script and telephone it through before the children arrived from school. I would then switch my attention to them, hear tales of playground squabbles, deal with homework and such. I would make their tea and enjoy it with them, then bath and bed, with enough time to read a story. Only then would I head back to work. I had often left for Television Centre before Michael returned in the evening. By the time I was back—never before 1 a.m.—he was fast asleep. We would wake next morning and share breakfast, family news and arrangements. But it wasn't easy.

Television was *Line Up*'s subject, and television in the sixties was at the hub of national debate. It wasn't something people did if there was nothing better to do: it was seen as the thing to do. Only three channels and still black and white, its technology was basic, but it commanded almost universal attention. Each morning on buses and trains, in offices and factories, people discussed the previous night's programmes. And because choice was limited, they found themselves all talking about the same issues. It was *Line Up*'s task to put those discussions on the box.

The BBC was a factory of programme-making. Every day pouring through the gates of Television Centre, streaming through the doors—there were no security checks, no barriers, no passes—came all the disciplines it took to get programmes on the air: make-up girls in the make-up department, costume designers in the costume department, set designers and builders in the design department, lighting men and cameramen in the studios; writers, editors, producers, directors all had their own offices. Later came the actors, presenters, musicians, dancers to green rooms and dressing rooms. Throughout the building there was a continual buzz of creative activity. There were obviously planners and schedulers, finance men, controllers and others who set the rules for what went on screen—quite severe rules about taste, decency and money—within which we operated. But they didn't set the tone, the mood of the building. It was the same at Lime Grove where Current Affairs operated, and at Kensington House, home of the Arts. The programme-makers dominated.

This provided a huge playground for *Late Night Line Up*. Regularly BBC viewers would hear at the end of a programme the voice-over announcement: 'This programme will be discussed later tonight on *Late Night Line Up*.' It built an audience, it built a following, and eventually it made us something of a cult. For not only did we talk television, we broadened out into music, poetry, world affairs, the

224

arts, film, and even our own brand of surreal happenings. Promoters and publishers knew that, with seven days of programming to fill, we would welcome their writers, pop groups, composers, stars.

Some of our guests brought with them their own playfulness. I remember the artist Marcel Duchamp arriving early to be interviewed by me. BBC Reception sat him in one of the foyer chairs where he watched with delight what was happening. Alecto Galleries were showing some of his work and had loaned us one of the pieces. It was called *Bicycle Wheel* and consisted of a wheel fixed into the top of a kitchen stool. It was the first of Duchamp's ready-mades and was one of the first expressions of what came to be known as conceptual art. I marvel now at their casual disregard of its safety, for it had arrived, and was standing, unwrapped and unattended, in the BBC foyer. When I came down to collect Duchamp he was smiling quietly to himself. 'Oh, I have been having such a good time. I have been watching the expressions on people's faces as they notice the piece and try to make something of it.' It seemed that delight was part of his personality. He smiled good naturedly, smoked cigars and would have preferred to talk about chess. My interview with him, about the nature of Dadaism, Surrealism and the nature of his found objects, is now lodged in Tate Modern.

In the same week that I interviewed Duchamp I also interviewed the American convicted spy Alger Hiss. His was and remains an intriguing story, with the suspicion that he was set up persisting to this day. His high-flying career as a lawyer, helping

225

create Roosevelt's New Deal, negotiating the post-war Yalta Agreement, setting up the United Nations, all these achievements went for nothing when in 1948, at the height of the House of Representatives' Un-American Activities Committee hearings, he had been charged with being a Communist, and spying for Russia. The first trial resulted in a hung jury; at the second, he was declared guilty. He served forty-four months in jail and came out to a career in ruins. But he persisted in pleading his innocence: articles and books about the case multiplied. It became a legendary trial. Dame Rebecca West referred to it as America's Dreyfus case.

Not surprisingly, he was keeping a low profile in London and only agreed to talk if I went to the Goring Hotel in Victoria where he was staying. I found a tall, lean man of impeccable old-world manners, gently spoken, thoughtful, not rushing to answer but fastidiously telling his story. He had fallen into poverty. He was working in a stationery store, earning very little. Yet apart from a deep outrage at his own fate, he seemed without rancour against the world. I left feeling sympathy for his plight, and still unclear as to how it had come about. Even today, the matter isn't finally resolved.

Every day through our modest little studio—so small it was originally intended for weather forecasts—passed just such diverse and interesting people. I tended to corner the classical musicians: Luciano Berio, Pierre Boulez, Karlheinz Stockhausen, William Walton and John Cage, who remained silent on the matter of his music, preferring instead to give me a recipe for Armenian chicken. Layers of salt, apparently. *Line*

226

Up took it in its stride. I interviewed the sixteen-year-old Oliver Knussen, called in at the last minute, when István Kertész withdrew, to conduct his own first symphony at the Royal Festival Hall. Pop music brought in rising stars such as the Kinks, the Bee Gees, Elton John, Fleetwood Mac, the Hollies and the Moody Blues and jazz greats such as Duke Ellington, Buddy Rich, Arlo Guthrie, Stan Kenton and Miriam Makeba. Rising comics tried out their style: Terry Jones and Michael Palin did sketches, and Barry Humphries came with an early version of Edna Everage: she was frumpy in those days, with straight, greasy hair and a felt hat. And Barry had a drink problem: I remember, but he won't, his hosing me down with the contents of a soda syphon at a rather boisterous after-the-programme party. America got wind of us: Woody Allen came several times, so did Barbra Streisand. Myrna Loy, Martha Gellhorn, Dick Gregory, Busby Berkeley, Lillian Hellman and James Baldwin all reminisced about their lives and times. Janis Joplin and Jimi Hendrix made their music, Joplin swigging great gulps of tequila in hospitality room BO55: a grim, windowless room that would drive anyone to drink. And often did. The Europeans knew they'd find a place with us: among them Günter Grass, Václav Havel, Marguerite Duras, Jacques Loussier and Georges Simenon.

Sometimes we were very serious: James Watson explained the double helix; Chinua Achebe pleaded the Biafran cause; Conor Cruise O'Brien extolled the United Nations. Sometimes we were simply surreal: on one occasion we staged a happening in which an actress played the part of outraged viewer and broke into the studio wielding

227

an umbrella. It made next day's front pages and proved our more serious point about how easy it is to create news. Another time we enacted a game invented by that whimsical spirit Ivor Cutler, involving much eccentric ritual but in fact being an excuse for everyone to splat me with custard pies.

We were among the first to ignore distinctions between high art and low. With an easy fluency poetry took its place beside pop music: Allen Ginsberg, Cecil Day-Lewis, then Poet Laureate, Roger McGough, John Arlott and John Pudney. We ignored BBC strictures about who was not to be interviewed. Oswald Mosley and Mary Whitehouse both had their say, in defiance of the BBC ban.

Why did they all come and keep on coming? Certainly the fee was derisory: I recall being in that same bleak BO55 when Sean Connery, offered a modest cheque, simply took his lighter to it and used it to ignite his cigar. No, the attraction had to be something else. Several important things were different in the 1960s. In obvious and practical terms there were few television channels, and even fewer programmes that wanted more than quickie anecdotal exchanges. Second, our outlook was unique: we indulged our guests at length, letting them expound ideas and theories in extended conversation. It was a time when such things found an eager audience: not large but committed. But, most significant of all, it was a time when change was quickening, new ideas were opening up. We seized the culture and caught up everyone in the talk.

And there was plenty of talk. Even when the programme was finished we adjourned with our

228

guests to the soon legendary hospitality room, for more talk and what became a regular late-night party. Our frequent contributors—the likes of George Melly, James Cameron, Jonathan Miller, Philip Oakes, Nicholas Tomalin, Willie Rushton, Clive James—would come along. No problem with the BBC's security men: we asked them too. And between us we drained the drinks trolley dry. Soon we were listed by *Vogue* as among the best party venues in London. I can recall—just about—getting home around three o'clock in the morning, and being up at eight to get my children off to school. It felt like a full life.

As the 1960s progressed we got more radical. History records it as a time of sex 'n' drugs 'n' rock 'n' roll, of the Summer of Love, of kaftans and beads, of Mary Quant and Biba. Photographers like David Bailey and Terence O'Neill, then young and lusty, photographed the beautiful people as they romped through the gardens of freedom trampling their parents' preconceptions in the grass. The photographs still look wonderful today.

But some things didn't photograph. And were more important. This was the decade of profound social changes enacted in laws that underpin the tolerance of society today. The 1960 acquittal of Penguin Books on charges of obscenity when they dared to publish D. H. Lawrence's explicit *Lady Chatterley's Lover* marked the start. My sister was in hospital at the time, having her appendix out. In triumph I took along a brand new copy: the nurses were all agog. Within just eight years many other things were different too: capital punishment was abolished in 1965; abortion was legalised in 1967, the same year homosexuality ceased to be a crime;

theatre censorship went in 1968; in 1969 divorce became easier. The decade of sex 'n' drugs 'n' rock 'n' roll had more serious achievements to its credit. The pictures just weren't as good.

The mood of the times was to challenge everything. So we did. One Armistice night we ran extracts from the new film *Oh What a Lovely War*, and I interviewed Spike Milligan about why he disapproved of the Cenotaph ceremony. His recollections of suffering shell-shock in the war were more poignant than any formal memorial. On the day of the investiture of the Prince of Wales we devoted the programme to the subject of Welsh nationalism. A top BBC voice charged us with 'being mischievous' and 'hell-bent on creating trouble'. Rowan's three-page response vigorously defended our 'right to provide a unique forum for people's views and attitudes that receive little or no coverage elsewhere'.

More and more we saw ourselves as the alternative television, the voice of those who wouldn't normally be heard. The war in Vietnam was bringing protesters on to the streets. We put them on television transmitting a full twenty-five-minute attack on American policy made by Americans, which had been refused transmission in the States. And as student radicalism swept Europe we brought it to Television Centre. Quite literally. At the height of the Paris troubles in 1968 we invited over to London some twenty of the ring-leaders, including Daniel Cohn-Bendit, Danny the Red. They filled the studio, and explained to Michael Dean what they were about. I turned up, too, to share the excitement. A cartoon in the press at the time showed two gendarmes on the streets of

Paris, one saying to the other, 'It's quiet tonight,' and the other replying, 'Yes, they're all over in London on *Late Night Line Up*.'

We weren't simply sympathetic to the Left: we were interested in chronicling all the changes that were afoot. In 1968 when Robert Conquest's book *The Great Terror* laid bare the horrors of Russia under Stalin, he came and told me the full story. The Left was no longer under any illusions about Russia: Solzhenitsyn's books about the gulags were reaching the West. But it hadn't given up its ideology. The talk was now of giving socialism a human face. It was a phrase that was beginning to be heard, if only in whispers, in Czechoslovakia. It was why *Line Up* wanted to be there.

In 1967 David Mercer's play *In Two Minds* caused a great stir. Produced by Tony Garnett and directed by Ken Loach, it was based on the theory that R. D. Laing had expounded to me years before: that schizophrenia might have its origins in a dysfunctional family background. It was the BBC's official entry for the Prague Television Festival. It provided an excellent pretext.

This was the year before the famous Prague spring, but rumblings could already be heard. David Mercer, who was involved with the Left, had acute political antennae. He had a way of being tuned in early to seismic political shifts. Armed with his list of contacts, we arrived in Prague and began making phone calls. It wasn't going to be simple. The Russian hold on its satellite state was rigid. I travelled on a Prague tram alongside an armed Russian soldier, one of the occupying force, being studiously ignored by the other passengers. We had been told it was likely our phones were

231

tapped and rooms bugged. Getting the interviews we did was a matter of outdoor meetings, changing rendezvous. The trickiest was with a young playwright whose plays, wry comments on the power of the state, were beginning to gain an international reputation. His name was Václav Havel. He was an apparently modest, even shy young man, rather chubby, and already a heavy smoker. But his seeming diffidence was deceptive: he had a quiet steely resolve that would see him through years of persecution and eventually give him the courage to lead the Czech people in their Velvet Revolution. But in 1967 he was still merely a dissident playwright, with a quiet smile and a quick wit. We came back to London in the summer of 1967 with a profile of dissident Prague before the West was really aware of what was under way. In January 1968 Alexander Dubcek became president and began to introduce democratic changes: a free press, an opposition. Brezhnev complained bitterly, and prepared to act.

In August of that year when Russian tanks stormed into Prague and brought its political experiment to an end those of us who'd been there and made many friends were horrified. Many of the dissidents I had interviewed on my visit managed to get out of the country. If they passed through London they contacted us and turned up again on *Line Up*. The film-maker Milo Forman went to America; Jiri Pelikan, the director of Czech television who had encouraged open and free discussion on his network, fled to Rome. But Václav Havel stayed. He was put under house arrest and from then on became the focal point for increasing dissent. Nineteen years later he became president of Czechoslovakia and, from 1993, president of the Czech Republic. Years later when he made an official visit to Britain in that role, he told me how in the sixties whenever he visited London and was quizzed by immigration officials about his purposes there, he proclaimed blithely, 'To appear on *Late Night Line Up*,' and was amiably waved through.

*   *   *

By 1968 America was at boiling point. Mainstream public opinion was swinging towards the anti-Vietnam-war demonstrators, who had been gathering strength throughout 1967. In April Martin Luther King, who had spoken out against the war, was assassinated. Robert Kennedy, who had declared himself an anti-war candidate for the Democratic nomination, was shot in June. Benjamin Spock, whose childcare manual I was now using for my own family, was convicted for counselling his protégés to avoid the draft. The Chicago Democratic Convention broke up after the pugnacious Mayor Daley of Chicago urged police to confront the huge waves of anti-war protest. That was in late August. By 4 September I was in New York for *Late Night Line Up*. We'd come a long way from just reviewing television programmes.

*   *   *

But something about the 1960s was not radical at all: its attitude towards women. True to the times, sexual harassment was a matter of routine. I took it

233

for granted. A quick squeeze, a salacious leer, an unlooked-for pinch, a remark on one's cleavage, speculation about one's sex life. Women learned to deploy a range of diversionary tactics, to duck and weave, to reject, repel and discourage without creating an 'incident'. It was a useful social skill. And I needed it.

Louis MacNeice's poem 'Bagpipe Music' celebrates 'a bit of skirt in a taxi', and in the fifties the acronym NSIT had stood for 'not safe in taxis'. Even so, I was surprised when, having gone to the House of Commons in a taxi to collect Douglas Jay, then president of the Board of Trade and a member of Harold Wilson's cabinet, I had to fend him off vigorously before we arrived at Television Centre. Sometimes it was more brazen than that. Mortimer Wheeler, who already had a goatish reputation, actually had his hand on my knee and creeping up my leg in the course of our live studio interview. On another occasion a film director I hardly knew made a direct offer: 'I want a mistress and I'd like it to be you. But my wife mustn't know. Can we come to an arrangement?' I didn't tell him I already had one.

And then Frank Muir invented the phrase that has followed me ever since: 'the thinking man's crumpet'. Asked by a print journalist, writing about *Line Up*, to summarise each of us, Frank delivered the defining phrase. It went into the headline. And has stayed with me. These were the days of mini-skirts and long, loose hair. For the first time in my life I was riding a wave of confidence, in myself as a woman with an exciting role in television and in terms of my private life. No doubt I radiated a sense that things were going well for me. I was also

234

capable of deploying flirtation as a tactic for getting what I wanted, and for getting on with people I liked. Then it didn't carry the heavy disapproval of the feminist ideologues.

How do I feel about it as a label? My response has changed with the eras. Initially I thought of it as no more than a larky joke, a teasing male put-down for someone they couldn't handle. As it persisted, I talked with Michael about the problem of being defined simply by my looks. He replied, soothingly and generously, by reading to me the lovely poem by Yeats, 'For Anne Gregory', which ends

> . . . only God, my dear,
> Could love you for yourself alone
> And not your yellow hair.

Then, in the early 1970s, having gone to support a feminist meeting in Westminster Hall, I was suddenly surrounded by a group of young women who demanded aggressively why I felt entitled to be there, and why I had not denounced in public the insult to which I had been subjected. Only then did I begin to take it seriously. Of course if you deconstruct the phrase, the 'thinking' belongs to the man and so does the 'crumpet'. I was being defined as no more than what today might be labelled 'toff's totty'. This was so clearly at odds with how I saw myself that I began seriously to care that it would reflect on any reputation I was building as a professional broadcaster. Throughout the seventies I tried to limit the damage. Whenever young female reporters—and there were more and more of them—came to interview me, I would ask them not to use the phrase. Apologetically they would explain it was mandatory: 'The editor [male] insists.' Then in the eighties when I was busy on *Newsnight* it was no longer relevant, and even when it persisted in the press, I could once again laugh it off. By the nineties the phrase itself was out of date, a quaint left-over from earlier values. And I was by then among the first generation of older women to be seen on the screen. Young women now ask bemusedly, 'What was all the fuss about?' It is itself, in a tiny way, a measure of how far, in language, attitude and behaviour, women have come since the sixties.

*   *   *

During the Summer of Love—1967—the laughter of the flower-power children in their floating skirts and exotic jewellery wafted in through our windows, and tugged at our ageing hearts. For someone like me, already with a husband, home and two children, the gilded caravanserai of youth's pleasure came too late. Had I simply been at home I might have missed even a glimpse of the passing cavalcade. But somehow shreds and patches of the whole hazy world of psychedelia and its messages of druggy pleasure lapped at the doors of the BBC and, for a short while, made its home in corners of *Late Night Line Up*. To open the doors of our office from the grey rigours of a BBC corridor was to enter another world. Secretaries in flower-speckled flowing dresses clattered at their typewriters. I favoured Biba boots, clothes by Ossie Clarke and the earliest Mary Quant, sometimes full-length Laura Ashley dresses, and wide floppy hats, festooned with scarves. There were no BBC suits in sight. Those not permanently welded into their leather jackets flaunted bright colours, cheesecloth, denim and coats of many colours. There was a dartboard and a game regularly in progress. Some people would be making plans to go to the rock festivals; a bolder group attended the Wet Dream Festival in Amsterdam. A number smoked cannabis. And did so regularly. On afternoons when rock groups were recording in Studio B, the air outside was pungent with the familiar smell. And then things went too far.

It was Rowan's birthday and someone baked a cake, lightly laced with cannabis, for the whole office to enjoy. By the time I arrived, there was not a crumb left. Instead I found heaps of giggling people, laughing at each other's remarks and indulging in sillinesses of all kinds. Others were nodding off quietly in armchairs. Rowan, however, was not amused. Not even remotely, not a glimmer. He knew we had pushed things too far and put the whole easy-going enterprise in danger. Several Riot Acts and dressing-downs later, we were, within days, being more discreet. But it had been a close call. It was soon after this that two newly recruited and startled young secretaries broke ranks and reported that someone had offered to sell them cannabis. This time the move was low-key, swift and effective. 'Hasn't someone from *Line Up* been done for drugs?' I was asked. By then he had already gone and it was easy enough to answer, 'No.'

Line Up had a following rather than a mass audience. It appealed to intelligent people who were interested in books, ideas, music and, above all, television. But it also had many enemies within the BBC. The BBC's mighty programme-making departments hated seeing the talent they had nurtured and brought to the screen unceremoniously dismissed—within hours of transmission—by guests invited in by, as they saw it, an irresponsible gang of mavericks answerable to no one.

The trouble was there from the start. Early in 1965 BBC2 transmitted a serial adaptation of Dostoevsky's *The Brothers Karamazov*. Following the final episode I interviewed David Magarshack, the novel's distinguished translator. Director of Television Kenneth Adam condemned our instant criticism. The memos flew. 'It's all right, perhaps, for *The Likely Lads* but you cannot dismiss a really serious adaptation like *The Brothers Karamazov* too frivolously.' And the controller of BBC2 weighed in alongside: 'Was it not predictable that anyone so closely concerned with a novel of this magnitude would have found a television adaptation unsatisfactory, and, therefore, be pretty sour in his reaction to it?' That was it. A gentle shot across Rowan's bows. The fact is that the concept of balance held no sway in our outlook. Today it would most probably be considered wise to have an opinion in favour balanced by an opinion against. We believed that an extended conversation with an individual of strong views legitimately held was fascinating in itself.

Whenever a television play caused a scandal *Line Up* was usually there aiding and abetting. There were plenty of opportunities: in just seven years, from 1965 to 1972, there were 231 Wednesday Plays and Plays for Today. Each major work by Dennis Potter, David Mercer, Alan Plater, Simon Gray and Charles Wood got the full *Line Up* treatment. Sometimes we did this with the happy collaboration of its producer and director. Tony Garnett and Ken Loach, responsible for so much of television's ground-breaking drama, never complained about us and, indeed, offered active help and contributions. But then, they, like us, were busy pushing back the frontiers of what television was allowed to do.

Up the Junction was expected to cause trouble. It answered the call of BBC Drama's aggressive new head, Sidney Newman, for 'gutsy, spontaneous contemporaneity'. But it was a political hot potato: it was about abortion, at that time illegal, and Nell Dunn's raunchy script involved the enactment of an illegal abortion on a kitchen table. *Line Up* was alerted. We gave it double coverage. On the night before transmission we broadcast an interview with Nell Dunn. On the night the play went out we devoted virtually all of a thirty-minute programme to it, including footage of Nell Dunn and Ken Loach answering calls from the public, and a report on the number and tone of calls to the duty office, which referred to the BBC being 'flooded with protests'. It was the latter remark that got us into trouble.

We had ignored a general ruling by the director general and the board of management that no reference should be made to numbers or tone of calls of protest received, a ruling made 'in a determination not to allow the lunatic fringes, who, as the Duty Log shows, are so often the majority of the callers, to dominate the front pages and so make our programme policy more difficult to

239

implement'. Then as now the BBC was touchy about the protests it received.

It was touchy, too, about the strong competition coming from the commercial channel. In the summer of 1968 three new independent companies were launched: Harlech, Yorkshire and London Weekend. *Line Up* invited three independent critics, Philip Oakes, Michael Findlay and Nicholas Tomalin, to review their first week's output. Nicholas Tomalin was witty and fulsome in his praise of London Weekend Television. BBC bigwigs would have preferred blander stuff: we were wrong to be promoting our rivals. 'It amounted to a puff for London Weekend Television and did not question the claims made by all three companies . . . they also knocked the BBC without being challenged.' The squall was quickly soothed by the controller of BBC2, who claimed it as 'a remarkable demonstration of the BBC's broadmindedness'.

The hero in much of this was David Attenborough, who had become controller of BBC2 in 1965 and was daily in touch with Rowan, tipping him off when the battle was getting hot. Huw Wheldon, controller of programmes who'd appointed Attenborough, backed him up declaring, in the face of one attempted putsch to have us abolished, that *Late Night Line Up* was 'working in an area which no other television network would dare to contemplate . . . It is always lively, sometimes brilliant . . . I am most reluctant to ask controller BBC2 to clip the wings of this important and inventive programme or to ask him to change its nature.' Instead he asked the departments to support us by supplying any clips we needed. In return he put *Line Up* on three months' notice that we should temper our criticisms.

We did for a while. But there was always a contradiction. The heads of BBC departments were passionately committed to their programmes and unable to understand how every night the BBC could be broadcasting serious criticism of its own output. They would demand that something be done. The discontent spread. Contributors began to complain, too. Drama producers found writers were hurt and upset when their efforts were dismissed virtually as the credits rolled. Some threatened to take their work to ITV. In 1969 Irene Shubik, one of the most illustrious producers of the Wednesday Play, personally requested that *Line Up* be forbidden to discuss *The Exiles*, by Errol John. Rowan told her it was none of her business. She appealed to the new controller of BBC2, Robin Scott, and he conceded. There had been just too many rows.

It's hard to realise, now that television has become a commodity, subject to the market forces of cost-cutting, ratings, consumers, marketing and competition, that there was a time when many of us saw it as a public facility, which came to us, in the case of the BBC, in return for the licence fee; it was a place where ideas could be presented in all sorts of ways and offered up for people to consider, an arena of democratic exchange in the interests of all. *Line Up* carried this to extremes, handing over some of its programmes to groups of people to speak as they chose. In February 1971 Tony Bilbow went down to the Guinness factory to ask a group of workers their views of the week's television. Half-way through, as things got noisy, one of them

241

declared, 'Well, you'll be cutting this, won't you, to suit yourselves? You won't let it go out just as we say.' It was a challenge we took up, transmitting the entire encounter with all its edges rough and its opinion raw. It was a real breakthrough. Far from being merely chaotic and untidy, which it was, it also had an energy and immediacy that in those days was new to the screen. It was even commended by the BBC board of management.

We were spurred on to do more. Other factories, other groups had their say. As they gained in confidence their say wasn't merely about specific programmes. Soon BBC policy was being examined and criticised. Popular participation was all very well, it seemed, when they approved of you but not otherwise: by November 1971 the director general had put it on record that he 'was concerned about the way in which *Late Night Line Up* raised matters of BBC policy behind the backs of management'. Television's managing director agreed: 'The television service was embarrassed by this and other incidents associated with *Late Night Line Up*. It was trying to devise ways of preventing repetition.' The writing was on the wall.

Line Up finally came off the air on 20 December 1972. Its last programme was devoted to a long interview with David Attenborough, our foremost champion, who was himself leaving the role of director of programmes, television, to return to programme-making. It was a celebratory wake for all of us. My lasting memory is of David, late into the night and relieved of the burdens of office, waltzing round the gilded figure of Ariel that sits at the heart of the doughnut-shaped Television Centre, and singing to the skies, 'I am free! I am free!' It was a fine end to what had been the eight-year run of an extraordinary programme, sprung from nowhere, staffed by radicals and enthusiasts, that had entertained and informed the public about every aspect of television, the most significant new medium since print that would shape their times and their thinking for the foreseeable future. In later years there would be attempts to re-create something like it, bring back its immediacy, revive the old spontaneity. They didn't work. The moment had passed.

But we had had our hour in the sun.

CHAPTER ELEVEN

FAMILY AND FRIENDS

I thought I could do it all. Each of the different segments of my life, the job, the children, the marriage and more, made different demands. I felt I was up to it. I relished having such richness in my life. But I was going it alone. The entire domestic routine was accepted as my responsibility. Wasn't that how it had always been in families like mine? I had learned to cook and sew, to clean and polish, and if I did it with less fanaticism than my mother, I still accepted it was my responsibility. I marvel at women today, liberated from the assumption that they must provide a clean and tidy home and three meals a day for their families before they even think of having a paid job. Anything I did was in the teeth of that assumption. My mother had always said, 'The rich have their babies and then

243

give them to others to bring up. We don't do that.' Although I disavowed much that she stood for, some of it stuck. So, yes, I would bring up my children, they would go to local day schools, I would feed, clothe and cherish them. I would be the mother of the Gracchi.

Naturally it was also for me to nurture the marriage. It was all very well for me to read Betty Friedan and feel ready to reject the feminine mystique. Putting it into practice was another thing. Michael's career was going well. In 1964, when he was just thirty-three, he became Head of Plays for BBC Television. A great opportunity. I saw it as my role to back him up, to provide the care and comfort that would support his working life. When we moved to our new home, I saw it as my responsibility to deal with electricians and builders, hunt for second-hand furniture, shop around for lamps and cutlery, choose rugs and china. And once they were all in place I became the perfect hostess, trimming the candles, stirring the Béarnaise and watching the soufflé rise.

As for the job, I had no long-term plans. No one spoke of my having a career. I overheard someone say, 'She does it for the pin money.' The dictionary defines 'pin money' as 'a woman's pocket expenses'. It then goes on to offer a more obscure historic definition: 'money gained by women from adultery or occasional prostitution'. Thus women's earnings were either trivial or sullied. Certainly for the first years of *Late Night Line Up* I was paid less than the other presenters, and only Michael Dean's indignation on my behalf got the situation remedied. We were a loyal band, probably less interested in money than in justice.

244

Once I joined *Late Night Line Up* I thought and lived very much day by day. Working on a programme that goes out daily gives you a shortened time perspective. An enterprise that can have its genesis in the morning, can develop its plans, shape up its project, embark on its fulfilment and reach completion all before the end of the day foreshortens your own sense of time. Life in miniature. So mine became like that, living in the immediate present. It was the only way I could cope. Day by day the engagement diaries of the late sixties and early seventies record . . . what do they record?

DIARY: AUGUST 1966, *Matthew has measles*.
For a mother of small children there is something close, even something sweet about the mild illnesses of childhood. In those days mumps was thought of as routine for children: they caught it, they stayed in bed, the doctor made a couple of easy-going visits and they got better. There were no jabs, no medical panics. Our attitude to measles was the same. Even when you had it in France.

In the summer of 1966 Michael and I with Harriet, then seven and Matthew, who was three, took a motoring holiday along the Loire valley in the white Cortina, moving from one Logis de France to another. One sunny afternoon we visited the château of Azay-le-Rideau; tall trees gave welcome shade to the avenue that approaches the fabulous building. We had a basket full of melons and pâté, crusty bread, a rug, sunglasses, sun oil— all the paraphernalia of a picnic. We also had a whingeing child. Matthew initially fell behind, we walked ever more slowly and he failed to keep up.

He held out his arms to be carried, he lay on my shoulder. Was he tired, irritable, just being difficult? Later I was to think back often, and guiltily, to how slow I was in realising that he was ill, his brow hot and his energy draining away. Rather late in the day the truth dawned. Abandoning all plans for the outing we drove to the nearest *pharmacie* and bought a thermometer. His temperature was soaring. By the time we checked into our hotel at Amboise he was lolling in my arms almost unconscious. The French *patron* was immediately helpful and sympathetic, no thought of rejecting us and our problem. To safeguard their other guests, they accommodated us in a small annexe at the rear of the hotel and called their doctor. He came within half an hour. By now Matthew was in a bad way. I cooled his head with a damp cloth as the doctor diagnosed measles.

What to do? The hotel extended our stay, fed us regularly, and as Michael and Harriet went exploring, I lay beside my son in a darkened room for four days. The spots covered his body, and clogged his eyelids. I knew of the risk to his sight, so the curtains were kept permanently closed. It wasn't light enough to read a book. I simply gazed at my sad little boy, hour after hour, watching the progress of his rash, the hot swelling red blotches, his little person too ill even to moan. I entered with him into the fever and sweats: I stroked him, held him, washed him. The French doctor came daily and administered medicine. On the third day, Matthew looked up, registered our presence.

Today the same events would follow a different course. We know more now, and there would be more concern and alarm. In those times, childhood ailments simply took their place in the woven intricacy of love and loving that defines being a mother. Our response depended less on public-health information than on what we knew from our own early years.

I recall, with something close to happiness, the episodes when I had measles, mumps and chicken-pox. It released in my mother a unique tenderness. The greatest treat of all was when, with great caution, she would carry upstairs on a black metal shovel a heap of burning coals glowing red from the living-room fire and set them in the small green-tiled fireplace at the foot of my bed. In practical terms it did no more than take the chill off the icy room but as the afternoon darkened and the curtains were drawn, the flickering of flames on the ceiling above my head was childhood's bliss. I lay on the rumpled sheets, the clamminess of a high temperature slicking my hair to the nape of my neck, and revelled in a near delirium of happiness.

I tried always to create such a sensation of comfort and care for my own children. It's what mothers do; it's what children remember. Their need is palpable. They seek and hold your gaze, following you as you move quietly and solicitously round their room and round their bed. They snuggle against you seeking the animal comfort of your body's texture and smell, they bury their head in your lap. Caring for a sick child is the essence of being a parent. It is when bonds are forged for ever. Compared to it, the real world and its commitments must go hang.

Thirty-five years later Matthew and I returned to Amboise, he now in his late thirties and a father of four. I wanted to tease out my memories of the measles episode. Could I recapture what it felt like, have the old sensations of concern and fondness? Experience again what it was to be a young mother? I knew that would feel good, recalling a particular kind of happiness. Today, like all the other Loire towns, Amboise is organised around its tourism: pedestrianised streets, ranks of postcard stands, too many T-shirts and souvenir shops. And more hotels. We went in search of the *logis* with the annexe, where my small son had been so ill. Was it this one? No space. Or this one? Wrong outlook. It seemed to have vanished. The château walls, the bridge and the riverbank were solid and present, and busy. Too busy to remind me of times past. My memories were wispy, intangible, suspect. I tried to force the memories forward; I stared hard at things that hadn't changed. I have always loved the broad steady throb of the river Loire, the moving depths of its water dappled in places where rocks break the surface into an intricate web of ripples, in a pattern that never changes. But my stares elicited no response, no sudden cry of recognition of this tree, that green island basking in the sun. I measured out spaces, gazed at windows, mansard roofs, glimpsed restaurant tables, pleading with my memory to come forward with some sentimental recognition. It refused.

Then I realised my folly and let go of all the effort. We had beers by the little old church; we took photographs of each other on the bridge; we ate lunch at a window table with a full view of the town, just in case a memory might sneak up while I was preoccupied with soup or cheese. We took time to explore the house of Leonardo da Vinci of which

I had no recall. We made our own day. Suddenly my present outing with my grown son to Amboise mattered more than the memories that had brought me there. One day I expect to recall it with just as warm nostalgia.

DIARY: 16 OCTOBER 1964, *election results.*
At one of those election-night parties, energised by shared hopes, Michael and I joined our friends Jim and Monica Ferman, whom we had known at Cambridge, at their home in Swiss Cottage to see the results come in. Jim—James Ferman, who would one day be the nation's film censor—was at that time directing plays for BBC Television. It was there I met David Mercer for the first time. He was then emerging as one of television's foremost playwrights. His television career had begun in 1961 when, with the confidence of the newcomer, he began with a trilogy, *Where the Difference Begins*, *A Climate of Fear* and *Birth of a Private Man*, plays that told of the generational and class conflicts that were becoming evident as children of the working class made their way up in the world. David's father had been a railwayman in Wakefield although, as a driver of steam trains, he was one of the working-class and union élite. David and his brother Reuben, a scientist, moved into different worlds.

We had all voted Labour, some with more enthusiasm than others. David was a Marxist and a good deal further to the left, I think, than the rest of us. But for us all it was a long, nail-biting night. The Tories had held power for thirteen unbroken years, the government mocked by *That Was the Week That Was* was now being brought down by the ludicrous Christine Keeler scandal. Harold Wilson won by a whisker, with an overall majority of four.

Some weeks later, David Mercer phoned and asked to come round. Michael was away, the children in bed. I agreed with hardly a second thought. We sat in the darkening room before a blazing stove, gazing into the red heart of the coals. I would later learn that he was much given to impulsive infatuations. This and his eloquence brought him many conquests. But the term 'casual affairs' won't serve. David was genuinely interested in how other people thought and experienced the world. Each attachment mattered to him. While he was with you, he turned the full force of his attention towards you. On that night, crestfallen, like a reproved child, he offered to leave. Instead I asked him to stay and talk.

What he was really good at was friendship. While his emotional life was often chaotic, his friendships were strong and true. And there was nothing exclusive about such friendships. He wanted his friends to know and share each other. Gradually I found myself drawn into the orbit of his circle. Television success and that of a West End play—*Ride a Cock Horse* starring Peter O'Toole—had made David suddenly affluent. He had wasted no time in buying a house in Hamilton Gardens, Maida Vale, and, rare for those times, called in a designer to create spaces of light and colour, big sofas, big lamps, strong primary colours. It was to become a magnet of sixties talk and conviviality. At all hours of day and night writers, actors, film-makers converged on the place. Tony Garnett, then producing a raft of outstanding Wednesday Plays—including several of David's— was there a good deal. So were David's neighbours, the lawyer Irving Teitelbaum and his wife Mo, the writer Roger Smith, a French actress called Maria, who bore David a daughter. Later there would be Lynn, who was initially still in the sixth form of her school. Finally there was the beautiful Israeli, Daphna, who became his third wife and, all too soon, his widow.

I, too, began to call round there regularly. I would drop in on my way home from *Late Night Line Up*. For a time I even had my own key. I would get there sometime after midnight to find lights blazing from every window of the tall house, the place busy with people drinking, a few smoking pot and arguing. How should society be organised? How should we live our lives? The two great questions bequeathed to us by those bearded old men Marx and Freud. It was the serious side of the sixties: fundamental questions of how society is organised were being debated across all classes, genders and countries. And we lived in a mood of rising expectations.

As the sixties progressed the talk seemed to get more frantic: civil rights, psychiatry, Cuba, Guevara, the Vietnam war. In July 1967, London's Roundhouse played host to *The Dialectics of Liberation Congress*. The show was a hit: it ran for two weeks and played to packed houses. I went along to join a throng being harangued by Stokely Carmichael, the black American radical who coined the phrase 'Black Power', whom I could hardly hear but whose bright yellow satin shirt—its full sleeves amply displayed by his sweeping gestures—made him, even in the shadows of the cavernous Roundhouse, a charismatic figure. When *les événements* burst on to the streets of Paris,

251

British supporters went across to join them. For the rest, there was a major sit-in at Hornsey Art College. There were radical magazines being written: the *Black Dwarf* edited by Tariq Ali, the *International Times*, the *New Left Review*. There was even the dotty proposal, put forward, I think, by Kenneth Tynan when Jean-Louis Barrault occupied L'Odéon in Paris in support of France's striking workers, that we—someone—should occupy the Royal Opera House, Covent Garden. As David ruefully remarked: 'In Britain, no one would notice!'

And somewhere along the way, I broke the demarcations of my different lives: I told David Mercer about my continuing affair with Harold Pinter.

DIARY: 20 APRIL 1965, *Francine arrives*.

How did I manage this complicated life? I couldn't cope with two children, a job and everything else without help. Nannies and housekeepers were for grander folk than I, so I opted for au pairs, a succession of them, arriving one after another at about the same time each year with the purpose of learning English in exchange for a little domestic help, full board and pocket money. All very well in theory. The practice fell often hilariously far short of expectations.

Gitte was the first and the best, although we weren't to know that then. Gitte had a magical gift: she could think into the mind of a child. It was like living with an angel, her low voice, her gentle presence softened for us the strain of having someone else enter the circle of our marriage. Michael and I were close, intensively so, in a

252

private, exclusive way. At home we wanted to be alone together. We had grown to think alike, to react alike. Now we had to accommodate not only a first child entering the circle but a stranger eating and sleeping in the same domestic cocoon of our home. Gitte made it possible, showing us through her love for Harriet that families needn't be inward-looking and enclosed. She invented games, created stories, amused and soothed, and wept when the time came for her to leave us, not turning round to wave goodbye, so great was the pain, as the taxi sped her away. A year later, when we saw the film *Mary Poppins* and the magical nanny flew away, out of the lives of the children, Harriet, at the time four years old, reminded suddenly of her own loss, stood in the cinema and screamed to no one and everyone: 'I want my Gitte back! I want my Gitte back!' Not many children are lucky enough to start life with their own Mary Poppins. We would never be that lucky again.

Maria was tall and clumsy, as though always surprised her limbs were so big. She had a loud voice, big laugh and a hearty willingness to please. But her purse was stolen on the Underground and she went home in sorrow at the wickedness of the English. Then came Francine, French and chic, who with her friend would try on my clothes when I was out. Michael discovered what was going on but didn't tell me until she'd left. Marguerite was problematic from the start, given to sudden bursts of energy and then turning glum and downcast. She brought home a boyfriend, waxen-skinned, pimply and equally moody. It was when the wastepaper basket began to fill with syringes that we realised she had to go. Then came Sabine, tall and blonde, fastidiously dressed; she brought her own crisp white aprons with her. But she set the house on fire. She left an electric fire switched on next to curtains and came back from classes one day to find the top of the house burned off and her exquisite wardrobe in cinders. She chose to leave of her own accord. As they came and went, mostly German, some French, an Israeli, strange idioms invaded the children's language: a three-year-old doesn't normally begin a sentence 'Notwith-standing . . .'; neither does 'otherwise' nor 'that being the case' feature in childish speech. It was time to try an English girl. Unhappily she came from the rural backwaters of Norfolk where they don't talk much at all. Within six months she was pregnant and went back home to her mother.

I bore all these adventures with resigned lightheartedness, knowing it was the price I must pay for being a working mother. I could expect it to be troublesome, awkward, stressful, this having-your-cake-and-eating-it. I might aspire to the freedoms of feminism, but it needed freer spirits, bolder figures than mine to press forward the revolution. I must grin and bear it.

DIARY: SEPTEMBER 1965, *Michael away in Munich*.
Michael's job as Head of Plays put him under enormous pressure. Increasingly he was travelling abroad, meeting writers and other television people. His boss was Sydney Newman, an ebullient Canadian who'd been poached by the BBC from the ITV company ABC where he had galvanised their drama with a policy of strong raw plays of contemporary life. Now he was doing the same for the BBC. He expected Michael to find and develop

new writers and producers and help to get their work on television. There was no shortage of talent, but the subjects were new and challenging. Michael backed them to the hilt, bringing to the screen a stream of single plays that made audiences and critics sit up and take notice. Others were taking notice too.

In 1964 Mary Whitehouse, a senior art mistress at a school in Shropshire, was seeing on television a whole lot of things she didn't like. In the name of her Christian beliefs and strong traditional family values she spearheaded a campaign against the 'filth and depravity' of BBC programmes. If she was a woman seeking a role, she had found it. The chairmanship of the National Viewers and Listeners Association fitted her like a glove—a rather smart one, in fact, of a pair that matched her handbag and her hat. Mary Whitehouse, suburban smart in a time of kaftans and beads, expressed the fears of middle England and spoke from a devoutly Christian perspective that was then much more widely shared. Her very ordinariness marked her out as a formidable champion. There were no convoluted intellectual dilemmas to cloud her judgement. When she protested from the centre of her own life and attitudes, thousands identified with her. She wanted television to present a Christian version of a good life: she admired *Dixon of Dock Green* in which, week by week, the friendly copper put right society's ills. She reserved a particular hatred for the Wednesday Play and Play for Today. Michael was in the firing line.

Nuns being raped in the Congo wasn't anybody's idea of a wholesome Christian life. *For the West*, by Michael Hastings, was a play about the Congo massacres, produced by James MacTaggart, just one of the thirty-two single plays he would produce for the BBC in 1965. MacTaggart's output was not only prodigious in quantity, it was outstanding in quality. Of those thirty-two plays he produced, four were by Dennis Potter, two by John Hopkins, with others by Hugh Whitemore, David Mercer, Nell Dunn, Christopher Logue and Troy Kennedy Martin. The MacTaggart Lecture, the keynote address of Edinburgh's annual television festival, was named in his honour. 1965 was his year, but *For the West* was not one of his best. All these plays were pushing the barriers, trying out new ways to express new ideas, but it was the use of violence in *For the West* that caused a public outcry. It could be argued that massacres are hard to write about without depicting violence, but even Sydney Newman, reminiscing years later, regretted its transmission: 'The play involved an act of gross cruelty to a child and I don't think anyone becomes emotionally or morally richer by seeing that sort of thing.'

We were on holiday in Ireland at the time, seeking escape and rest in the solitude of the Kerry hills, kicking sand along wide strands, staying in farms where the children could play with animals and get their clothes dirty. The BBC tracked us down even there. Without mobile phones or even, at some of the farms, phones at all, they found us. The Director General required an immediate response. When would we be back? Please see me. It was a call to the headmaster's study. Or that was how it felt.

Michael cared about good writing and good writers. He enjoyed the creative collaboration,

256

talking about scene structure, dialogue, character, casting. That was where the rewards lay. It was what he was good at. But fighting battles with organised lobbies was not his strength; nor were the competitive egos of BBC management. He faltered. The scripts piled up around him, but he refused to delegate. He became stressed and his health began to suffer.

There was strain in his private life, too. In Venice I had unwittingly opened a letter into another private life than mine. And I had handed it back and let the matter rest. I never enquired further. Michael, likewise, respected my privacy. But now there were indications that his contained life was no longer contained. Nor was it happy. Nor was it the only other life. Our marriage, so carefully poised and shielded from pain, was about to spiral out of control.

DIARY: 16 SEPTEMBER 1967, *Music Makers at Gospel Oak*.
The steadying hand of routine held me firm, kept me functioning. Children thrive on routine, and I thrived with them. While I was caring for them, attendant to all the trivia of daily life, they were caring for me. Out of that daily trivia, something worthwhile was being created. The modern habit of cynicism requires me to disclaim this even as I write it, but my share in shaping my children's lives was the most creative thing I have ever done.

The Music Makers were a group of parents, teachers and children who came together on Saturday mornings at Gospel Oak School to play together. My children were both learning: Harriet the piano and clarinet, Matthew, the piano and

257

flute. I was one with thousands of other parents keen to supplement the standard state education with all the extras that would make for a civilised life: music lessons, ballet lessons, acting lessons, visits to galleries and museums, outings to castles and stately homes, concerts and theatre visits—the whole package of middle-class cultural aspiration.

I remember it now: sitting in the parked car in Weymouth Mews while the children took those musical briefcases—the ones closed with a metal strip suspended in two leather straps—up the mews stairs to a half-hour piano lesson with the formidable doyenne of piano teachers Barbara Kirkby Mason, who wrote the books from which they practised. I recall the dancing-class showcase afternoons, sitting glumly through the displays of gawky, clumsy children parading as fairies and cygnets, in the hope that one's own might break the mould and emerge as the occasion's one true swan. It was not to be.

I have a fond memory of Harriet returning from drama classes conducted in the living room of George Melly's house with questions about a strange painting that hung above them as they writhed on the floor pretending to be snakes or frogs. The picture was clearly bewildering to a child. It was the naked body of a woman, which also looked like a face. Which was it? It was, in fact, by Magritte, *Le Viol*—The Rape. George Melly, famous as a jazz singer, had always been a keen collector of paintings. And there really was nothing to explain. The painting *was* both a body and a face. Art was like that, I explained, probably a more enduring lesson for her than the drama class.

DIARY: ANNIVERSARY, 29 JUNE, *Mother's death.*

We all resolve to do better than our mothers. In my case I wanted to do things differently. She had been a formidable smacker. In being a parent who didn't smack I learned many things. First, in the short term, smacking is easiest. A sharp slap, a quick bout of tears and it's over and done with, a lesson learned. And it may be. But something else isn't over. And if smacking happens often, it becomes the defining form of the relationship. Second, children are unbelievably provoking, driving the patience of parents to the limit, testing their strengths and weaknesses, exploiting their hesitancies. Every parent will reach the limit of their tolerance. I did. Twice: once when Harriet ran out into the street into the path of an approaching car; again, when Matthew's prolonged fit of sulks was ruining a holiday for us all. Third, the rewards of not smacking are slow to be realised but rich and enduring in their influence. I recall the exhaustion of having to summon up a reasoned case in response to 'Why should I?' rather than the peremptory 'Because I say so!' Oh, how often I longed for that 'Because I say so!' But it's not something you'd ever say to an adult, and the sooner a child learns the nature of reasoned argument the better.

My sister Susan and I had been my mother's power base. And she'd hung on to it rendering us timid, lacking in confidence well into our adult lives. This was something else I wanted to do differently. Better to start early. Out of the interminable family arguments emerged the two strong personalities of my daughter and my son. At the age of thirteen Harriet was given a dress allowance, a modest enough sum but it came with gentle indications of what I would find appropriate. She sped off triumphant and came back with her first purchase: a second-hand white satin wedding dress. The second item for this progressively eccentric wardrobe was a full-length fitted silk coat worn by film actress Lizabeth Scott in a 1930s movie and found in some obscure sale of showbiz costumes. Evidently she was destined to be her own woman. And not just in clothes. From early on she showed considerable musical talent: the piano, the clarinet, even the violin. At the time the Inner London Educational Authority had in its gift scholarships for those showing musical ability. Harriet was awarded one such scholarship but defiantly turned it down. To my pleading words, 'Why not give it a try?' and 'One day you'll be glad you did . . .', she offered her firm rebuttal: 'Do I want a career in classical music? No. Would I rather spend my time doing something else? Yes. Wouldn't the scholarship do more good to someone who wanted it? Yes.' She clearly knew her own mind. And has done ever since.

DIARY: 10 JULY 1968, *Matthew: parents' day.*
In the 1960s and 70s many people had an optimistic sense that a great educational enterprise was under way: the move to comprehensive education. I was thoroughly in favour, believing, simply on the evidence of my own life, that there were plenty of bright children not getting the start in life they deserved, and if educational resources were shared fairly then both the children and the community would be better off. We naively reckoned without

the strength of Britain's private schools, which continued to cream off many of the best teachers and, in return for big fees, kept class sizes low.

None the less, numbers of public school-educated parents who could afford private education chose instead to send their children to comprehensives as a matter of principle. There were also public school-educated teachers who opted to make their careers in state schools. It was a time of high hopes and the founding of many fine schools. Harriet went to Camden School for Girls, founded by the Victorian pioneers in girls' education, Miss Beale and Miss Buss, at the very moment when it was changing from being a grammar school to a comprehensive. Matthew would be less lucky. His own state school, St Marylebone Grammar School, which had been founded in 1797, wasn't allowed to go comprehensive. It was simply abolished, closing in 1981 just as my own grammar school, Stockport High School for Girls, had closed in 1974. Suddenly a policy that was wiping out the good—the grammar schools—before soundly establishing a worthy replacement seemed to me folly. In despair I abandoned my loyalty to state education: Matthew finished his schooling at Latymer Upper School in Hammersmith. I was exercising my choice to select the best for my child. But it was a choice I could make only because I had enough money to pay.

One day Matthew, too, would make his own choices. And not as I expected. Failing to pass his A levels at a standard that would gain him the exact place in the exact university and course he preferred, he refused to go to university at all. To cheer him up in what he saw as his failure, I called him to join me up in Edinburgh where I was reporting on the Festival for BBC Television. We found him a job washing dishes in the basement of the Festival Club—incidentally, alongside George Melly's son—and in their spare time they shared the delights of the fringe. Then he decided to take ship and sail from Leith docks to London, on a two-masted brig where untrained young people were being taught the rudiments of the sea. He phoned two weeks later from the London docks to say he wouldn't be coming home. He was staying with the ship. They would sail to Cornwall and then across the Atlantic. This was what he really wanted to do. He had, in effect, run away to sea. Another resolute young person. Not doing what I wanted them to do, but being the sort of people I wanted them to be.

DIARY: JUNE 1962, *Venice*.
Throughout the 1960s Michael and I returned often to Venice. The diary records our journeys, visits to Padua, outings to the Lido, dinner at La Colomba with the actor Barry Foster and his wife Judith. They were days of sunshine and casual happiness, made up of the innumerable trivia, the petty ordinarinesses that, taken together, amount to something significant—a family's continuing and substantial life.

But there are many things the diaries don't record. Many blanks on the pages. There are no entries at all for the other life I was living.

CHAPTER TWELVE

THE SECRET

The secret persisted. Somewhere among the school meals and the music lessons, the glasses of sherry before Sunday lunch and the unpredictability of long days at *Late Night Line Up*, the secret kept its place.

Something happens to secrets. They have a life of their own. They are born in heat and panic, in intrigue and excitement. But something happens. They shift and mature. They become wayward and uncontrolled, then fall back into banal routine and are all but forgotten, taken for granted and almost betrayed. Then, out of the blue, they rear up and demand to be revealed, pressing the case for their legitimacy, scorning to be kept from the limelight. Then, just as suddenly, startled by the imminence of catastrophe they shrink back in horror of being known. So the trajectory of our secret—the life Harold and I led together—took its unpredictable course.

*   *   *

In scene one of *Betrayal*, the former lovers Emma and Jerry meet for a drink in a pub two years after their affair has ended. They exchange rather tender if strained pleasantries; Emma is now seeing a writer called Casey, a fact that makes Jerry, who is Casey's agent, a little tetchy. They enquire after each other's marriages and children. Emma's son is now five, her daughter Charlotte, thirteen. They recall the episode in someone's kitchen—whose?—when, many years earlier, Jerry had thrown Charlotte into the air. Gradually they speak of how they once used to meet, of how Emma recently drove past the very house, parked and went up to the front door. Jerry felt a sudden irritation, he says, at hearing gossip about Emma having occasional drinks with Casey, whereas the two of them had had an affair for seven years and no one had had the faintest idea. No one knew. Only the two of them. So no one had gossiped.

*   *   *

In the case of Harold and me, more and more people were getting to know. It was unavoidable, given the lives we were leading. One of us was now in the full flowering of a career as an internationally renowned playwright. This was the decade when Harold was producing much of his greatest work, not only *The Caretaker* but *The Collection*, *The Lover*, *Tea Party*, *The Homecoming*, *The Basement*, *Silence* and *Landscape*. In *The Basement*, made for television in 1967 and produced by my husband, Michael, he played the part of Stott. He completed four screenplays, *The Servant*, *The Pumpkin Eater*, *The Quiller Memorandum* and *Accident*—and saw each of them made into a film. He also wrote screenplays for the film versions of *The Caretaker* and *The Birthday Party*, and directed a stage revival of the latter for the Royal Shakespeare Company as well as Robert Shaw's play *The Man in the Glass Booth*, both in London and New York. Michael and I were at all of the first nights, and many of the parties that followed. No reference was ever made between us to the secret. It was simply there.

Harold was constantly on the move. Letters reached me—often taking days and circuitous routes—from Milwaukee, Berlin, Jamaica, Venice, Taormina, Boston and New York. Over and over from New York: from the Algonquin, the Regency and Hampshire House. Often he would remark on the whirligig of our lives, always placing us in context as the still centre. In the midst of it all I seem to have been some place where he felt centred, without stress. A place to come back to.

In my own sphere, I was on something of a roll. I was now on *Late Night Line Up* some three nights a week, as well as a medley of other programmes during the day. As the only woman presenter on *Line Up* I attracted a modest amount of media attention. Most of the articles in newspapers and women's magazines were, predictably, about my clothes, my looks and my domestic arrangements (not all of them!), but there was an approving theme of 'We shall be seeing more of . . .' And that was just the problem. If my face was becoming known so, too, might my visits to Burghley Road.

And yet it was to Burghley Road we kept returning. We brought our different concerns there. Harold would talk of his plays and their productions. Then for the first time, in 1968, in the play *Landscape*—a title I had suggested to him— the lead part was no longer played by his wife Vivien but instead by the actress Peggy Ashcroft. It signalled a relaxing of what had been until then a fierce mutual interdependency. That interdependency was why I believed, even when the marriage became unhappy, he would hold on so tenaciously. It was why when it ended that it did so with such explosive power. But it was not a situation I ever commented on.

I brought to Burghley Road an interest in the politics of the sixties. Other writers—David Mercer, Dennis Potter, Trevor Griffiths, John McGrath—were writing of contemporary issues. Harold rejected all my efforts to engage his interest. He maintained a firmly neutral public face. In the mid-sixties the magazine *Encounter* published a symposium in which leading figures in the arts expressed their views on whether or not we should join what was then called the Common Market. Harold sent one sentence, declaring he didn't care one way or the other. In 1967, when Che Guevara was captured by Bolivian soldiers and shot, he became instantly a world icon. Numerous writers—including Graham Greene, Pablo Neruda, Robert Lowell, Christopher Logue, Frederic Raphael, Susan Sontag—offered tributes to him in a volume called *Viva Che*. Harold did not. He refused to engage with such issues in private, and he would not commit himself in print.

I would ask why, and we would discuss his concerns. He disliked the oversimplicity that afflicts so many movements for change. But I recognised there were limits in what you could say to Harold, in how far you could press a different point of view. On one occasion I reached those limits. I asked directly why he did not write in a way that showed engagement with the broader world. I made some suggestion, I can't remember what it was. What I do remember is that he reached for my wrist, held it firmly as if emphasising the point and, speaking in the tones of a parent implying 'I don't want to have to say this again', simply and slowly spelled it out: 'It—is—not—what—I—do.' And, of course, he was right. It wasn't what he did. It was, at the time, what he had deliberately chosen not to do. Later, of course, things would change, and change with startling force.

It was while they were working together on the film *The Servant* that the American director Joseph Losey asked Harold, casually, no doubt, but pointedly too, 'How's your affair going?' Apparently David Mercer, who was also working with Losey, had spoken of it. In sudden anxiety and outrage at a confidence betrayed, Harold wasted no time. He phoned David as soon as he could and demanded that they meet. David was summoned for a drink at the Hoop in Notting Hill Gate: they hardly knew each other, and it was an odd coming together. David, cross-examined by Harold, declared he had been too drunk to remember what he had said to Losey or to realise what he was saying. He was given to regular bouts of drinking and was fluent in the abject apologies that followed. On this occasion, too, he was full of remorse, offering no excuses, no explanations, just regrets. His directness, almost childlike, appealed to Harold.

So the secret was out. It was not only out: it had come into the pub and was enjoying a pint with the boys. And I had no place there.

Once the skirmish about 'the affair' had been dealt with, David and Harold realised they had other things to say to each other. It was the start of a strong and important friendship. They shared a meticulous regard for language, and the responsibility of the writer towards it. And it's impossible that Harold did not begin to listen to David's views on world affairs. Over ten years later, when David saw *Betrayal* at the National Theatre, he wrote to Harold, man to man, with no reference to their long-shared secret: 'It's, of course, a major work . . . this writing of silk and steel and many other fleeting textures . . . is the voice of a real master . . .' Then after castigating the critics who saw *Betrayal* as nothing more than a tale of adultery among the chattering classes, he went on:

> It really is true that only the writers can redeem the language from the depredations of all who exploit it for purposes extraneous to truth. Your work, your mode of awareness in drama, is exemplary in this respect. And not only the language, of course, but the moral essence of a culture which it embodies.
>
> I felt quite humble coming away from the Lyttelton—but excited and rejuvenated, too, as one can only be in the presence of a fine artist's work.
>
> Thank you for it.

There were soon other men who knew the secret too.

The critics' early squib about *Betrayal* being about nothing more than adultery among the 'chattering classes' of North London came closer than they knew. In 1964 Harold and Vivien had moved back to London from Worthing into a tall, stately house in Hanover Terrace, Regent's Park, some five minutes' drive from my family home in Primrose Hill, and only fifteen minutes from

268

Burghley Road. Then, in the spring of 1967, we had notice that the Burghley Road house was to be sold.

I wrote the devastating news to the address of an actor in New York, whom I didn't know. I didn't even know what he looked like. His name was James Patterson and he lived on FDR Drive. That's was all the information I ever had. Peter Hall's production of *The Homecoming*, starring the original cast, including, of course, Vivien Merchant, had been on tour in Boston and, in the early months of 1967, opened on Broadway. The Pinters moved to New York for the run of the play and Harold searched out someone he trusted via whom I could send my letters. He came with Harold's recommendation: Patterson was in on the secret.

In 1968 Harold and I moved from Burghley Road to a flat in South Hill Park Gardens at the heart of Hampstead. A risky move in terms of secrecy but the only arrangement that could be managed within an ever-broadening circle of sympathetic friends. The secret was beginning to flex its muscles.

This was the time when politics in America was getting rough: Martin Luther King and Bobby Kennedy both shot dead, anti-Vietnam protests everywhere. In Britain confrontations were more decorous. There were literary confrontations: censorship still restricted writers. In mid-1968 Calder and Boyars were prosecuted for obscenity for publishing the American novelist Hubert Selby Jr's *Last Exit to Brooklyn*. The jury found them guilty. The verdict was overturned on appeal but John Calder had to bear costs. In the theatre the

Lord Chamberlain was in his dying moments as censor. Harold caused a stir by refusing to allow his play *Landscape* to be performed with one word— 'fuck'—cut from its text. It was allowed to be spoken on the Third Programme, but not heard from the stage until the Lord Chamberlain's role as theatre censor was abolished in 1968.

In all this turmoil my suggestion to Rowan Ayers that I visit America to report more closely what was happening there wasn't entirely without personal motive. We decided I would make a three-week visit in September. It wasn't a random date: I knew Harold would be there alone at the same time. The secret was ready to flaunt itself on the streets of New York.

Except it wasn't to be like that. Not at all. It was not at all as we had planned or imagined it would be, and the planning had been meticulous. On the flight across, after several strong drinks, I had confided at length in my *Line Up* producer, Jim Smith, exactly what was going on, and how I would need his collaboration in fixing time when I could be free. I was building an expectation that I would have more of Harold's company than ever before. I was meeting up with a BBC crew in New York. Peter Bartlett and Peter Edwards had only recently been filming the landmark programme about the royal family. For that occasion they had been kitted out in appropriately country tweeds or dinner jackets as events required. Now, almost by way of relaxation, they were being sent with us and could relish the easy informality of how we worked and the casual *Line Up* attitude to life in general. Better keep the secret from them, I suggested. They were all housed in some regular but drab BBC accommodation downtown, but I had booked myself into the relatively swanky St Moritz Hotel, along Central Park South but, more importantly, in the next block to Hampshire House where Harold was staying. I arrived to find two dozen red roses in my room. No need to ask who had sent them.

*   *   *

New York hit me like a brisk warm breeze blowing in from some exotic desert. This was my first visit to America: I was thirty-five years old and voracious for the strangeness of it all. I had stored in the mythologies of my mind all the glamour and candour that I knew largely from American cinema, and early cinema at that: *42nd Street, The Barkleys of Broadway*—even *King Kong*. I was startled by everything: the man swirling the pizza dough in the window of the restaurant, the glass of iced water placed on your table before you could ask, big yellow taxis, small dark bars, straight streets, tall buildings—it was all obvious stuff, but for me as fresh and surprising as seeing my first elephant.

And this was the time the American writer Ariel Dorfman calls 'the fanatical sixties'. Everything was political. Right then America was pulsating with politics: the politics of race, of anti-war protest. I arrived on Labour Day, catching the gaiety of its New York parade. I couldn't wait to plunge into the torrent of talk and argument that was in the air. And I was lucky.

To be in New York on the breaking wave of a love affair is to relish all the things in the city that reflect back your own sense of heightened

271

immediacy. I stood a long time before Rembrandt's miraculous painting *The Polish Rider* in the Frick Collection, I strolled the medieval cloisters imported wholesale from France and displayed at Fort Tryon Park. But as the weeks went by, when I wasn't working, I was doing this on my own. Harold was caught up in his rehearsals, but more than that he was caught up in being a lionised figure in New York's social life. We snatched at every moment. But there were receptions he couldn't refuse, dinner parties in his honour. He couldn't conspicuously opt out—that was made clear enough. And then the blow fell. A telegram from Vivien announced her surprise arrival from Britain. Harold's great fear, that Vivien might find out about us, now took over and ruled all his decisions. It governed what I had hoped would be our time and our space together. We wouldn't be able to meet any more. The secret had turned poisonous and was now eating its own. I had become its victim.

*   *   *

The excitement of work was there when I needed it. Jim Smith and I had arrived with little more research than a sheaf of phone numbers for contacts of friends and fellow journalists. Soon we were embroiled in interviews and filming. In the evenings we took to haunting a club called Revolution. 'Hey Jude' was being played a lot that year. We danced and drank. My spirits lifted. They were lifted, too, by the people I interviewed. At that time active in New York there was a clutch of radicals who wanted change. Together they represented part of an exhilarating burst of liberal ideas into American politics. I returned with their testimonies to be shown on *Line Up*, giving a vivid picture of American attitudes at that crucial date. Unhappily the BBC exercised a scorched-earth policy in those days, dumping and destroying reams of programmes we might treasure today, mine among them.

First up, strangely, was Mayor John Lindsay, a Republican but with such progressive ideas that his own party soon deserted him; when he finally came to pitch for the Democratic presidential candidacy, the whole political procession had moved on. He had something of the glamour of the Kennedys—tall and lanky, he wore the easy confidence of his wealthy Yale background—but months earlier he had confronted riots breaking out in New York, as in many other American cities, and sent in Task Forces that had calmed the trouble and restored order to the angry streets. In 1973 he bowed out of politics for good. Towards me he was gracious in a patrician sort of way. I was useful media fodder. I found him rather chilly.

Tom Hayden, then a student activist, was altogether different. When I met him he was intense, like a coiled spring, full of outrage at his arrest a mere week or two before. He was in a hurry, but eager to talk with someone easily persuaded to take his side. I realised as he sat there—dark unruly hair, open-necked white shirt—that the apparent casual style belied the steely resolve of the purposeful young American political animal. Hayden would have a long political run as state senator for California until his dignified retirement in 1999. I might have guessed as much

273

in 1968, when he was a major mover in bringing together thousands of anti-war protesters at the now notorious Democratic Convention in Chicago. By that year American casualties in Vietnam had reached thirty thousand; many conscripts were burning their draft cards, others had fled to England, others—such as Bill Clinton, from the well-heeled middle class—sought out legitimate ways to avoid the draft. Not surprisingly America was in uproar, and Hayden was one of those leading the field. He had been charged—as one of the Chicago Eight—with conspiracy to incite a riot, and later endured a four-month trial of legendary idiocy. Judge, plaintiffs and witnesses all behaved with comic waywardness. Accused Black Panther Bobby Seale was bound and gagged in court then sentenced to four years for contempt, thus reducing the Chicago Eight to the Chicago Seven. Defence witnesses—who included Timothy Leary, Allen Ginsberg and Arlo Guthrie—weren't always helpful. One of them, Norman Mailer, proclaimed, 'Left-wingers are incapable of conspiracy because they're all egomaniacs . . . we can't even agree on lunch!' And so it proved. The defence attorney, William Kunstler, was himself charged with contempt by Judge Julius Hoffman, frantic to impose order on his turbulent courtroom. Among the seven, those who called themselves Yippies— the Youth International Party, founded by Abbie Hoffman and embracing anyone who shared its aims—were deliberately insolent, lounging around, putting their feet up, chattering, throwing kisses around the court. Only Hayden kept his cool. I could see, on the day I met him, the impressive seriousness of the man. What I couldn't see was

274

that he was soon to marry Jane Fonda, or Hanoi Jane to her detractors, a woman seeking a role and finding a husband.

When I met Gloria Steinem, who was soon to take America by storm as the feminist founder of *Ms* magazine, she was still in pre-feminist mode, still the chrysalis from which the powerful butterfly of militancy would emerge. She had been one of the city's leading journalists for a decade already. She had famously gone under cover as a Bunny waitress at Hugh Hefner's Playboy Club and published the article in *Show* magazine. But she chafed under the burden of being given girlie assignments. By the time I met her in New York she had reported on the assassination of Martin Luther King, covered the presidential campaign of Senator George McGovern, and was steeped in Democratic politics, seen as a powerful campaigner and high-profile journalist. It was intriguing to catch her just as her thoughts were sharpening around the issues of women. Her arrival at the BBC's New York offices was dazzling. She looked every bit the glamorous New York princess: exquisitely dressed in a tiny bright-coloured mini-skirt, beautifully coiffed and groomed, she was the epitome of the prevailing male fantasy of a successful woman. But her mind was already resistant to being treated as a doll. We spoke of the problems we both had in being taken seriously. It emerged later in her writings that we had interesting things in common: our mothers had held the promise of bright achievers, hopes dashed by domestic duties that pitched them into deepening depression. I didn't know that then, but such family background was moving us both towards feminism. My interview with her was high seriousness itself. We spoke of American discontents and the nature of protest simply as serious journalists. Being women didn't come into it.

When Martin Luther King was shot in Mississippi, radical black protest took a leap forward. The Black Panthers sprang into action and one of the people they attacked was the writer William Styron—who had made a splash with his first novel, *Lie Down in Darkness*, at the age of twenty-six, and would go on to write *Sophie's Choice*. In 1967 he had published *The Confessions of Nat Turner*, in which he, a white Virginian, told in the first person the story of Nat Turner, black leader of the 1831 slave rebellion. The imaginative act of a white man seeking to describe how it felt to be a black slave invited the scorn and contempt of current black leaders. The title of Julius Lester's book, *Look Out, Whitey! Black Power's Gon' Get Your Mama*, which was published in the weeks after we arrived in New York, expresses exactly how blacks felt, deploring the fact that Styron's arrogance had been hailed as 'literary achievement'. 'Styron's novel is no different from the many editorials by white writers and politicians telling blacks that violence is wrong.' It was time to let Styron, a veteran of the Second World War and the Korean war, speak for himself. We flew to Martha's Vineyard, summer haunt of rich Americans and especially successful writers, to meet him.

It is always good to visit writers in their homes. The domestic setting, the hints of writing routine, the status of the author in his own household, the fluency that comes more easily at home all help to make the job easier. Besides Styron wouldn't budge—and we could well see why. His house by the sea was full of sun, air and family. It opened on to the shore and a drift of sand came indoors on everyone's bare feet. His wife Rose offered that instant and generous welcome that is so specially American, and made me feel tight and cramped in my English ways. Their expansiveness grew: I was asked to stay the night with them and was accommodated in a pleasantly ramshackle garden house below big-leaved trees. Americans rate writers highly, ascribing to them a persistent if sometimes ambiguous power, and I, as a journalist, was given conditional membership of the tribe. The other three BBC people—more operators in the world of television—went off to find local lodgings.

Meanwhile I was walked along the seashore to meet the Styrons' neighbour, Lillian Hellman. Years later I would interview her in London. She made then an interesting point I have since had reason to bear in mind. Speaking of her personal life I remarked casually, 'Now, you had an unhappy marriage so you divorced--' She interrupted: 'No, that's not correct. I had for many years a very happy marriage: then it went wrong, then I divorced.' A fine distinction that was to apply in my case, too.

The interview with Styron about *Nat Turner* went well. The talk spilled into issues of current black protest, the rise of the Black Panthers, events and police violence at the recent Chicago Democratic Convention where Styron, along with other writers, had been in attendance. The talk continued over dinner. I couldn't help but notice that the meal was cooked and served by black staff. This incongruity struck me with such force that I couldn't contain myself and, once the staff were back in the kitchen, asked whether this situation—white writer identifies with black rebel while waited on by black servants—didn't offer a certain awkwardness. 'Oh, no, no,' they reassured me, 'they've all been with us for years! They're like part of the family.' I am sure they were. Styron's position at the head of a traditional Virginian home made his novel seem to me all the more remarkable.

After dinner, William decided I should see more of the island and go visiting. It was a bright, star-lit night and we drove off along straight, deserted roads to remote beaches and homes. I had had plenty to drink, so my memory of our call on another writer in his isolated house has a hallucinatory quality. All I remember is that he was shaggy and tousled, slumped in a leather sofa in a huge open-plan room lined with books. Several large whiskies later, my capacity to lock his name into my memory had fled. But we talked books, reviews and books, the life of writers, their lives and books again. But who was he? Had I spent the evening in the presence of some towering figure of American literature or, lubricated by alcohol, exaggerated the whole thing? I would never know. On the way back we stopped, so that Styron could show me the longest beach on the coast and the best surf. We walked on the sand as the tide thundered. There was a rather tender embrace in the dunes, but I discouraged more. 'Why? Are you faithful to your husband?' he asked.

'No, I'm not,' I heard myself say. So now I was

sharing the secret with virtual strangers.

*   *   *

I travelled back to London without seeing or hearing any more from Harold. I was desolate. Somewhere within Kennedy airport there is a long tunnel, white-tiled, severe and bleak. It was my route home. I have a memory of walking along it for hours. There were no other people, or if there were I don't remember them. It was night. There were bright fluorescent lights in this tunnel. Its white tiles were tawdry, clean without being clean, glaring and ungenerous. I was dressed in dark clothes, dark against the white, and I was burdened with extra luggage, toys from FAO Schwartz for the children and gifts of music for Michael.

I had been changed by what had happened, by my false and vague hopes for some intangible happiness. My memories of the white tunnel are at once vivid and vague, without place or location. I was moving through my life as in a dream, sensing my aloneness and also that something else was coming into being, something new about me that was different and beginning to feel strong. I was pleased with the work I had done, the encounters I had had with others making something useful of their lives. All so sure of themselves. I wanted to be like that.

> Man's love is of man's life a thing apart,
> 'Tis woman's whole existence.

Byron's old maxim was ringing true. Admittedly he mixed with some odd women: the crazy Caroline

Lamb, the obsessive Annabella Milbanke, the insistent Claire Claremont. But here was I playing true to type, gripped by the vagaries of my emotional life, tossed back and forth on a rollercoaster of feelings, making a mess of things that had once held so much promise. All this turbulent passion was getting in the way. In the way of what, I didn't yet know. But I was becoming more and more aware that there was more to life than this. There was work and purpose. Most of all, there was myself.

Although the flight arrived at Heathrow at an unearthly hour, Michael had got the children up and brought them to meet me. My little family of three huddled together at the end of the line, waving and smiling. No white tiles here, just the frowsty carpets of the arrivals area, its noise and dust. And the spontaneity of their welcome. I had brought Harriet an Alice in Wonderland doll, long gold hair and china blue eyes, for Matthew some brightly-coloured toy of tracks and trolleys, for Michael the Russian recording of *Eugene Onegin*. Their exclamations of delight and pleasure were just what I needed. It all felt so enduring and secure.

But it wasn't.

*   *   *

Back at *Late Night Line Up* the pace seemed to quicken. By doing the sort of things—making filmed profiles, short documentaries—that other departments regarded as their territory, I felt we were yielding our unique place on the network and risking making more enemies. I thought this was putting the future survival of the programme at risk, and said so, forcefully and often. But Rowan had a strong conviction the programme needed to develop and his talented people be given a chance to push new ideas further. He resented my interference. We agreed to differ and I got on with the new remit, which involved me in more travel, more filming.

In February 1969 we flew to Lausanne in Switzerland to spend a week with Georges Simenon. 'We' consisted of the usual team, myself, a director, and a camera crew of three—cameraman, sound man and electrician—but on this occasion an entire second camera crew. The director, an Australian called Tony Wheeler, had fancy theories about the nature of film-making, the need to break with conventional routines, and set up a critique of the process itself. The second camera team was there to film the first in action. This was post-modernism *avant la lettre*. This was, after all, only 1969.

Simenon submitted himself to the experiment with amused collaboration, relishing the risk of its not working: 'It's like one of my novels, a bit here, a flashback there, and in the middle of it I think, Will it all fall into place?' Having given up five days of his time for us, he was soon in discreet control of what we did.

We were given a tour of his immaculate house—another writer's home, which yielded plenty of clues. It was an obsessional life. His custom-built desk housed a series of shallow drawers each containing a set of tobacco pipes all cushioned, aligned in order and facing the same way. Each day he smoked a different pipe, moving through the

281

sequence of drawers until on reaching the bottom he returned to the top. Beside the bedroom was the medical facility, like a miniature operating theatre: a tall narrow bed, overhead light, oxygen supplied, diagnostic instruments, a cupboard full of drugs, and a copy of the *Lancet*. At one moment he absented himself to go and get a flu jab.

A waif of a teenage daughter was sometimes in evidence, pale and seemingly awestruck by her father. His wife, he explained to me, had had a nervous breakdown five years before, was at first in a sanatorium, but now lived in a hotel with her own suite and her own staff. He talked about it quietly and exactly. The tone of his discourse was steady, controlled, unemotional.

We filmed continously, breaking off at noon when a maid, in navy dress and crisp white apron, brought us a tray of drinks. Simenon drank only Evian water. Later I walked with him in the snow, taking the route he followed every day: 'When I'm working on a book I walk silently, ignoring even close friends who pass by; when I'm not writing I greet everyone.' With us he greeted a postman who passed on a bicycle.

After five days we took our leave: he proffered pink champagne and we drank to the next novel and the success of our film. He enquired whether Tony the director was satisfied, if he had found what he wanted: 'After all, I have nothing to hide. I'm not complicated or mysterious.' We left knowing there was something extremely strange about Simenon and he had offered a brilliant and complete front to the world and our cameras. Our television profile, which might have been thought worthy of the archive, did not survive the BBC's spring-cleaning.

*   *   *

Early in 1969 *Late Night Line Up* planned six long-interview programmes in which I talked with leading writers of the day. John Osborne was one, David Mercer another. Harold also agreed: he had been interviewed on *Line Up* before but not at such length. This time he was relaxed and funny, the Pinter whom not many know, the raconteur at his ease, fluent with phrases and comic timing. By now this was one of the rare occasions on which we could meet. Time was running out on us.

*   *   *

In scene three of *Betrayal* the lovers are in the flat they share, discussing how things have changed, how difficult it had become ever to be there together. Jerry complains that Emma is now so busy with her job that she isn't free in the afternoons. Emma protests it's a job she likes, that she wants to do. And Jerry concurs, that, yes, it's good. But she isn't free. Emma, for her part, complains that Jerry is always out of the country so even if she is free he's in America. It is the final, sad denouement of their affair. Once it had been impossible to meet, but they had. Now it was finally impossible.

*   *   *

And so it was over. I wasn't free in the afternoons and Harold was frequently abroad. Within a year of my return from New York we had abandoned the flat. Yet it wasn't over.

Some time in 1970 I was busy late at night in Television Centre. *Line Up* was due to go on air within the hour. A letter was brought from reception to the office, addressed to me 'Private and Personal'. It contained the following poem, unsigned:

> All of that I made
> And, making, lied.
> And all of that I hid
> Pretended dead.
>
> But all of that I hid
> Was always said,
> But, hidden, spied
> On others' good.
> And all of that I led
> By nose to bed
> And, bedding, said
> Of what I did
> To all of that that cried
> Behind my head
> And, crying, died
> And is not dead.

The secret had triumphed. The play *Betrayal*, when it arrived at my door eight years later, proclaimed the same. But back in 1970, moved by the poem he had sent, I knew there still remained more unravelling to be done. We met in the Taverners pub alongside Lord's cricket ground. And we talked. I talked of how Michael and I were now separated, and divulged for the first time that I had

284

told him what had been going on between us. The crucial revelation was that I had told Michael of my affair not in recent days as our marriage collapsed, but long before.

A thoughtful silence fell. That same night Harold phoned Michael late, and demanded he come round to see him. Michael—such was the authority of Harold's command—agreed and went round to Hanover Terrace. Michael explained, for it was implied some explanation was due, that his own behaviour had been such that he had felt no right to censure Harold for his. Harold suggested that Michael, the conventionally wronged husband, was in some way to blame for having kept secret his knowledge of our affair.

*   *   *

Scene two of *Betrayal* takes place in the evening at the home of Jerry, Emma's lover. Jerry has called Robert, her husband, urgently to his home. It is one of the most remorseless, painful and sadly humorous scenes in the play. When I read it, part of its plot was immediately familiar.

Robert admits that he knows of Jerry's affair with his wife. She has told him about it. Jerry is bewildered that Emma should have chosen to tell her husband of the affair the previous night, just as their marriage was in trouble. But no, Robert explains, she didn't tell him then. In fact, she told him several years earlier, and he has known of the affair between his wife and his best friend for years. This is the ultimate betrayal that lies at the final uncoiling of the play's web of deceit.

In the play the bond between the two men—

285

Jerry the lover and Robert the husband—is of an altogether different intensity from the professional acquaintance between Michael and Harold. Harold wrote into the play the sort of powerful male friendship that he enjoyed with those men closest to him. Not quite incidentally the play is dedicated to the playwright Simon Gray, one of Harold's most loved friends with whom he regularly played squash, as do the fictitious figures Robert and Jerry. It is one of the bonds between them.

*   *   *

Some five years later, early in 1975, Harold and I met for a drink. Nothing unusual in that. We had kept in touch from time to time, pleased to see each other as friends, rather than close and confiding. He knew that for two years I had been living with Jack Emery and that we planned to marry. But now he had news for me. I knew it was important news by the way he hesitated—a pause long even by Pinter standards—then turned and looked seriously at me. He told me how he had come to know the biographer Antonia Fraser, and they were close. I was the first person he had told. I took a deep breath. There was another pause.

Antonia is one of the great beauties of her generation. Tall and blonde, she had made slaves of the *Line Up* editors whenever she appeared on the programme. I had met her briefly on those occasions, but knew her not at all. What I did know was that she was a successful biographer and reviewer and also the high-profile wife of a Tory MP, Sir Hugh Fraser, by whom she had six children. Clearly there would be difficulties ahead, if there weren't already.

I made clear my delight in their happiness. Then, as we talked, I found myself expounding what perhaps to Harold must have sounded like advice, circuitously expressed, perhaps, but advice none the less. I spelled out the story of the secret we had shared. Of how that secret had changed and magnified, shifted and divided, becoming known to more than the two of us, extending its sway into places even Harold hadn't imagined. I talked of how secrets have their own direction and can damage where none was intended, how they can turn on those who have engendered them and take their revenge. What I said was in part explaining the past, but also indicating something about the future. It was a warning.

Harold and Antonia's secret didn't last long. But no one could have dreamed it would be so universally and violently exposed. Harold told the new secret to Peter Hall, who was directing his play *No Man's Land*. He also told his close friend Peggy Ashcroft. And he told Vivien. And it wasn't a secret any more. Vivien's reaction made evident why Harold had been so insistent that she didn't find out about us. He knew his wife well. He knew her better than anyone. He knew her nature in all its particular detail. He had observed her behaviour, watched her reactions, sensed her anxieties, loved her as his wife and seen her star in his plays. Now she took centre stage in her own right. And she made a move no one could have expected: she began talking to the papers.

By the opening night of *No Man's Land*, 23 April 1975, journalists had already picked up rumours. Three days later Jack and I were married in the crypt of St Mary-le-Bow Church in the City. The ceremony—as befitted a second marriage for us both—was for close family and friends only. But the same night we had a big party for far more. Harold came alone. And dropped a bombshell. He had spent the day packing his bags, his books, clothes and things. That very day he had moved out of his home. Vivien and he had separated and would never be reconciled. He had moved into the Grosvenor House Hotel. In all the gaiety of the celebration I was only dimly aware of Harold being cheerful, jovial, talkative throughout the evening. But later I do remember: he was the last of all our guests to leave. On my wedding night, Harold, who had just left his wife, stayed drinking with us both until the early hours. We had moved into a life without secrets.

Vivien, who never knew about my affair with Harold, let rip at Antonia. 'Actress Tells All' was the tone of Fleet Street's headlines. Their love affair had all the ingredients that excited the press: beauty, talent, success, fame. Vivien's pain and anger were out of control. The press loved that too. It destroyed her judgement. And her chance of survival. After the divorce, Vivien's spirit was broken. Her career declined. Her health deteriorated. When she died in 1982, I attended her funeral. I wondered, sorrowfully, what part I had played in bringing her to such a sad end.

*　　　*　　　*

With *Betrayal* opening at the National Theatre in December 1978, it seemed the story was finally over. But the secret lingered. When I had first read

288

the play I was fearful of scandal, and all the emotional wreck and damage that might go with it. Many people knew by now what had happened and how the play had drawn on such events. But some sense of loyalty stopped the gossip spilling over, getting out of hand. The affair was seen as something in the past. Other lives and loves had clearly superseded it. So no one talked. At the party after the play's first night, only Lord Longford, Antonia's father, broke ranks, claiming in a voice louder than I would have liked, 'They tell me this play is all about you, Joan.' His comment was quickly hushed over.

For two decades the much-abused chattering classes displayed tact, discretion, even affection in keeping things to themselves. Then in 1995 Harold phoned and asked me to talk to Michael Billington, drama critic of the *Guardian,* who was collecting material for his biography. 'What shall I tell him?' 'Tell him the truth.' So I did. Now cushioned by the confidence and security of a more stable life and grown children, I felt the newspaper fuss that greeted the biography's publication as no more than a sudden eccentric irritation. Our affair had provided the superstructure of events from which *Betrayal* had sprung. Now the account of *Betrayal* had taken its rightful place in a serious study of Pinter's life and work.

And the secret was finally over.

CHAPTER THIRTEEN

TELEVISION TIMES

In 1970 I published a book about television. It was called *The New Priesthood* and was co-authored with Nicholas Garnham, then a television director and today Emeritus Professor of Media Studies at the University of Westminster. The title indicates the high-minded tone of the enterprise. It derived from Coleridge's definition of the role of the clerisy in his national church: its duty, the quotation ran, was 'to preserve the stores and to guard the treasures of past civilisation, and thus to bind the present with the past; to perfect and add to the same and thus to connect the present with the future'. Phew, and I thought we were just making television programmes. Our introduction went on in equally elevated tones: 'The tradition that underlay the original Reithian concept has died and a new society is in the process of giving birth to a new and more egalitarian tradition, a new definition of the role of cultural priesthood.' This was our definition of what was meant by public-service broadcasting, combining Reith's sense of values with a greater regard for individual tastes and preferences. That remains my view today.

The glossy jacket was designed by Jonathan Miller and it showed a television set with four knobs labelled BBC1, BBC2, ITV and ?. The question mark indicated the expected arrival of Channel 4. There was much debate at the time about the purpose and ethics of television, and our book was made up of some eighty interviews with leading figures in the television of those times. Only three of them were women: Renée Goddard, head of scripts at ATV, Irene Shubik, co-producer of the Wednesday Play and Stella Richman, the recently promoted controller of programmes at LWT. There were other women working in television, of course, but these three were among the most senior. Today the tone of that debate, our attitudes and concerns at the time, stands as a snapshot picture of television in a bygone age, its aspirations and fears thrown into vivid contrast by all that has happened since.

It hadn't been easy for me to get permission from the BBC to do this. The corporation insisted on a rigorous control of what its employees wrote and said about it. Now here was I intending to perpetuate in print the kind of critical talk about television that had got *Late Night Line Up* into so much trouble. I was not a member of staff and, indeed, until 1967 had been on only three-monthly contracts routinely renewed. Even after five years on *Line Up* some in the BBC were still hostile to my writing the book at all: 'Surely,' Leslie Page, then assistant controller, TV administration, advised his colleagues, 'no one would regard either Joan Bakewell or her co-editor as being remotely qualified either by experience or intellect to produce a book of any substance or importance of this kind.' The mood was not encouraging. Still, all the leading television figures of the day agreed to be interviewed, as—to his lasting regret—did Lord Reith himself.

It was a strange encounter. He was then eighty-one years old. He had been the BBC's first and monumental director general, from 1923 until 1938. By the late sixties he could scarcely be said to be in the swim of current events. None the less he was willing to talk. At least, initially. We arranged to meet in the bar at the House of Lords around teatime, when there would be few people and not much drinking. I took along my cumbersome tape-recorder and set it up to catch the fleeting comments of his frail voice, uttering its staccato opinions charged with as much disapproval as he could muster. It didn't occur to him to be helpful. He simply sat, his huge rangy figure folded away like some tired vulture, refusing to meet my gaze and turning his head away to look out blankly towards the Thames. He was really talking to himself, and reiterating, as he must have done regularly over the years, his utter hatred of television.

The interview, duly subbed, was sent for him to approve its publication. I received back a curt note from his secretary saying he had now decided he did not want his views to be included. Something gave me the courage to challenge his decision. I wrote back a stinging letter, declaring my outrage: we had had an agreement on which he was now reneging and I had always thought him to be a man of professional integrity. His response was as mild and submissive as a child's. He conceded my point entirely. He agreed his views could be printed but asked that they be reported as indirect, rather than direct speech. He did not want quotation marks round his judgements.

He told me how much he hated television. Indeed, its development was one of the reasons for his leaving the BBC and he believed his fears had been fully justified. He regarded it as trivial and inconsequential; the quantity of it appalled him. He would have liked drastically to restrict the hours so that programmes would have to compete in quality for fewer opportunities. He blamed television, he told me in exhausted tones, for the decline in our intellectual and ethical standards, which he saw as an absolute tragedy. None the less he was proud that the BBC had pioneered television back in the late 1920s. He regretted that its monopoly had ever been broken by ITV. He regarded Lord Woolton, who had steered through the ITV Act, as 'doing more ethical and intellectual harm than any other man of his day'.

He was a man steeped in regrets: for himself, for the BBC and for the country's moral decline. Yet this huge figure, crumpled by age and disappointments, sitting opposite me in the late sunlight of his life, who felt his ideas had been so rejected and ignored, need not have worried. His mark sat on every page of our book. In 1970 his presence might have been long gone from the counsels of the BBC but his influence in setting television within a moral context of what was good for the people and the nation lived on some forty years later, in the views of contemporary broadcasters. As with F. R. Leavis, Reith's puritanical bigotry—his contempt for so much and his lack of tolerance for tastes other than his own— had established a commitment to standards that schooled generations of broadcasters to follow the moral high ground. Even today I can see no argument for preferring the moral low ground.

What shines from the pages of the book are not the standard facts of television history but the amazing confidence and pride of the entire industry. This was the heyday of the programme-makers, a community united by common aims, which were to fulfil our public-service duty to make the best possible programmes. Audience research existed, of course, but only, we sensed, as an afterthought to check how many viewers there were. Consultants and managers were still in the future. Focus groups were unheard of. Audiences were taken for granted, and our task was to shape and—implicitly—to improve their taste.

We were to be the judges of that taste. There survived from our grammar-school and university backgrounds a wish to pass on our own enthusiasms. Humphrey Burton spoke of seeing himself 'as a proselytiser, seeking converts for that substitute religion known as art'. 'Missionary is too big a word for it,' declared Melvyn Bragg, 'and propaganda is the wrong word.' And John Drummond, another doyen of the BBC Arts Department: 'I don't think we're here as educationalists. We're here as enthusiasts to share that enthusiasm. And the fact is it works.' Indeed, it did. Arts programmes were plentiful on both BBC1 and BBC2, with viewing figures to match: for the ballet *Coppélia*, seven million; a biography of Kathleen Ferrier, six million; *Rigoletto*, four million; Ken Russell films, six or seven million. These were the days before the ratings war hotted up. It didn't need to: people were avid to see all that was new to them, and in those days most things were.

That is not to say ratings didn't exist. There was clearly a culture divide between serious programming and light entertainment. Each sneered at the other. 'All the channels are excellent at these new documentaries,' complained Dennis Main Wilson, father of some of television's greatest sit-coms, 'but I'm sure 50 per cent of the nation don't understand them.' Tony Smith, then editor of the BBC's *24 Hours*, later a mover in the setting up of Channel 4, and subsequently president of Magdalen College, Oxford, gave me a rigorous definition of where to draw the ratings line: 'I look at our weekly figures avidly, obsessively, trying to put on half a million here, a million there. But I wouldn't put on television anything that isn't appropriate to *24 Hours* in order to do that.' Such integrity ruled out any pandering to ratings: 'A programme that is put there simply because you know people will watch. Isn't that analogous to pornography?'

These high-minded Reithian sentiments could prevail—as they did throughout the seventies—because television had little to worry about in terms of money and audiences. These issues existed, but the debate was elsewhere. Television was then at the forefront of the country's cultural life. The people I interviewed spoke in alarm of how one day television might be like water out of a tap, a background interest in people's lives and homes. And the example they pointed to with fear and dread was the USA. Over and over again US television was cited as the nadir to which we must not fall: evening schedules full of quizzes and poor comedies, laced with nasty commercials. British television must never go that way. Billy Cotton Jr, then head of Light Entertainment, later controller of BBC Television, put it dramatically: 'In the BBC I can argue with someone purely on the basis of the content of the programme. He can't say to me, "Look, I agree, but the sponsors or advertisers won't buy it." If that ever happens you're a commodity, not a broadcaster.'

ITV, which had broken the BBC monopoly only fourteen years before, was still widely seen by BBC people as tainted by commercial values. Many deliberately used the term 'commercial' rather than 'independent' television to convey their disapproval. Barry Took, then a comedy consultant to the BBC, was particularly severe: 'Commercial television is making money. They're nice people, and they're good administrators and they're making money. Like the Westminster Bank. But we're making show business.' Between this interview and its publication in our book, he moved across to become head of Light Entertainment at LWT! Sometimes the opportunities were too good to resist.

These were boom years for television news and for current affairs across all three channels. Serious programming was in the ascendant as it would never be again. Even the broadcasters thought there might be too much of it. *Tonight, 24 Hours, World in Action, This Week, Gallery, Panorama*—for some ten years the air had been choked with talk and serious coverage of current events. And then there were the documentary series: *Man Alive, The Question Why, Yesterday's Witness* alongside such mould-breaking interviews as John Freeman's *Face to Face*. These were times when people were using television to learn, to make up for education cut short and no chance of going to university. Could there be too much of it? The fear, much argued over at the time, was that the audience, regularly

296

confronted with crisis reporting on every side, would either grow bored and turn away, or become neurotic, alarmed, as rival programmes told them in ever more vivid terms that life was increasingly hazardous and unstable. The insight was prescient: since that time both reactions—apathy and panic—have come into play and there is little the broadcasters can do about it.

Above all, British television in the 1970s was enormously self-contained. The BBC, employing twenty-three thousand, was serviced and staffed to produce 85 per cent of its own programmes while ITV's quota of permitted foreign imports was 14 per cent. There were no more than one or two independent companies. The entire industry was focused on native talent and professional skill. There wasn't even much enthusiasm for selling our programmes abroad. BBC Enterprises sold in eighty-two countries and made £1.9 million in 1969, but they hadn't found a market for Kenneth Clark's prestigious *Civilisation* series, considered the sort of thing the BBC did best. And when it did sell *Cathy Come Home* there was much talk of its having given a poor impression of Britain abroad. Billy Cotton again: 'I see no reason why the BBC should emphasise selling programmes, if it means they've got to change their standard to do it.' None the less 1970 was the first year when the BBC actively went out seeking co-production. It was an unobtrusive signal of what would one day change the nature of programme-making. The book we had written, while setting in aspic the mood of the times, also held clues to what the future of television would be.

It was into this bear-pit of competing egos, close-knit allies and potential defectors to the other side, of male hierarchies and departments that I would soon have to make my way. And I was singularly ill-equipped to do so. My contract with *Line Up* would end in July 1972, so I would be out of a regular job. What was more, I was approaching forty: a dangerous age. Women broadcasters, being relatively new, were mostly young. No one yet knew to what extent and for how long a woman over forty would be acceptable as a television journalist. No one had done it yet. It was daunting to think that I—'the thinking man's crumpet', who worked for 'pin money'—might be one of those to pioneer that particular track. But there was worse. My marriage was by then beyond rescue and I had decided to get a divorce. I found myself alone with two young children to care for, the mortgage, a bit of a reputation but no income, no career plan, no pension. It was a bad time.

I can spell it out like that, the problems I faced. I can list them all with chilly accuracy. Set them down as matters to be resolved. But it was not how I lived them. Nor how it felt. Emotionally I was confused and unhappy, drifting deeper and deeper into bewilderment and despair. The diaries of the time—little more than a scattering of engagements and reminders—tell of more than the daily round. The writing gets wonky, there are inks of various colours (everyone in public life knows just how serious coloured ink can be), I write across the pages, overlap margins, ignore the lines, go in for capitals and exclamation marks. Even as I was presenting a serene front to the world, the diaries were giving the game away. And so were the actual entries: I was regularly seeing a doctor in Harley Street, who prescribed lots of drugs. I had regular appointments with Largactil and Seconal. I went for occasional sessions of psychotherapy with the psychoanalyst, Nina Coltart. And I kept on smiling, smiling and talking to teachers, smiling and paying the bills, smiling and cooking meals, smiling and making programmes.

In the final years of *Line Up* I had fallen into an intermittent and turbulent affair with one of its producers: Jim Smith, who had been with me in New York and knew all that had gone on there. He and I would dream up film projects for *Line Up*, which would involve our being officially away together for a couple of days at a time. 'On location' was known in television to be a sort of sexual no man's land where the rules of conventional behaviour were allowed, even expected, to relax. And so it was. But two of the projects we embarked on had significant consequences for my life. One brought me a house of my own. The other introduced me to my future husband.

The Northcott Theatre, Exeter, seen in the late sixties as one of England's liveliest regional theatres, had as its dramaturg a young writer called Jack Emery. The theatre served the whole of the South-west, and Jack had developed a policy of creating plays built round the histories of such figures as John Wesley, Judge Jeffries and the Duke of Monmouth, and the key roles they had played in the communities of the area. These plays then went on tour to theatres, halls and schools

299

with a good deal of success and popular acclaim. It was an era when theatre was breaking away from its traditional building-based role and involving itself in the lives of ordinary people. Peter Cheeseman was pioneering the idea at the Victoria Theatre, Stoke; Ann Jellicose was doing something similar in Dorset; and John McGrath's 7.84 Company was touring to remote communities in Scotland. It was a story of taking drama to the people whom we thought worth telling. The theatre's director, Tony Church, was an old friend of mine, and we had acted together at Cambridge. I was looking forward to seeing him again. But in the event he was too busy. Instead he sent along Jack Emery.

I remember little of the interview, but I was later to remember Jack. He was then in his mid-twenties, full of energy and enthusiasm, as yet untouched by life's disappointments. He was tall and willowy with long blond hair, jeans and hippie beads. He spoke with intensity and excitement about his plays and his ambitions for them. Away from London, away from my personal turmoil, I found his company and eagerness a breath of fresh air. Then I got into the train for Paddington and forgot all about him. Three years later things would be different.

The decision to buy a house of my own, in my own name and with my own money, feels now like the first totally independent thing I ever did. Everything else had been in some way conditioned by my wish to please my parents, to please the men in my life. I had always had a stand-off relationship with money. My parents had paid for virtually everything until I married, when my husband took

300

on the role of family breadwinner. Student holiday jobs, even my early broadcasting, were seen as extra to the main financial axis of the household, which was a male responsibility.

But now that so-called pin money was stacking up. I had cash to spare. Money of my own. I decided to buy a house in the country, well away from London. I found what I wanted in the little seaside village of Cawsand, which, with its twin Kingsand, nestles in a wooded, sandy bay across Plymouth Sound, on the border between Devon and Cornwall. The house is in Armada Road, named, it was said, because Drake's fleet, fresh out of Plymouth Hoe, had hove to in Cawsand Bay before going out to meet the Spanish. Other quaint anecdotes added to the village's charm. The local pub boasted an old plaque on which an elegant handwritten script declared, 'In this inn, Nelson and Lady Hamilton enjoyed many romantic interludes.' (When the pub was modernised the new landlords not only ripped out the eight-foot mahogany bar but replaced the romantic plaque, declaring its claim couldn't be proved!)

I wanted my children to come to know something about the countryside. They were growing up as thoroughly London street children, playing hide and seek among parked cars, banging door knockers and running away, shop-lifting the occasional toy from a local—understanding—newsagent's. The only chance they had to roll on grass was on Primrose Hill, rendered hazardous by a multitude of local dog-walkers. On rare visits to a place called 'the country' Harriet complained her shoes got dirty. This wouldn't do. Now I planned they would have their school holidays by the sea, all

301

fishing nets and rock pools, cliff walks and steaming bowls of mussels freshly harvested from the beach.

I wore dark glasses for the auction, and a cream leather coat. I must have looked like a mobster's moll. I swaggered into the auction room of the Plymouth hotel, exchanged a conspiratorial look with the estate agent appointed to bid for me, then sat stiffly, transfixed with fear, on a small gold chair, staring straight ahead. The auctioneer's hammer hovered aloft. Regulars must know the routine: bidding goes sluggishly at first, then quickens as the rival parties engage, then slows as they reach their limits; numbers thin out before the final two take it slowly to the kill. I had no idea. I thought the sluggish opening meant we had it in the bag. Inward smiles of self-satisfaction. Then the bidding quickened: my heart thumped so loudly I thought they'd hear it. We reached my limit. Bidding stopped, but not in my favour. The room held its breath. No one fidgeted. It was my call. The dark glasses were suddenly a menace. I would go one bid further, but how to let the man bidding on my behalf know. There was no eye-contact and I was too frozen by fear to take off the glasses. The awesomeness of it—my bidding with my own money for my own property—paralysed me. Suddenly, as the pause gathered dust and the hammer grew heavy, I gave an extravagant and neck-wrenching nod. My bidder got the message. The bid flew, it hovered unchallenged, the hammer cracked and suddenly I had my own place in the world.

The cottage had cost £5,500, deposit by cheque £500. I caught the train to London, feeling I'd won some kind of independence.

*   *   *

Back in London, my contract with *Line Up* finally ended, I was soon battling for work—and for any prospect of a regular income. The divorce had been as civilised as these things can be. I had cited the most significant of Michael's women friends. He refrained from any mention of Harold. But in acknowledgement that I, too, had contributed to the breakdown of the marriage I gave up any claim to alimony. Michael left the home we shared near Primrose Hill, and I took it over. We were both keen to safeguard the children from too much shock and hurt. They stayed in the same home and went on attending the same local schools. There was minimum disruption. Indeed, for them there were positive benefits. Michael, who had for years been something of an absentee father, was roused by his fear of losing his children into being fulsomely attentive. There were outings and treats, holidays on Hadrian's Wall, visits to Scotland and Cornwall. I began to realise that divorce need not be the catastrophic failure and shameful end of everything that I had feared. Somewhere at the bottom of my gloom I saw how life went on, rearranged and restructured, and that children need love more than they need legal contracts and orthodox patterns of behaviour.

*   *   *

I ricocheted around for a while, trying to find my bearings. Women were on screen a good deal more in the 1970s. By the end of the decade Angela Rippon would have become a BBC newsreader; similarly Anna Ford at ITN. But a man's decision put them there. Grace Wyndham Goldie, head of Talks and Current Affairs, and rightly hailed as one of the most formidable women in the early years of the BBC, has a lot to answer for: she preferred to appoint men. And said so. Professor Asa Briggs, the august official historian of the BBC, quotes her rumoured remark: 'I don't want too many women on my staff. They burst into tears. It is a tiresome thing that women do.' And she acted appropriately. Like Margaret Thatcher, she enjoyed power for herself but appointed men to serve her. What was more, those she'd appointed as young men years back—Alasdair Milne, Donald Baverstock, Michael Peacock—were creating a climate of highly competitive, thrusting journalism that was to make their reputations. Already there were women working on *Panorama*: Catherine Dove had been the first, producing mostly items about the arts, but although promised an arts series of her own she was overtaken by the ambitious Huw Wheldon on his way to creating and editing *Monitor*. Dove left for ITV. Perhaps women weren't pushy enough. But others would follow, Revel Guest, Anne Tyerman, Margaret Jay, and they, too, would forge successful careers. But none was an on-screen reporter. I knew I had no place on *Panorama*.

Instead I made do with the crumbs that were on offer, which did nothing to encourage me to think women's place in the world was shifting. Under the generic title *Times Remembered* I was invited to interview the widows of Famous Men, and, in a later series, women who had worked for Famous

Men. The women themselves were impressive: the powdery and genteel Lady Tweedsmuir, widow of the novelist and Governor General of Canada John Buchan; Valerie Pascal, whose husband Gabriel, the volatile Hungarian film producer, had made Shaw's *Caesar and Cleopatra*; the toweringly tall Lady Baden-Powell, wooed as a teenager by the fifty-year-old Baden-Powell and founder of the Guides; Oscar Deutsch's widow, designer of the art-deco interiors of her husband's Odeon cinemas; Lady Dowding, whose husband masterminded the Battle of Britain and believed all his life that his dead pilots were talking to him from the spirit world; Carl Jung's housekeeper, Churchill's cook. These women, and others, were often strong, intelligent, resourceful. But there was no denying that they were either grand or dependent, usually both. They had subsumed their lives in those of their men, either as wives or servants. The programmes didn't do much to encourage new attitudes.

Nor did many in the BBC. While still on *Line Up*, I had gone to see Derek Amoore, then Head of News, to put to him a question then being increasingly expressed among feminist groups. It was easier for me to do this than most, because I clearly had a job of considerable weight already and didn't want any other. Why, I wanted to know, were there as yet no women reading the news? And was there any prospect of it happening? Derek was uneasy with women. He made silly flirtatious remarks, which, given his authority, he could push beyond the bounds of discretion. He also wore dark glasses and drank a good deal. Not an easily approachable man. By the time I arrived in his

305

office, he was already well into the whisky, which I declined. I was serious; he was awkward. He pranced around, waving his tumbler. I sat and listened. What I heard wasn't encouraging. Women, he predicted, would never read the news. Their clothes were too distracting, their voices were too shrill and their temperament would render them tearful at bad news. A son of Grace indeed.

He wasn't the only BBC figure to have problems with women. Robin Day was another. He was a thoroughly serious and professional journalist who, in office relationships, was scrupulous. Socially he was a menace. There was no subtlety in his manner: at office parties he would attack head on. 'Do the men you interview fancy you? Do they stare at your legs? Do they stare at your breasts? Do you sleep with many of them?' I might have enjoyed a serious conversation with such an outstanding broadcaster, but his awkwardness and his gauche attempts to cover it defeated us both. Whenever he loomed in sight, I made myself scarce.

But there was one area where women journalists were being given something of a chance. General Features produced a clutch of programmes, of which the most outstanding was *Man Alive*, whose editor was also head of the department, Desmond Wilcox. He recruited and promoted several women reporters, most prominently Esther Rantzen who became his wife. Desmond had appeared a number of times on *Line Up* on occasions when *Man Alive* was to be discussed, which was often. He was fluent and amenable. But he was displeased by our book *The New Priesthood*, taking exception to an anecdote told at his expense by the film-maker Tony Palmer. He threatened to sue for libel: the paperback edition was pulped.

Desmond was a small, ebullient man with a noisy ego, who thrived on being cock of the walk, but drove away any rivals from his own particular farmyard. You were either within his coop or outside it. I was destined to remain outside. A number of his producers attempted to recruit me. I had done a number of single reports for the annual BBC1 *Holiday* programmes and was wined and dined by its editor, Tom Savage, who said he wanted me to have a permanent contract with the show: he just had to clear it with his boss. The contract never materialised. Again, I was recruited by producer and director Eddie Mirzeoff as a reporter for his documentary about Westminster School. Dates were pencilled in my diary, meetings were planned, when word came that Desmond had insisted they find a 'less well-known face'. It was an argument I couldn't challenge.

Years later it occurred to me, rather fancifully, that I might have been blacklisted. In the early 1970s I had been called in by the head of Presentation, the modest, rather timid Rex Moorfoot. He had addressed me almost apologetically as he delivered in rather elliptical terms what was clearly a warning. He advised me to 'be careful'.

'Oh, why exactly, Rex?'

'Well, it's thought by some in the BBC hierarchy that there are those on *Line Up* who want to overturn the government of the country. Their sympathies have been noticed.' I replied that we lived in a democracy, believed in its freedoms and

307

reserved the right to be critical. We parted amicably enough and I thought no more about it. I accepted then and, reconsidering the matter now, I believe that the rather hippie, wayward conduct of *Late Night Line Up* was probably more to blame for my struggles than any political witch-hunt.

However, in the mid-1980s when details of the BBC's vetting procedures came to light in the *Observer*, I was intrigued. BBC contact with MI5 had been strong during the Second World War, but with the transition to the Cold War the vetting had increased. The feeling grew that anyone with left-wing links posed a security problem. Whenever someone joined the BBC they were referred for clearance. It wasn't always given and it was considered enough explanation to say, 'There were security considerations.' In 1965 Stephen Peet, a senior producer in Documentary Features, was so treated and persuaded his MP Kenneth Robinson to lobby the Home Office for a retraction. The broadcaster Michael Rosen, then a general trainee, was told in 1972 'better if you go freelance': security reasons again. By 1975 MI5 had set up a special desk for dealing with 'subversives in the media'. They objected to Anna Ford joining *Man Alive*; they blocked Richard Gott from the editorship of the *Listener*; they tried unsuccessfully to recruit Jon Snow of ITN to spy on his colleagues. They objected to the film director Roland Joffé, and the drama producer Kenith Trodd. On many such occasions, the BBC's departmental heads kicked up a fuss and the bans were lifted. Desmond Wilcox did so for Anna Ford. Tony Garnett threatened to go public unless Joffé could direct *The Spongers*. The BBC conceded. A clutch of renowned writers—Simon Gray, Dennis Potter, Colin Welland—protested to the BBC about Kenith Trodd. The BBC relented and he went on to produce *Pennies from Heaven* and win the year's top BAFTA award.

Some twenty years after these newspaper revelations, at his eightieth birthday party I asked Rowan Ayers whether he thought, given the sustained left-wing slant of *Line Up*, that I had been blacklisted: 'Almost certainly,' he said, with a grin. Of course, now under the Data Protection Act I could check out the facts. But I don't. I prefer to leave the matter a mystery.

*   *   *

My virtual disappearance from any regular BBC television was remarked on in the press. A cartoon by Michael Heath reduced me to tears. It showed a wistful dad gazing at discarded sixties memorabilia in an attic trunk, while a toddler enquires, 'Dad, who was Joan Bakewell?' I was beginning to wonder myself. Was I really just a flimsy bit of sixties nonsense, notorious crumpet that had now had its day? I resolved it should not be so. I took encouragement when people I respected lent a hand. Julian Barnes, then television critic for the *New Statesman*, ran a Bring Back Bakewell campaign, giving a generous mention of whatever modest appearance I now made. But clearly I had to look outside the BBC if my career was to have any substance.

*   *   *

309

I found a new home and new opportunities at Granada. All freelance broadcasters need a mentor, someone on the inside of the broadcasting institutions who believes in you and will promote your interests. David Attenborough had been one such, but he was gone. Rowan Ayers was now heading up Community Programmes. Denis Forman, then director of programmes at Granada, would be the next. Denis was and remains a remarkable spirit. Undaunted by having lost a leg in the Battle of Monte Cassino, he forged ahead in the post-war years, first as a seminal influence in the development of the British Film Institute where he was at different times chairman and director, then as a force for good in shaping the enlightened policies of Granada Television. He joined in 1955, and from the mid-sixties to mid-eighties Granada's programmes were his concern. With his encouragement, *World in Action* became a flagship for tough investigative reporting that was also entertaining. It set the standard. Denis was always about standards.

Now, in the declining days of *Line Up*, he and his director of programmes, David Plowright, invited me to join Granada hook, line and sinker, taking up a whole range of opportunities with them. But such a major commitment meant moving to Manchester. It came at the very moment my divorce had left me a single parent with two children at school. While I toyed with the notion of commuting, hiring nannies, or even moving the children to new and strange schools in the North, I knew in my bones I couldn't do that to them. Life had given them enough shocks. So I said, 'No,' to the big offer. A clear case of 'the path not chosen', it remains one of the big what-ifs of my working life. Instead I made occasional visits to Granada as a freelance to present a series called *Reports Action*.

The culture of Granada was abrasively different from that of the BBC. It had been founded by millionaire socialists Sidney and Cecil Bernstein and had no doubts about its political allegiance. Or its style: a formidable Francis Bacon hung in the foyer of the Manchester building. There were good paintings everywhere. And from the start it had a reputation for radical programmes. Not surprisingly, Granada attracted radical programme-makers. Gus Macdonald's career was to have perhaps the broadest reach: born in Glasgow, he first made his mark as a leader of the ship-building apprentice strike on the Clyde, then moved through programme-making to television's top management, thence to the House of Lords and became a minister of state in Tony Blair's government; I caught him when he was in charge of Granada's local broadcasting. But there were others of a left-wing temperament, too: MPs Margaret Beckett and Brian Sedgemore appeared regularly on a local programme, Jack Straw worked on *World in Action*. And there was Jim Walker.

Jim made *Reports Action* a surprising popular success. Its flowering was brief and golden—just six series—and it was cut down in its prime by the malaise of the time: the excessive power of the unions. But for a short time it commanded my loyalty, my enthusiasm and my energies. Its origins were not auspicious. It sprang from a worthy idea already finding expression in numerous small local programmes tucked away in the schedules of ITV's different companies and commanding little

311

attention. Granada brought the idea into the open, shook it vigorously and set it before the national audience at six fifteen on Sundays. It was the first secular programme to break the God slot, the ruling that programmes between six and eight on Sunday evenings should have a religious content. Churchmen objected, and the Church of England's representative on the religious advisory committee, the Revd Donald Reeves, claimed it was not explicitly religious. Jim Walker had an answer to that: 'Look,' he said, 'you're talking to an atheist here. The only bit of the Bible I like is "By their works shall ye know them." Will that do?' I heartily agreed. We all agreed. This was a programme made by people of missionary zeal. Perhaps that qualified us as religious. In the end Jim won the day, and the relentlessly do-gooding *Reports Action* continued doing its good.

Reports Action was a child of its time. It was born of the mid-seventies just as the steady prosperity of the post-war period was running out. The once-and-for-all turn in economic fortune came in 1973 when OPEC (the Organisation of Petrol Exporting Countries) quadrupled the price of oil, then at the end of the 1970s more or less trebled it again. There would be no going back from this sudden jolt into a new world order, and a sense of crisis was in the air. Out of this was born the environmental movement, concerned at the rapid increases in global pollution. Television caught the mood. This was when *The Good Life* was launched, a comedy created round a young couple, played by Felicity Kendal and Richard Briers, trying to live a self-sufficient life. It was against such a national background of concern and the idea that we must

312

take responsibility for each other that *Reports Action* could survive.

I co-presented the series with Bob Greaves, a man who, while slender and agile, gave the impression of being roly-poly and cuddly. He was the acme of the local news reporter: formerly Granada's local news editor, he stepped before the camera and found his place in the community. Everyone in Granadaland knew him: his waxwork stood between Raquel Welch and Sophia Loren on Blackpool's Golden Mile. His good humour and spontaneity spilled from the screen. He had already co-presented the local version of the series with Anna Ford, who had now joined *Man Alive*.

I was drafted as the show went national, live at peak time. It was totally different from anything I had ever done. It would focus my life ever more clearly around the work I did and the role I had as someone in the public eye. At last life was becoming more fun. And *Reports Action* was central to that. It was aggressive, hectoring, active. If you were talking you were walking. We strode around the studio, delivering fast-paced patter, and mottos like 'Don't view it—do it', and 'Don't sympathise—mobilise.' This was not late-night sophistication: here I was in the mainstream of popular entertainment. So what exactly was *Reports Action* up to?

The idea was to provoke the public into action to help themselves and others. Each week we would launch several appeals, and invite people to phone the studio at once if they were willing to help. We had target objectives and scoreboards in the studio, and banks of people at telephones taking calls. So, an appeal for discarded fridges would turn into a game in which the scoreboard clicked away while we launched the next appeal. This time it might be for visitors to go one-to-one visiting at psychiatric hospitals, or for drivers to take a lonely granny out to tea. Soon we were inviting people to turn up at specific locations. A reasonable crowd, a pop group and the WRVS serving hot soup answered our call to clear the rubbish from Loch Lomond. Unhappily we had made the film report when there had been a drought and the water level at the loch revealed tin cans, old tyres, loads of dross. By the time our helpers turned up, there'd been heavy showers and we all had to wade out in wellingtons.

The idea took off. I found myself helping to clean canals, working with archaeologists on their sites, learning to ride a motorbike to demonstrate a safety flag we were giving away. I was out of doors in all weathers; the mini-skirts of *Line Up* days gave way to a whole new wardrobe of bulky sweaters, jeans and boots. We urged skilled tradesmen to volunteer to do repairs for the elderly. We gave things away, too: fifty thousand kidney donor cards, tins of chemical to remove graffiti from walls, red pennants for cycle wheels to reduce accidents, kits to test for river pollution. And then we went too far, offering kits to help anyone wanting to give up smoking. We anticipated ten thousand requests; 450,000 people applied. Phone lines were jammed not only in Manchester but in our ten other regional call-in points. We had to call on ASH, the anti-smoking campaign, to help us out. We were tapping into some hidden need in the public to be of use, to help others. Support was welling up. We pushed it further.

Soon we were inviting people to come together to help each other: housewives clubbed together to save money by buying food in bulk; young able-bodied groups met to befriend the less able. We invited people to swap homes for free holidays. And all this was done at breakneck speed, the scoreboards clicking away to reach targets. Bob and I were described as jolly PT instructors, bullying and chivvying a response from the viewing public. We each had our favourite successes: I was delighted when we found adoptive parents for a handicapped three-year-old. And amused when a man who asked for three hundred pairs of discarded spectacles to send to leper hospitals in India received twenty thousand! We were soon in the *Guinness Book of Records* for the scale of our achievement.

The response was not only extraordinary but unpredictable. Disappointingly only a few hundred were willing to take the housebound out to tea. But some three thousand volunteers phoned in offering to visit people in psychiatric hospitals. Some called long after the programme was over. The comedian Peter Cook even phoned me at home at 2.30 a.m. asking to be included in the hospital visit. And he was. By now the series was well established, with audiences of eight million. So we pushed the idea of community help still further: we invited people to spot factories belching smoke and report them; to spot boarded-up houses that could be used for the homeless; to complain to their councils if sports facilities were inadequate. By now Clive James, then television critic for the *Observer*, was declaring, '*Reports Action* might well end up governing Britain . . . The thought occurs that Bob

315

and Joan could take over the country far more easily than Arthur Scargill.'

The name is significant. This was the late seventies when the unions were exercising their power to the utmost and pushing their demands further at every concession. Granada was a strongly unionised company and I knew at first hand how constraining this was. Whenever we went filming with a television crew, their union's deal was such that within the working day they had the right to an hour-long lunch break at a pub or hotel offering a three-course set lunch, with choice of starter. Travel to and from the location counted outside the hour. If we were filming in November in the North, when it doesn't get light enough to film until 10 a.m. and is dark at 4 p.m., this made for a short filming day. This union practice set severe limits, but we lived with it. But then they moved in on the studio.

On the day of transmission the banks of telephones in the studio and in the regional centres were an important part of the programme. Many of the calls needed expert advice and handling, so where possible they were answered by people from the Community Service Volunteers who had been involved in setting up the different appeals. But as the programme's success grew and the calls escalated, many of the phones were answered by secretarial staff who were members of NATTKE, entitled to double pay for working on Sunday. Gradually union representatives among them began to cast a jealous eye towards the jobs done by unpaid volunteers. Eventually they demanded that those jobs, too, went to paid NATTKE members. It added an intolerable burden to the already stretched budgets. When Granada refused, the union blacked the series. I wasn't privy to management negotiations, or aware of what must have been going on backstage. But of the outcome I was in no doubt. *Reports Action* ended. It was over. The great experiment in public generosity and goodwill had been destroyed by greed and self-interest. It was at this point that my left-wing sympathies reached their limit. I was furious that so much good could be so wilfully destroyed.

We had tested the idea that human nature could be motivated to give willingly of time and effort without consideration of financial gain, and that society as a whole could benefit from such an impulse. Whole areas of the voluntary sector had become involved. Round Tables and Rotary International set about fetching and carrying; self-help groups sprang up, creating communities of common interest. Most remarkably, this was all done without money. It was not any kind of telethon, where people phone and pledge sums of money, then stay put. It was active participation. People gave and volunteered their services for free. Others received help and comfort without having to pay. Unhappily it was the professionals—the union pressure to increase their hold on jobs—who defeated us. The spirit of self-help that was changing social attitudes collapsed before the forces of self-interest and money. The show was axed in January 1979. In May of the same year Margaret Thatcher became prime minister. She didn't believe there was such a thing as society. But she did believe in money.

317

CHAPTER FOURTEEN

ARTS MATTERS

The freelance life was all very well, but I realised that if I wasn't watchful it could become a bit episodic. A solid job with a clear role in an established institution helps define who you are. If you're a freelance you define yourself. I had been late, as it was, coming to the serious business of work; now I wanted something more in focus, something with which I could identify. But I still wouldn't consider a career in the terms that the male world defines it, a predictable journey through ambition, promotion, power and pension. I needed something else.

In the 1980s I would find it. It would grow from interests seeded long ago, in the libraries and theatres, the cinemas and art galleries I had sought out as I was growing up. It concerned an arena of human experience that involves people in high-risk, unpredictable enterprises, in explorations of what it is that makes us human, in attempts to convey to each other our sensibilities and weaknesses, and in so doing push ourselves to dare new and extraordinary things. I mean the world of the creative spirit. In institutional terms it is referred to as 'the arts'.

So far in my life, my most sustained emotional commitment had been to and with my children, whose lives as they grew up, despite the rough and rocky days of adolescence, had come right. By 1980 Harriet was twenty-one. In her days at Camden

School she had fallen in with a group for whom learning wasn't 'cool'. I had fretted and nagged, and we had quarrelled, so she had taken off in her mid-teens to live with her father's new family in Hampshire. It was a happy move. At Havant Sixth Form College she began to enjoy learning. Finally she came back to live with me and attend a London crammer. She worked under great pressure to catch up and win a place at the Courtauld Institute. There, she blossomed. Now she was a young woman—with crazy hair and freaky clothes—taking off into her generation and its concerns. Matthew wasn't far behind, making his own way and decisions. The nest would soon be empty. My first priority would no longer be the well-being of two young people. I could now begin to think exclusively of my own professional interests and preferences. What this released in me was an almost frenetic energy and drive, as if the stopped-up ambition of a lifetime—a lifetime of by now over forty years—was suddenly released, and I could let rip doing what I wanted to do. I had left it late, I had made that choice, but I refused to let that discourage me.

I was encouraged in this by the happiness I had found some years earlier in my second marriage. The young man, Jack Emery, whom I had interviewed for *Line Up* years before in Exeter, had cropped up again in my life. We bumped into each other on a train, exchanged phone numbers. I visited his one-man show at the King's Head theatre in Islington. We went to a party or two, the cinema. He wooed me with flowers, gifts of scent, attention, care. I was charmed. He was twelve years younger than me—in his late twenties as I was hitting forty—but why not have a fling, a straightforward, uncomplicated fling, with this tall, attractive, available young man?

In my time alone, since separating from Michael, I had spent the summer holiday taking the children to Malta where a colleague from broadcasting, the zoologist Desmond Morris, and his wife Ramona, were busy spending their windfall fortune from Desmond's book *The Naked Ape*. They had a lovely house there and a fine yacht. It was their intention, Desmond has written since, to spend it all as soon as possible, then return to Oxford and work. This they did. The year of my second visit, 1973, Jack flew out to join us for the weekend. Things were getting serious. He was filling an important space in my personal life, a space left empty by all that had gone before. I wasn't consciously in search of a man. He was just suddenly there. And *making me happy*.

Within weeks he was speaking of marriage. I spelled out my refusal: I had already had my children and he, as a younger man, might want his own. I didn't want any more. Our lives didn't match. I refused to consider it. But we went on being happy together. Jack was about to take a job at Peterborough's theatre, the Key, but before he did so he was invited to visit the Adelaide Festival in Australia with his one-man Beckett show, then take it on to other Australian venues. He invited me to go along too: six weeks without my family and with no obligations other than to be what the papers called 'his travelling companion'. Michael generously moved back into his former home to care for the children, by now in their mid-teens, and I left for Australia. I had never enjoyed such freedom from responsibility. I felt lightheaded, reckless. The tour was full of success, sun and the easy friendships of the Australians. By the time we returned, we were planning to marry.

We were married in church, the second time for both of us. Only the signing of the register had to be done elsewhere. Jack's father was a Baptist minister and although our own doctrinal beliefs had lapsed we both felt that the sacredness of the place and the liturgy gave weight to our personal commitment. I had always been bewildered that divorcees, serious about a church ceremony, had found their way blocked by Church authorities. All you needed to do was find the right vicar. We were lucky because in the Revd Joseph McCullogh, of St Mary-le-Bow in the City of London, we already had a friend who was sympathetic to us. Indeed, it was he who suggested he conduct the ceremony. 'But you're not allowed to,' I protested.

'Allow me to know what I am and am not allowed to do.'

And that was it. We agreed. Apparently as rector he had much discretion in what he chose to do, and Joseph, very much an eccentric individualist in the diocese, liked to please himself. His parish was perforce a topsy-turvy place: as he had no parishioners at the weekend, he held services on weekdays.

In April 1975, Joseph married us in the Norman crypt. My father, now living alone in a cosy retirement of Cheshire golf, Spanish holidays and occasional world cruises, had known of my rackety life, but kept any misgivings to himself. Now it seemed I was to be settled once more. Humphrey Burton, who with his wife Christina had cared for

321

me 'at times of crisis, composed and played his own anthem as a small congregation of friends gathered to wish us well. As I took my first step down the aisle on my father's arm there appeared to be few of them. In fact, I could see hardly anyone. There was an eccentric explanation: Harriet's necklace had snapped, scattering pearls across the flagstones, and our helpful guests were out of sight, scrabbling on hands and knees to retrieve them for her.

This time I was resolved there would be no infidelity. I had made that clear. This marriage was my second chance, a fresh start. I felt I was returning to something new and untarnished. What I didn't realise at the time was that I was also returning to my earliest emotional ties. I knew already that Jack suffered intermittently from depression. There had been episodes, even in the euphoria of our coming together, when he would retreat into silence and a place of emotional isolation I could not reach. Believing the myth that the love of a good woman might do much, I expected our happiness to dissipate whatever troubled him. Besides, didn't I already know how to handle depression? Depression, after all, had haunted my mother's life, and my childhood home. Perhaps unconsciously I recognised how it worked and was even comfortable with it.

*   *   *

I had begun my involvement with the arts back in the days of *Late Night Line Up* when our guests were often writers, painters, dramatists and creative people generally. Then, in 1974, I had deliberately added to their number. I helped to create an artist, conjure him from thin air, invent him. His name was Anton Krajny and he was a hoax. A hoax that got out of hand.

In 1974 Scottish Television invited me to write and present a documentary about the Edinburgh Festival. They partnered me with the boisterous, good-humoured, Scottish light-entertainment producer Clarke Tait; an unlikely pairing, he suspicious I might be a *Private Eye* pseud, I fearful he would not understand High Art. Both sets of fears were groundless. We got on famously, arguing, shouting, laughing, teasing, working long and hard for what we believed in. We also became friends.

Not everyone joined us. One researcher in particular offered the programme little help, arriving daily simply to cadge free seats for concerts and shows. He always got them: the rest of us were too busy working. Clarke and I seethed with rage. It was not until the post-programme party held in my Edinburgh flat that we had our revenge. The parasitic young man arrived casting high-flown judgements to left and right, spouting arty jargon about this play, that concert. Clarke and I, on our knees with tiredness, rose to the occasion.

'Tell me,' Clarke began, with an endearing chuckle that alerted his friends to mischief, 'what did you think of the Krajny exhibition?'

'Krajny?' Alarm registered behind the glasses. 'Krajny?'

The hook was in: Clarke played the line. 'You must know Krajny, for God's sake, man! Anton Krajny. His exhibition was the talk of the Festival. Don't tell me you hadn't heard?' Clarke's belligerence dared him to admit ignorance, Sir Toby Belch to his Malvolio.

'Oh, Krajny, yes, of course.' He blinked nervously. 'Yes . . . Krajny . . . well, actually in my view . . .' The bogus opinions poured forth. And Anton Krajny had sprung into life. News of his existence rippled round the party. Others gathered round to enjoy the fun, courting his views, pandering to his vanity. Cruel? Probably, but Krajny came to symbolise the hypocrisy of much Festival chatter. As such he soon garnered a substantial following well beyond the party.

The myth grew, too. Anton Krajny turned out to be a reclusive Polish surrealist minimalist, sometime performance artist, friend of the Pope and colleague of Lech Walesa. From then on, an annual Krajny Dinner was organised during each Edinburgh Festival. Its speakers over the years have included art figures as diverse as Richard Demarco, John Drummond, Paul Gambaccini, Owen Dudley Edwards and Douglas Rae. On each occasion it opened with a formality known as the Piping of the Scrotum (in fact pig's offal), paraded on a silver salver ahead of our procession through the streets of Edinburgh.

It was six years before the press heard of Krajny, and then they were intrigued. It seemed there was no silliness they wouldn't swallow. There were mentions in *Harpers and Queen*, the *Radio Times*, the *Sunday Times*. Krajny's antics multiplied: he'd been seen in New Mexico and Bolivia. A spoof television documentary almost caught up with him, but he was always just turning a corner, vanishing down an alley. Then, in 1980, the story went big. A front-page banner headline in the *Glasgow Evening*

News declared, 'Top Pole Flees to Safety': 'A dissident smuggled out of Poland is on his way to Scotland to claim political asylum . . .' a three-column exclusive. In no time at all the London papers and television companies were on the trail. This was serious: journalism was our bread and butter and we'd been leading the press by the nose. It was time to run for cover. The phones rang: we didn't answer. We lay low, only confirming through devious contacts that there was really no story, no follow-up. We escaped censure and giggled conspiratorially at our luck. We never knew what our researcher made of it all. He might even, we imagined, have been its unwitting source.

The hoax became an established part of Edinburgh Festival folklore. It was reported in books, written up wittily by Owen Dudley Edwards in his *City of a Thousand Worlds*, a terrible warning to cultural pseuds. However, the final warning came to us, the perpetrators. In January 1981 I received an invitation from the Francis Kyle Gallery in London to the private view of work by Anton Krajnc. With it, a poster of a beautiful work of art. I went to the show: there were more beautiful lithographs. The man—Anton Krajnc—was indeed a real and accomplished artist, with a name near enough to our own invented hero. Not surprisingly he wasn't pleased at our distracting recollections of the other Anton. And the thought occurred that if the name had been identical he might well have sued.

*   *   *

It felt as if my life was lightening up. And settling

down. It settled even more when in the late seventies I was given an important chance in radio. I was invited to become a co-presenter of the current-affairs programme *PM*. As would happen increasingly, I owed my opportunities not to the male hierarchy of the BBC but to independent-minded women who were making their confident way into the higher echelons of BBC power. I had no experience of current affairs, and I had worked in television rather than radio: it is not true that if you can do one you can automatically do the other. The risky decision to try me out was made by *PM*'s then editor, Jenny Abramsky.

Jenny was and remains a force to reckon with. In 1999 she became Managing Director, BBC Radio. She stands a mere five feet tall, and when she was pregnant, as she was throughout much of 1979, she looked virtually spherical. As if to make up for her stature, she projected a powerful sense of exactly what she wanted from her programme and expected from her presenters. Her dark hair framed strong, intelligent features, and an expression of total concentration. She would cup her hands over her ears to read a government document or significant report, and emerge minutes later in total command of its content and its weaknesses. In working mode she had little time for social niceties, but when something went right, she would break into a broad smile that lit up the entire office. I worked always to earn Jenny's smile.

The presenting was regularly divided between two pairs. My regular partner was Gordon Clough, a wise old owl of a reporter, privately oppressed by tax bills, with a passion for crosswords and one of the most mellifluous voices on radio. He it was who as early as 1980 pricked up his ears when the navy announced plans to pull *Endurance* out of South Georgia and commented, 'There'll be trouble there.' It was two years before the Falklands war. Susannah Simons, with a warm giggle to her throaty voice, usually partnered Robert Williams, a reporter invalided out of front-line radio service in Belfast. The programme format was that the men had the leading role, the women the secondary. This wasn't an issue: the men were obviously the senior journalists. But the day came when, from necessity rather than choice, Susannah and I were to present together: the first time, someone in the office noticed, that women had taken both roles. There was a brief discussion as to whether it was worth remarking on the fact on air, but the women's view prevailed: no, we would make no mention of it. Women now held their own place on radio without it needing to be the subject of comment.

*   *   *

It is hard to recall now—in the light of what was to come—the excitement with which the return of Peter O'Toole to the Old Vic was greeted at the start of 1981. It was fifteen years since he had been seen on the London stage. I knew how high expectations were because Jack had been appointed associate director of the Old Vic Company in January of that year. For the next eighteen months the wayward fortunes of that enterprise were to dominate my domestic life. The actor Timothy West had taken on the Artistic Directorship at the Old Vic after an awkward

327

negotiation with the Arts Council, which insisted, as one of the conditions of continuing its grant, that existing Artistic Director Toby Robertson step down and take a sabbatical. Tim, an outstanding actor with a thriving career, had never run such a company before. He arrived to find that, contractually, Peter O'Toole had signed up to play Macbeth on condition he had full artistic control. He had unrealistic notions of casting Meryl Streep as Lady Macbeth and John Gielgud as Duncan. So far so bad.

Jack was in charge of marketing and created a subscription scheme, by which people buying tickets for several productions got them at a reduced rate. In those days it was a pioneering idea in London theatre, and full-page ads in the Sunday magazines making grandiose promises brought an avalanche of bookings. Indeed, the success of the marketing gave the season's debut such a high profile that when things went wrong there was nowhere to hide. Certainly not from me. I was reporting for *PM* at the time: domestically I was neatly placed to get wind of the disaster as it unfolded; professionally I was in early with a scoop when the scandal broke.

Something went wrong almost from the start. The two macho actors—Tim and Peter—were not good collaborators. Peter forbade Tim any right to attend early rehearsals, which were in the hands of film director Bryan Forbes. Word leaked out that there were tensions. It reached Jack, and so it reached me. It was my unhappy role to keep mum and keep smiling.

The first night on 3 September was a crescendo of awfulness, like embarking on the *Titanic* when you've already seen the film. Tim, in an unwise pre-emptive strike, had inserted a single sheet announcement into each programme, declaring that the production of *Macbeth* was under the total artistic control of Peter O'Toole. It gave the press their cue. Editors around Fleet Street were alerted even before the curtain went up. Tim then retired to watch the show from the shadows at the back of the dress circle as Peter fulfilled the by now wide expectation of proving a disaster. The performance was so bad the audience began first to titter, then to laugh outright. The staging was wooden, the set old-fashioned and O'Toole himself disappointed all the high hopes people had had. After the show Tim offered little more than brief thanks to the cast and vanished. For Jack and me the ordeal was different. We were among the critics and media people, bravely having drinks with them in the interval, stonewalling their increasingly insistent quizzing on how this could all have happened. At the after-show party Bryan Forbes asked discreetly, 'It wasn't all that bad, was it?' He had his answer in the next day's papers. Banner headlines: 'West disowns *Macbeth*.'

The catastrophe was a terrific hit. The rush for tickets was unprecedented, with queues stretching right down the street. On the quiet, the *PM* team got its own allocation of seats. Everyone but the company seemed to be enjoying the disaster. There were cartoons, jokes, it became a national laughing stock. In fact its success steadied the finances of the Old Vic Company: *Macbeth* made a profit of £20,000. There were five more plays in the season, each of which had a moderate success, pleased its audiences, went on tour and made no public waves at all.

By Christmas time when the Arts Council grants were to be announced, there were said to be massive cuts on the way. The Tory government went ahead with axeing an unprecedented £1.4 million from their arts budget, leaving the Arts Council to supervise the fallout, which it did by cutting the entire grants of forty-one arts organisations. The Arts Council meeting at which it endorsed such cuts took place on 17 December. I remember the date vividly because that evening we had a dinner party among whose guests were Sir Claus Moser, Marghanita Laski, and Richard Hoggart. Claus, then chairman of Covent Garden, bounced in, in jubilant mood, declaring with relief that he'd been tipped off that the Royal Opera House's grant was secure. Solicitously he asked after the Old Vic. Jack replied, cautious but worried, that so far they had heard nothing. Meanwhile our other guests, Marghanita, who happened to be deputy chairman of the Arts Council, and Hoggart, who sat on it, held their counsel. It was a grim evening. Next day our worst fears were realised. The entire grant was withdrawn. Within six months the Old Vic Company went bankrupt.

There is much discussion about the causes of depression. Current thinking seems to indicate a combination of genetically inherited disposition, some sort of chemical component and the impact of life events. It was certainly the latter, the Old Vic debacle—protracted as it was over eighteen months—that plunged Jack into a prolonged period of depression. Things weren't helped, I was to realise later, by the fact that he had embarked on an affair with a working colleague that had got emotionally out of hand. I was not to uncover it for three more years. Meanwhile the depression persisted.

*   *   *

How much does adultery matter? It has always occurred, even within the strictest societies. It had been part of my first marriage. Indeed, it is so potent a feature of human behaviour as to be part of the given, almost as though the basic instinct is so strong that we should accommodate rather than condemn it. And many do. None the less it is widely disapproved of. Religions inveigh against it; some communities punish it. It is the one circumstance that in a single word justifies divorce. Of all the degrees of permissiveness that we now accept, adultery is still for many a stage too far. We simply don't know how to deal with it.

We almost forget how sensationally painful it is—that moment when the uniqueness of the relationship is suddenly over. It has all the impact of a sudden death. Indeed, it is a sort of sudden death. At its most extreme the emotional shock can drive people to breakdown, even revenge on a terrible scale. Crazed by grief and loss they can go wild, damage themselves, damage others, take life, take their own. Short of that, there is a quietly endured unhappiness, the collapse of trust, the sense of failure. Yet ignoring the evidence, the realities of life, many of us still persist in vesting all our hopes and dreams, our sense of identity and purpose in this one overarching bond. It comes to embody the best we can achieve, it defines who we

331

are. When it works, it gives us the best of life. But when it is fractured—carelessly or calculatedly—the sun dies.

There are wives who are reconciled, though with sadness, when their men stray. There are, perhaps, fewer men who would concede the same to their wives. If a casual fling grows into a serious attachment, things move a step closer to the end. People can choose to stay married and live towards some benign, often deeper understanding that will see them through into a calmer old age together. Or they can separate on the instant, and divorce. When the time came, I would choose to go on, keen to mend, eager to salvage. But it doesn't always succeed. In the long term mine didn't.

* * *

In July 1981 I rejoined BBC Television. I had been almost ten years outside its broad encompassing embrace. As a freelance I had popped up now and then in film and holiday programmes. Invited by Julia Mathieson, one of an increasing band of women producers, I made a series of ten-minute films about fashion, and a single documentary called *Arts UK OK*. But to sustain the steady income that my household now needed, I also had a parallel career in journalism, as television critic for *Punch* and then *The Times*. The new BBC commitment meant that these would have to go. But the priority seemed right. I had big plans for what I wanted to do.

The new job was to be called BBC Television arts correspondent. The role hadn't existed before and was created for me by BBC Television's then director of programmes Brian Wenham, a cultivated but waspish man, known as Wenham the Venom, in collaboration with George Carey who was editor of *Newsnight*. Today the BBC has a raft of people who regularly report arts stories and entertainment, so it seems odd that the arts had at that time no place except within the Arts Department. My brief, which had been formulated and agreed after much discussion, was not simply to report on arts stories as they arose but to try to change the existing culture of the BBC's News and Current Affairs departments so that arts would be as automatically assured of a place on the news agenda as sport. The project would in the end be a failure, but there were successes along the way, and some enduring achievements.

I knew what a wealth of theatre, music, dance and art now flourished around the country. It was an often repeated statistic, but worthy of note, that more people attended the theatre than went to football matches. Yet this was in no way reflected in our television coverage. I was also aware that the philosophy of Margaret Thatcher's government was to withdraw state subsidies as much as possible from a whole range of public arenas. Why not privatise the arts, too? I could see there would be interesting conflicts ahead. I also knew that unless a sustained and viable case for the arts was regularly set before the public they could easily fall into the assumptions of many politicians that the arts were merely the icing on the cake, when other more basic needs had been taken care of, somehow the prerogative of toffs and snobs. I believed, on the contrary, the arts to be intrinsic to a civilised society and something in which everyone had a right to share. There was no time to be lost in making the case.

I hit *Newsnight* running. My first move was to engage with the unions—the Musicians Union and Equity—to persuade them of the need to renegotiate the terms on which extracts from rehearsals and performances could be used. Existing arrangements with the BBC were too constricting. Something like one minute of performance was allowed before fees kicked in at a rate we couldn't afford. I made the case to John Morton of the Musicians Union and Peter Plouviez of Equity that if the arts were to get publicity they would have to be willing to make it easier for us, the broadcasters, to afford regular and consistent reporting. The deal was done with the BBC. Two of the earliest reports I made benefited directly by it. The first, a new play by Julian Mitchell called *Another Country*, told the story of the schooldays of Guy Burgess and starred two young actors new to the public, Kenneth Branagh and Rupert Everett. The second concerned the transfer of Peter Shaffer's play *Amadeus* from the National Theatre to the West End, and the issue, which has remained troublesome ever since, of whether directors, already paid once to direct a play at the National Theatre at the taxpayer's expense, should then garner further income by a West End transfer. My director David Wickham set the new style. Gone was the clumsy sense of a theatre production awkwardly caught on a camera somewhere in the stalls. David took the camera on stage, in and among the actors, putting on the *Newsnight* screen extracts that looked more like television drama than a snatched news report.

David, who had come to Current Affairs via News, brought to bear his instinct for aggressive reporting on the hapless world of music and dance. He caught something of my fervour for campaigning. Soon we were on the road together to Barlaston Hall, Staffordshire, a beautiful but then derelict Regency house, attributed to Sir Robert Taylor and now owned by the Wedgwood company, who reckoned there was nothing to be done but pull it down. The house was badly affected by subsidence from underground mining, so any cost of rescue would be substantial. So, we had two targets: the Coal Board and Wedgwood. Nothing daunted, we brought in a cherry-picker crane—one that allows your camera to reach up high, over walls, and look down inside at the sorry state of an exquisite interior. We called on the fine tradition of a fine industrial name, we expounded the uniqueness of the architecture. We gave it all we had got.

Somehow Barlaston Hall was saved. I don't want to know how. I am sure there were many voices, much pressure. But every time I catch a sight of it from a train speeding through Staffordshire I smile happily thinking of worthwhile work and a job well done.

We weren't as lucky at Beverley Minster. In the early 1980s there were plans to build an estate of modest houses directly below its south walls, ruining, the conservationists maintained, a view of the Minster unspoiled for centuries. A local row had broken out and we were soon in the middle of it, teasing out the reasoning on both sides, and presenting a dilemma that made the film worth watching. In the end the houses were built.

Were we personally partisan? Yes. Was our reporting fair? I think it was. The BBC's commitment to balanced reporting was the air we breathed. It was so familiar that we didn't need consciously to call it to mind. We knew, as Victorian children knew the catechism, the dogmas of our craft. We had a sense, even without any discussion, of how the images we used, and how we juxtaposed them, would be read by the viewer, how they would be judged by our peers and, possibly, revised by our editors. This was the shared code of programme-making ethics that prevailed in the 1980s.

But, of course, reporters and correspondents have their own views. They are not cyphers. I was strongly convinced that the arts were of value, and allied my loyalties accordingly. I stood amid the golden corn of a field in Shoreham to point up the extent to which a proposed motorway would damage the landscape that had inspired Samuel Palmer's vision. I took time out from a holiday in Greece to report on Melina Mercouri's passionate case for the return of the Elgin Marbles. I reported in 1982 how Scottish Ballet was beginning a scheme to give the sons of dock-workers a chance to learn classical dance, some eighteen years before the film *Billy Elliot* told a similar story.

Sometimes an item from the eighties replayed today recalls with an eerie strangeness the serious issues of the times. Talking about his play *The Normal Heart*, American playwright Larry Kremer set out the scale of the Aids crisis in America: 'Forty of my friends have died or are dying of Aids.' We forget, from an awareness of today's drug treatments, just how the deaths of young men were sweeping through communities. And year after year I quizzed a sequence of Tory arts ministers about the low levels of government funding, and harassed the Arts Council about its policy decisions. This didn't always endear me to the chairman of the Arts Council Sir William-Rees Mogg, who was also vice chairman of the BBC.

In the mid-eighties *Newsnight* editors, and a sequence of producers appointed for a term or two to the Arts Desk, championed this new attempt to give the arts a higher profile in the BBC's daily reporting. In my first year I made some fifty films, in subsequent years well over forty. And one story begat another. Interest infiltrated the entire team. Over some six years I was able to establish and sustain as broad and regular a coverage of the arts as any serious current-affairs programme before or since. It was not to last—and the indications came early.

*   *   *

In 1981 I was asked to join the jury for the Booker prize. I was ideally placed to have coverage of the shortlisted books and authors on *Newsnight* on the day they were announced, scooping the next day's papers. It was the idea of the scoop rather than of the books that impressed the editor.

Every jury has its own dynamic: prizes are the hazardous outcome of the shifting relationship between diverse and sometimes wayward egos. Ours was no exception. Malcolm Bradbury, a chairman of pipe-smoking affability, described us as 'two academics, two practitioners of writing— and a chairman in both camps'. The academics

337

were the critic Hermione Lee, and Samuel Hynes, professor of literature at Princeton University; Brian Aldiss, a writer of science fiction with many books to his name, dwarfed my credentials as an occasional journalist. Throughout the year I would read almost a hundred books. That alone would have been taxing enough, and I was combining it with a full-time job. I was putting myself under enormous pressure. But somehow that was what I wanted, craved almost. I felt driven by the sense that I was somehow behind, that the years of the family and my confused emotional life had damaged my capacity for sustained concentration.

Malcolm was a rigorous chairman. He insisted every single book was discussed, at least briefly, before our longlists of first twenty, then twelve, then the final seven. The winner would emerge on the afternoon before the formal Booker dinner. Hermione was the most conscientious, arriving at each meeting with an impressive page-long typed synopsis and critique of each book under discussion. I built up a box file with a card for each book and comments long and short. Sam was the most concise: his notebook appeared to have little more than a line for each book, and a yes or a no. Each to our own style.

Perhaps the seemliness of our deliberations kept the lid on some explosive differences. But ten days before the final judging it all proved too much for Brian Aldiss, whose passion and excitement finally erupted in a *Guardian* article laying bare much of our talk. He and I—as the non-academic wing—had spoken on the phone throughout the summer and it became clear he preferred novels that were 'big baggy monsters' (Henry James's phrase) to novels of anorexic excellence (Brian's phrase). It was clear that in his judgement there were three of the latter on the shortlist: Muriel Spark's *Loitering with Intent*, Ann Schlee's *Rhine Journey* and Ian McEwan's *The Comfort of Strangers*. He was also passionate for D. H. Thomas's *The White Hotel*. He couldn't contain his fears that the 'wrong' book might be chosen.

The *Guardian* article broke all the informal but assumed rules of confidentiality. The rest of us were thrown into confusion, seeing it as an encoded attempt to press the case for *The White Hotel*, which, since high summer, had been making the running in the press. The close and personal collaboration of our earlier meetings had been blown apart. When it came to the final decision Malcolm Bradbury, as chairman, deftly maintained the appearance that all was as before. But he didn't know about the meeting between Sam Hynes and myself.

Sam was on secondment from Princeton and currently renting Hans Keller's cottage in Hampstead. We sat in the garden in the late sunlight discussing what to do about *Midnight's Children*, the book we both favoured. We concluded that the decision was somehow being hijacked, and felt entitled to do something to redress the balance. We planned our strategy. We knew that Brian was passionately for *The White Hotel*, that Malcolm was very impressed by it but as chair was putting on a display of ambivalence. That left Hermione Lee: she had voiced some strong reservations about *The White Hotel*, speaking of its flawed structure and inner coldness. However, she was genuinely undecided and, so we judged, open

339

to persuasion.

We made our plans accordingly. We agreed that at the final meeting of the judges we would remain meek and quiet at the outset as Malcolm expounded the merits of each of the shortlist of seven. We would be firm but unaggressive in rejecting each one, with regrets, until the final two, *The White Hotel* and *Midnight's Children*, remained. Only then would Sam take the initiative, offering in pretty laid-back mode an exact critique of *The White Hotel*, along the lines Hermione had expressed. I would add mild but brief support. But no fireworks. As his points were taken up, Sam would then suggest that, perhaps as a basis for further debate, we might take an initial vote, on paper, just to see how the land lay, no commitment, no knowing how each was voting. The bait was laid. The trap sprung. And that was exactly how it happened.

We gathered in the board room of Booker McConnell with only an hour to decide before the grand dinner at London's Guildhall. The discussion went as we had planned. It was clear from the start that Malcolm had expected *The White Hotel* to win, but there he was holding the votes in his hand: three for Salman Rushdie, two for D. M. Thomas. And suddenly the deed was done. 'Well, is that it, then? Do we need to go further?' Sam and I feigned a little bemusement, as though it was as much a surprise to us as to the others. But suddenly it looked as though *Midnight's Children* had been the winner all along. It felt right. All at once everyone was speaking of what a fine winner it was. We adjoined swiftly, changed into our evening clothes and joined the glittering audience, to none of whom we whispered the secret: indeed, waylaid by BBC Television, I rather archly hinted that speculations about *The White Hotel* might not be disappointed. We left it nail-biting to the very end. In 1993 on the twenty-fifth anniversary of the prize, *Midnight's Children* was declared the best of the previous winners: the Booker of Bookers. When the *fatwa* was declared against Salman Rushdie, its author, in 1989, a protest from his five Booker judges led the letters of support for him in *The Times*.

As for my minor *Newsnight* scoop, it was nowhere, dropped for more important matters, in fact a minor government reshuffle. I could live with it. All journalists steel themselves against changing agendas. But gradually arts coverage within Current Affairs had to fight ever harder to earn its place. And it was a losing battle. In the end John Birt's revolution finished it off.

Meanwhile, outside the BBC I was caught up in other advocacy for the arts. I took a hand in shaping institutions that would, over time, begin to raise their profile. In 1981 the Society of Arts Publicists, the people I was meeting on a daily basis, came to me and explained they wanted a higher profile for themselves and the arts generally. I agreed to help. I rang the theatre impresario Robert Fox, who supplied several crates of wine for our re-launch meeting at the ICA. The push was on for more media coverage. Meanwhile across town, beginning at the National Theatre, I was meeting with other arts people—from the unions, theatre, film and the orchestras—to institute a credible arts lobby. In late 1985, I chaired a meeting from the stage of the Old Vic at which individuals, performers, artists and organisations, cheered on by messages of support from the likes of Peter Hall, Simon Rattle and Claudio Abbado—resolved to work to create a higher profile for the arts and spread the word about their significance and value to a broader public. Slowly what is now the National Campaign for the Arts took shape. Today it represents nearly five hundred organisations and over a thousand individuals. Finally the media itself took notice of what was going on. In the mid-eighties, interested journalists formed themselves into the Association of Arts Correspondents. Now, with this and the other organisations holding seminars, producing information papers and hosting luncheons, the infrastructure was in place to make the case in support of the arts. When the National Lottery came along in 1994 people understood why the arts deserved a slice.

*   *   *

In 1984 the Poet Laureate John Betjeman died. Who would be the next? *Newsnight* despatched me to find out, interview them, proclaim the news, and thus scoop the field, which was rife with press speculation. When my editors weren't neglecting me they were making extravagantly impossible demands, but at least this was exhilarating and I said I would try. Most of my enquiries were by phone and, sadly, I kept no record of the gossip exchanged, tips given, favours courted or brush-offs endured. But there was one person whose opinion I sought who found it difficult to hold a conversation on the telephone because he was growing increasingly deaf. I had already corresponded with him in search of photographs of his close friend as a young man. The friend was Kingsley Amis. The poet, of course, was Philip Larkin.

In a rather Larkin way, we did indeed speak on the telephone. But briefly. I phoned the library in Hull where his assistant told me he never took calls. 'Then please tell him I shall be referring on television to his possibly being the next Poet Laureate.' He came to the phone at once, an extremely courteous, even gallant voice and manner. We spoke only for moments as he explained he would rather I sent a letter. I did so. In it I referred first to the loan of his photographs, then continued in what reads now as a cloyingly winsome tone:

> All of which brings me to the hidden purpose of this letter, which is to sound you out on the subject of the Laureateship. Unfortunately it is not up to me to offer it, merely to ask whether, if you are considering saying 'yes', I could come to Hull and interview you about it as soon as the decision is made.
>
> In the meantime may I, in all modesty, urge you to consider accepting such a position. You may say, rightly, it is none of my business. But I am aware—perhaps even more than you can be—of the large number of your admirers who would rejoice in your acceptance.

His reply was thoughtful rather than dismissive. He clearly enjoyed teasing me.

> . . .Thank you, too, for your flattering remarks

343

about the Laureateship. Your suggestion, innocent enough at first sight, becomes increasingly improper the more I contemplate it. You mean that after I have been asked if I will accept the Laureateship, and have written back to say that I will, I then tip you the wink and you come up with dozens of witnesses (cameramen, call girls, etc.) and record me talking about it, which is then relayed to the nation on the day the honour is announced? The security risks seem vast. And won't the Prime Minister's letter end 'I must ask you to regard this communication as confidential', or something like that? And shan't I get thrown into the Tower of London in consequence?

In any case, I doubt if you would be put to the trouble. Every candidate has his drawback, and mine is that I ceased writing poems about seven years ago. The country cannot have a dumb Laureate.

I persisted, no doubt urged on by eager editors:

Dear Philip Larkin,
Thank you for your letter and the consideration you gave to my letter. I am sorry you found it to be 'improper'. In fact I thought it was so worded as to allow you yourself to decide if and how you might co-operate with my proposal. Certainly the idea that I should arrive in Hull at the head of troops of 'call girls' is your idea entirely. I don't think the Poet Laureateship is nearly so much fun! . . . [as for the programme] I have completely changed my plans. I want now to

344

do an item for *Newsnight* that would profile a number of our leading poets—those, you might say, who could be considered to be in the running. There is nothing subversive in this, no breach of security, no leaked poems. The Prime Minister herself would smile upon its innocence. I am thus confident that you might be more willing to take a small part . . . nature and duration to be specified by you.

Incidentally does ceasing to write poems mean you cease to be a poet? Ministers of religion remain so even after retiring from preaching . . .

By now he had had enough of this coy wooing:

Dear Mrs Bakewell
Thank you for your letter of 11th June. Clearly call girls was wrong: what do I mean? Call boys? Continuity girls? I meant simply the intimidating entourage associated with most television occasions . . .

I am sorry, but I shall always shrink from proposals to appear on television, whether to talk about the Laureateship or anything else. I realise this must seem very strange and even ungracious to you, and I apologise, but at my age [he was sixty-two] one still clings to the ideal of not doing things one doesn't want to do, even though that of doing things one does want to do vanished years ago. However, I should watch the programme you outline with great interest; don't forget Charles Causley.

With all good wishes . . .

345

He died of cancer some eighteen months later. His close friend Kingsley Amis was devastated. He was also being harassed by reporters who wanted his comments. At the time Kingsley was living just round the corner from my home in Primrose Hill and we met, not frequently but occasionally, for drinks or a meal. He phoned to ask me to get him off the hook. He would agree to talk to no one but myself, and a sound recording only, no cameramen or such, and then the BBC could use the tape when and where they liked. I agreed.

It was clear Kingsley simply wanted to talk, and I was sufficiently distant, neither close family nor one of the literary establishment, to provide the right neutral emotional climate. He sat hunched in his wing-backed chair, wearing old-fashioned brown carpet slippers, one foot for some medical reason mounted on a cushioned stool. He talked for over an hour, the forgotten tape spooling on, as he unburdened his grief. He spoke of Larkin's work, of course, but also of his jazz, his women, his humour, his remoteness, his meanness. Kingsley deeply resented that he had never been invited to stay with his friend in Hull. Such was the intimate distance between them that he had never invited himself. He was by turns funny, angry, sad and always eloquent. It was a man speaking of his love for his friend in almost Roman terms. He would never again, on hearing the post thud on to the doormat each morning, descend the stairs with a rising hope that there would be a letter from Philip. He had done it every day of his adult life so far, and would now do it no more. It was a remarkable testament. And, as is the way with broadcasting, it was edited down, shared out, and reached the

346

public in scraps and pieces. It doesn't survive.

* * *

I spent six years on *Newsnight*. As the years went by, and I raised my head from my desk to look around, or came rushing through the door hotfoot from a story, I became more and more aware of something different about the office. Different from my time in the 1960s. There had been a major shift in the way women were present. By now there was a goodly scattering of impressive women on the screen: Angela Rippon, Sue Lawley, Anna Ford, Judith Chalmers and more. But this was different.

It wasn't a question of numbers, although that mattered, or of roles, although that was significant. It was some more fundamental cultural reality. It seemed to me that there came together in the *Newsnight* of the 1980s a critical mass of women substantial enough, both in intelligence and responsibility, to make the difference. Many were producers, Helen Jenkins, Jenny Clayton, Gill Hornby, Fiona Murch, Elizabeth Clough, Ros Erskine, Kathy O'Neil, Jane Ellison, Jackie Ashley, Diana Milward; some were editors-of-the-day, Lorraine Heggessy, Jana Bennett; some were newsreaders, Jenni Murray, Linda Alexander; and some presenters, like Olivia O'Leary. They were not women looking to succeed in a man's world. They were there to change it from a man's world into the shape of the future.

None had yet been editor, or deputy editor. None, except as holiday relief or when the men were at party conferences, had been the lead presenter. In the eighties each *Newsnight* had two presenters, the central leading figure—always male, primarily John Tusa, Peter Snow or Donald MacCormick—flanked by a newsreader sidekick, always a woman. We, the women that is, spoke of this role as that of 'programme wife'; we also noted that the succession as editor was defined by what we called the 'favoured-son syndrome'. Thus presenter and editor were gender-determined. Within this family, I belonged as some benign elder sister, one who'd been around for some time but was delighted and a little bemused by the confidence and authority of my younger siblings.

Meanwhile word reached us from another department of the BBC that women were becoming uneasy about the male culture in quite another sense. The rumour was that a bunch of young researchers and secretaries were discussing their colleagues over a drink in the BBC bar, when a number of the women alleged that a particular senior executive had made approaches to them in which the conversation turned to corporal punishment and the suggestion that they might be spanked. Several were said to have made an uneasy exit from the situation. The rumours reached women throughout the BBC. They also reached *Private Eye*, who published them.

For over a year *Private Eye* made frequent and teasing references to the executive in question, naming him and adding the nickname 'the spanker'. Then in the summer of 1984 it published an article alleging that he had made 'greasy overtures concerning corporal punishment' to a number of female BBC employees. The alleged spanker issued a writ for libel. Eleven days later he resigned from his job, but the writ stayed for another eighteen months and was only dropped, he explained, for financial reasons.

The reason the story reached *Private Eye* at all was that certain of the women concerned thought the matter should have been dealt with more thoroughly by the BBC. Whether or not their allegations were true, they had taken them to Personnel; they had even made them to a BBC doctor. But they felt the allegations were not taken seriously enough. After the story was made public, the scandal had the effect of bringing the BBC's treatment of women into the media spotlight for the first time.

By the end of 1984 Monica Sims, Head of Children's Programmes, had been commissioned to draw up a report on the place of women in the BBC. It dealt with why there were so few of them in top BBC jobs and was delivered in April 1985. Thus it was that in the 1980s the lot of women changed most radically in broadcasting. In 1982 the *Newsnight* producer Helen Jenkins, as tough and robust an individual as you can imagine, was asked by the then editor of *Newsnight*, David Lloyd, a telling question. He needed urgently to send an experienced producer to report on the massacres then coming to light in the Lebanon's Sabra and Chatila refugee camps. Would Helen, he asked, be prepared to go? Or would she rather he send a man? He got a dusty answer for his thoughtfulness and Helen was on the next plane to the Lebanon. Since then it has become routine to see women in the front line, at war zones, surveying disasters. But it began in the 1980s.

Everyone who was there remembers the meeting. It was held at the end of July 1987 in Studio D at Lime Grove. The entire Current Affairs group was rounded up to hear significant news from John Birt.

Things had been getting sticky for BBC Current Affairs ever since the 1984 programme *Maggie's Militant Tendency*, an edition of *Panorama* that looked into alleged extreme-right connections of certain Tory MPs. Neil Hamilton and Gerald Howarth had sued. By 1986, the year the case came to court, Norman Tebbit had become chairman of the Conservative Party intent on getting tough with the BBC. In the autumn of that year he attacked Kate Adie's reporting from Libya. In September Douglas Hurd named Marmaduke Hussey as the Tory choice to be chairman of the BBC. Hussey moved quickly to settle the *Panorama* case out of court and Current Affairs were suddenly aware they were under attack. The Tory strategy found ready support in the Tory press, who ran a sustained campaign of vilification suggesting the BBC was in a state of collapse. In truth, it was making serious programmes the government didn't like. *Real Lives*, a balanced attempt to look at the situation in Northern Ireland, had been denounced for being uncritical, precipitating a rare strike of television's journalists; a First World War drama series, *The Monocled Mutineer*, which had been declared in a BBC press release to be totally factual, turned out to be a dramatised version by Alan Bleasdale based on a true story. The anti-BBC press was up in arms. In February 1987

Special Branch raided BBC Glasgow and seized material intended for a programme about Britain's Secret Society. Within six months of his arrival, in January 1987, Hussey moved against the director general: Alasdair Milne was sacked. The pressure was building. Then in the spring of 1987 John Birt was brought in from London Weekend Television as deputy director general to take over BBC Journalism. Now he was presenting his new plans. Not surprisingly, no smiles greeted his arrival.

I had been away from the office rumour mill for some time, not only out on the road making stories but also engulfed in a major crisis in Jack's life. For some time he had been working as producer, with David Aukin, at Leicester's Haymarket Theatre. He had taken a picturesque flat in a barn in Leire, and we met when we could. Then Jack left Leicester and went as producer to help Frank Dunlop run the Edinburgh Festival. Again we met when we could. Life was taking on the patchwork arrangements that are now the common lot of two-career marriages. In June of this fateful year, Jack went down with a virulent form of pneumonia. It got worse. He was in intensive care at the Brompton Hospital, critically ill for some three weeks and convalescing for several more after that. It was hardly surprising I went along to the meeting ignorant and scarcely engaged with what was about to hit *Newsnight*.

Studio D is a vast and gloomy space of echoing blackness. At its centre, brightly lit as a stage set, were our new bosses: the fashion-conscious supremo John Birt, Tony Hall, a compliant producer from the *Newsnight* ranks, a newcomer Samir Shah and Ron Neill, formerly one of us, a

351

Scotsman responsible for the hugely successful launch of the BBC's *Breakfast Time* and now sitting uneasily with the managers. There weren't enough chairs for us, the audience, all to sit. I was among those who shuffled around in the shadows, brooding and apprehensive.

Slowly and remorselessly Birt made it clear that the broadcasting world had changed. It is at this point that everyone's memories of events diverge. Rather like the witnesses to a road accident, everyone has their own vivid account and, keen journalists though we were, they don't always tally. What is common to all our memories, however, are three enduring impressions: first, that John Birt told us in no uncertain terms that we were not doing a good job, that *Newsnight* did not give value for money, it had too many film stories and not enough analysis; second, that Charles Wheeler, the only journalist among so many with the shorthand to take notes as Birt spoke, gave Birt a hard time; and third, that Birt totally failed to carry the meeting with him. We dispersed, bewildered and angry. This was as talented a team of people as you were ever likely to find in broadcasting being substantially rubbished by their supposed leader.

What we failed to realise was how thoroughly and implacably the new world of managers had arrived. This meeting, with its conviction that through efficiency and with better and more targeted resourcing we would produce better journalism, hinted at what was to come: the entire Birtian management revolution. In management terms we, the makers of programmes, were now 'product'; he was there to transform the process.

Ten days later I was at my desk in the *Newsnight*

352

office when I took an unexpected call from my agent. How odd. He usually conducted our business when I was at home. But this was urgent: he had just been informed by BBC personnel that my contract was not to be renewed. I was being sacked. My job was being abolished. I was poleaxed. I was so shocked I began to shake visibly. My producer, Jenny Clayton, took me out of the building for a stiff drink and a lot of sympathy.

What had gone wrong? It was an inappropriate question. That wasn't how things were any more. My values were old-fashioned: I expected merit to earn reward, and those who do a good job to be cherished and encouraged. Instead, I was one of the victims of the whole reshaping of programmes that had now engulfed the BBC. My role, as an arts reporter operating at the heart of Current Affairs, was incongruous to the newly focused planning. My contract had come up for renewal at just the moment when such changes were being implemented. Now was the time for me to go.

I might have been made aware of all this then had anyone in the News and Current Affairs hierarchy ever spoken to me about it. But no one did. Not a single editor, head of department or deputy offered any explanation. Or sympathy. Or thanks. Only Graeme Macdonald, then controller of BBC2, sent a note on my departure expressing his regrets. There would be no traditional BBC leaving party for me. Instead, when I had worked out my contract some months later, a few close friends at *Newsnight* organised a delightful dinner party at L'Escargot to mark the occasion.

The news of my departure hit the papers while I was reporting from the Edinburgh Festival. It was

353

on the front page of the *Sunday Times*: I had photographers on my trail. And it was from the papers that I first learned of other BBC plans, by now long laid, to create a regular late-night arts programme made by the Music and Arts department. The talk was that it was based on *Late Night Line Up*, to which it bore little resemblance: in reality it was a high-brow review programme that successfully restored the arts to the ghetto of arts broadcasting: it was called *The Late Show*. It dealt solely with the arts and won itself a cult following that often included me. But the bold experiment to drag arts coverage into the mainstream of news and current affairs was thereby formally declared dead.

Not surprisingly, many of the organisations whose struggles I had charted were distressed at this change of policy. They had believed, with me, that the arts merited a regular place on the news agenda: the Opera House, the Old Vic, Sadler's Wells, the British Council, the Theatre Managers Association, the Orchestras Association, the National Art Collection Fund, the National Campaign for the Arts, even the arts minister Lord Gowrie wrote to me of their regret and outrage at this turn of events. Resolved not to be mean-spirited about the matter, I wrote to the man in charge of this great new arts venture, Alan Yentob, offering to put my range of contacts and experience at the service of the new show. He never replied.

I don't believe my going was any part of the larger Birtian plan: I was simply a casualty. Under Birt, new specialist reporters were brought in supposedly to strengthen the analytical resources of the BBC. None had any brief to know about the arts. None did. The arts had always had to fight its

354

way on to the news agenda. Now it had fallen off entirely. And I had fallen with it. It was a huge disappointment.

CHAPTER FIFTEEN

THE HEART OF THINGS

Within a month of being dismissed from the heartlands of BBC Television I found myself back inside by another door. I was having breakfast with Olga Edridge, the editor of *Heart of the Matter*. I had been driven from the raw jungle of *Newsnight* and Current Affairs and was now being invited into the sunlit pastures of the Religious Department. Never was the distinction between carnivores and herbivores more appropriate. Former colleagues commiserated: 'Religion is such a backwater!' but I recognised a backwater with the potential to become mainstream. I was being invited to write and present BBC1's *Heart of the Matter*, a series that went out eighteen times a year at around ten thirty on Sunday nights. Its brief was to confront the moral dilemmas arising from current events.

At the end of the 1980s nothing could have been more timely. Greed, affluence and self-interest—the hallmarks of the decade—were inflicting damage. Society wasn't growing any more harmonious. Many groups and individuals who had been beguiled by rising expectations were growing discontented and beginning to speak out. Surely there was more to life than this mood of rivalrous, even bullying, competition. Throughout my twelve

355

years with the programme I saw issues of morality steadily coming to the fore of social awareness, whether it was the purity of food, the integrity of politicians, the nature of family life, or the decisions concerning war. Morality was being taken seriously. Sadly, despite its frequent success in touching the public's conscience, by the late nineties *Heart of the Matter* had, through the indifference of a BBC management preoccupied with popularity and ratings, been allowed to run its course. Yet in a small but important way we had contributed to the changing mood of the times.

Those twelve years divide quite neatly into three eras, which, taken as a whole, chart the slow marginalisation and final demise of the Religious Department as a programme-making entity in its own right. Under the first of the three regimes, and its editor Olga Edridge, *Heart* was made within the BBC in its London television headquarters. Religion was parked at the top of the East Tower, a sixties block, where through huge plate-glass windows we watched the setting sun and the aeroplanes moving like somnolent black fish in the blue sky as they descended into Heathrow. This was within the establishment, a part of it, at the centre of things. I enjoyed the respectability of a place in the car park, queuing for sandwiches at the food trolley, spending long hours, even overnight, in the cutting room where the editor had a nude calendar on his wall and dropped his cigarette ash into the Steenbeck editing machine. We made the programmes on film in those days.

But within *Heart of the Matter* things were not traditional at all. Olga ran a radical and surprising office. Of all my editors she was the one who brought me closest to her editorial role. Confident in her own skills as an editor/film-maker, she allowed me freedom to write as I chose, and together we relished seeking out the most offbeat and original stories. There was certainly a personal agenda. Olga was no BBC apparatchik: she had a whole life beyond the BBC and knew probation officers, lawyers, feminists, gays and campaigners of all dimensions. She had links with radical Christian groups in America. We would pioneer stories about gay priests, the campaign for the ordination of women, the plea by black lawyers that a black defendant should not face an all-white jury, the case for conjugal visits in prisons, the issue of euthanasia and how a doctor in Holland helped the dying on their way. We covered the poignant case in Argentina of a child of the disappeared being reclaimed by her birth family from her adoptive parents; we were in Boston to hear how a member of the Christian Science Church had refused medical help for his dying child and been charged with murder. We flew to Berlin the moment they took the first axe to the Berlin Wall, and sought out the churches where dissent had been secretly nurtured.

Each time we aimed to be ahead of the debate in searching out challenging opinions and counter-opinions. Often the stories related to specifics of religion. The Church of England had a higher profile in those days. And plenty of rows. The issues of women priests and homosexual clergy cropped up time and again. We had an exclusive of the first official wedding between homosexuals recognised by law in Europe. It happened in Denmark and one of the men was a priest—two stories for the price of one. We followed a frantic schedule, making six thirty-five-minute documentaries, including two foreign stories, within just eight weeks. Each series was a wild roller-coaster ride.

Olga is half Greek with flashes of temperament that call to mind the implacable passions of Greek drama. She also had a powerful impulse to teach and, as one of those overseeing the BBC's graduate-trainee intake, she would pick off talented newcomers, attach them to *Heart* and then allow them, scarcely knowing even the rudiments of documentary-making, to make their own programmes. It was her way of supplementing our meagre budgets. The *sine qua non* was that she herself would assist at every stage, shepherding and directing her flock, and at the end they would get an on-screen credit. In line with her principles she would recruit women where she could. She chose to employ Asians and blacks long before the BBC had formulated a policy about such matters. In March 1990 we flew to Stockholm to snatch the first ever long interview with Nelson Mandela after his release from prison, granted to us because Oliver Tambo's son was on our team: Tambo had been Mandela's law partner, and President of the ANC.

All this was high-wire activity. There were risks, and inevitably occasional errors. Given that we made over a hundred programmes, carelessness was remarkably rare—but some were quite serious. On the eve of the Wembley concert celebrating Nelson Mandela's seventieth birthday, his twenty-sixth year in prison, the Revd Alan Busak, a supporter of Mandela, was coming to London and we were to interview him. On the pretext of this religious visit, other Mandela sympathisers would also travel to London. An open telex to South Africa, sent by one of our inexperienced researchers, tipped off the authorities to this plan, and the named people had to go into hiding. On the domestic front another trainee quoted in a *Heart of the Matter* press release an insulting remark made by Dennis Potter of William Rees-Mogg, only recently vice chairman of the BBC. Not tactful. And the press were gleeful. I was on the phone with regrets instantly, but the mistake had been made. We looked careless.

At the start we were answerable only to the head of Religious Programmes in Television, John Whale, who had been most recently editor of the *Church Times*. He was unfamiliar with the grammar of television, but extremely concerned with the grammar of the written word. He would correct my scripts, not for their theology or ideas but for their punctuation, being fussy about capital letters and the difference between colons and semi-colons. Not a matter of prime importance for a spoken commentary.

In the days before Birt's Producer Choice policy took hold, many of our costs—staff, offices and facilities, BBC film crews—were taken care of for us. We never knew what they were. There was no pressure to maximise ratings, though we ourselves took note of how well we were doing. And in those days having a regular slot at around ten thirty on Sunday evening, with a strong brand and plenty of publicity, we frequently had audiences of around 2.5 million and occasionally over three million. Thus while we were not going out at peak time, we felt in many senses secure at the centre of the BBC's public-service role and its profile in the public's awareness. Over the decade that would change.

*   *   *

The exhilaration of working on *Heart of the Matter* wove itself in and out of my personal life. At both ends of the family things were changing. My half-way place between the generations, between my own father and my grown children, would make one of those primordial shifts. Within the same year, 1991, I had to face his death and the birth of my first grandchild. I would move up the family tree to become the elder of the tribe, the matriarch. By the millennium I presided over a harvest of grandchildren, finding myself newly defined by my place in their lives.

My father had enjoyed twenty-four years of retirement. He had reached the top of his particular tree, as managing director, then chairman of Simon Handling Engineers, the engineering group he had joined as a young foundry apprentice, then draughtsman over forty years earlier. As his career moved up, his politics moved right. His small stature filled out into a rubicund Pickwickian presence, proclaiming Tory doctrine with defiant bravura the more to outrage me. Of course we argued, shouted, wagged fingers, traded insults. Not for us the ominous silences: we had had enough of that in our family years ago. So we rowed and argued, and knew it was part of a deep, untroubled attachment, an understood and private love. I knew his story and he mine. I was his first-born, bearing the burden of his ambition, supported in all I wanted for myself and finally making him proud of what I had done. More intimately we had suffered together the pain of my mother's melancholy and her deep sadness within a life he did all he could to make joyful. He had been close and forbearing when my own marriage failed. He loved me with a particular love, but he loved us all and we him. Now he was going.

The call came in August 1991: he had collapsed at his home, in Poynton, Cheshire, and been taken to hospital with pneumonia. He was eighty-eight, yet I had somehow believed he would live for ever. So had he. At the age of eighty-five he had bought a new car. He regularly played golf, nine rather than eighteen holes being his only concession to age. He was a spry, even wilful character. I refused to think of him as frail and dependent. And, indeed, after a precarious twenty-four hours he was sitting up, a colourful tide of family and friends livening the ward and lapping around his bed. But the recovery stalled. He couldn't take food. And his jaunty eye, which sparkled with the old charm when golf-club cronies and their pretty wives jollied and petted him, glazed tiredly when the tray came round. Did he know?

We never spoke directly of his dying. We talked of what was happening in oblique language hinting at shared awareness. In the past at other deaths we had talked of how it might be. The half-jovial 'It'll be my turn one of these days', and more thoughtfully, 'Don't let them mess me around, will you, Joan?' I had said then, 'Don't worry. I'll be there going through it with you.' And that moment was not far off.

As the days wore on he would ask over and over, 'Is the baby born yet?' He was waiting. At the other end of the country a young couple in the full bloom of health and scarcely a year married were waiting too. My son Matthew's wife Sally was about to have their first child. The autumn series of *Heart of the Matter* had begun and I was in Aberdeen, reporting on the problems of whistleblowers in the offshore oil industry. And I also was waiting. The call came at ten thirty at night: my first grandchild, a boy, Thomas. The next morning I flew to Heathrow and drove with Jack to the cottage hospital in Dorset where a room was already filling with flowers. My father went on waiting in his hospital bed.

Suddenly there were difficult decisions to make, practical matters to decide. *Heart* was planning to visit Canada. I sat by the bedside holding his leathery hand in mine. I talked quietly with the doctor in the adjacent visitor's room. The provision of coffee and the reluctant start to the conversation signalled alarm. But what 'alarm' is there with death already in sight? I asked how long. The words stuck in my throat, literally. They came out huskily: 'No, not immediately. He'll probably live until Christmas.' I decided to go to Canada. I had baked him a bread and butter pudding, a particularly good one, rich in eggs and cream. It pained him to turn aside my gift. 'I just can't, but thank you, thank you.' It was the last thing I gave him. And his last words to me. I left the hospital desolate and packed for Hudson Bay.

In the 1970s the Québec government had embarked on the largest hydro-electric scheme the world had then known, with the admirable idea of providing clean energy in abundance for themselves and a surplus for export. They would do this in what appeared a vast and virtual wilderness but was in reality the territory and trapping lands of the Cree and Inuit who lived there. Now trouble was stirring. The Cree had craftily used some of their compensation money to send their young people away on university courses in native politics and environmental conflict. They had returned to make things sticky for Hydro Québec. A perfect dilemma for *Heart of the Matter*: clean energy versus native rights.

It's only when I am on the plane that I realise I am taking my father with me. A rich, somehow joyous melancholy has settled on me in which I feel in deep, almost continuous communion with him. I know the withered hulk of his many years is tossing among the sheets to find some comfort. But here on the plane his alert and enquiring spirit, deeply rooted in my own identity, is pulsing in my mind. I land hugging my sadness to me.

There is no road here. We descend under lowering skies to an untidy settlement with a scattering of native homes. The plane carries a mix of television folk, engineers—big burly men with beards and noisy voices come to work on the project—and a few neat, silent people with native features, the women wearing delicate moccasins of stitched sealskin. One has a child wrapped in a shawl. A world on the brink of change, inevitable, painful, and remote from my own cares. We film inland at Chisasibi, a settlement funded by Hydro Québec to house the displaced Cree. It is awful, with an alien Western-style shopping mall that has quickly grown shabby and strewn with litter. Young Cree are getting drunk. We hear of their myths and their belief that only the Creator owns the land. We hear, too, of their resolve to resist change, to keep their traditions alive.

One night as we contemplate the destiny of the dying Cree, there is a call from England. My father's condition has suddenly deteriorated. My sister's voice is flat, devoid of hope, resigned. I stand in the overheated corridor of the little wooden hotel, a million miles from what really matters, and let the phone line hang limp.

There is one important interview I need to do, back in Montréal. Others can mop up the rest behind me. I am febrile with conflicting tensions: keen to be gone, but with a chaotic energy that I discharge at the hapless Hydro Québec executive delegated to answer my questions. Suddenly I see him as more than himself: he is the destroyer of virgin forests, and vast waterways, of ancient traplines and rare lichens, of quavering Cree poetry and luscious Inuit heritage. I am fierce. I am angry. I attack and accuse. I rage and harangue. The interview is an aria of outrage and distress. Then I flee to the airport, subsiding into my seat. I am full of grief.

By the time I arrive my father has lost the power of speech. His eyes move slowly without purpose. When I come into range he responds with everything left in him. The eyes refocus, his shoulders hunch, he makes a sound. I am there. And he knows I am there. Our pact, never formally agreed, always understood, is fulfilled. I am going through it with him. And then there is a last dramatic twist to his life.

The new family drives north. With particular tenderness my son lifts his newborn son into the lap of his dying grandfather. On the baby's lip, a bubble of saliva, glistening and fresh as life itself. Above him, my father's face, sagged with age and illness, takes on sudden energy. He rouses himself as far as he can and rocks the small bundle where it lies: my father, myself, my son, my first grandchild: four generations, two of them at the extremity of their years. My son smiles, I smile. This is what life is. There is no sadness at all. No tears. I feel my father is liberated into his death.

The next day the light in his eyes dies.

*   *   *

In June 1991 Olga and I, filming in Florida, got an unexpected phone call from London. We were told that it had been decided over our heads that *Heart of the Matter* would no longer be made within the BBC but was to go out to an independent company. The 1990 Broadcasting Act laid down a new requirement that the BBC put a quota of its programmes—a minimum of 25 per cent—to independent programme-making companies. Suddenly there were lots of them. Stephen Whittle, the newly appointed head of Religious Programmes, Television, decided *Heart of the Matter* would fulfil his quota at a stroke. It would also guarantee him a clean sweep of new talents to make the series, which he claimed needed 'refreshing', a weasel word for saying you want the old guard out and replaced by your choice of new. Olga would cease to be editor—a personal and professional loss for me. But I was treated as part of the BBC package, being touted around for competing bidders. By the time the shortlist was down to four, I was even allowed a modest say in deciding my future. Our choice fell on Roger Bolton Productions, a company newly minted specifically to bid for *Heart*. They were to run it from the start of 1992 until March 1995.

The Bolton regime was an entirely different entity from the BBC. Here we were in a small office at the heart of Soho, joining the cappuccino and ciabatta society of independent companies, up antique winding staircases given a lick of paint, in small eighteenth-century rooms, loaded with paraphernalia of faxes and files. I moved from the volatile Mediterranean orbit of Olga Edridge, cushioned by access to BBC reference and record libraries, into the austerity of a tiny office and the severe northern puritanism of Roger, who had grown up within an evangelical sect of the Church of England, knew his Bible with a stark literalness and had a piercing sense of logic that put hairs seriously in danger of splitting. He already had a fine track record—as editor of the BBC's *Nationwide* and *Panorama*—with a reputation for high-mindedness and taking a story to the brink. The controversial *Death on the Rock*, about the shooting of three IRA suspects in Gibraltar, had been his, and had landed Thames Television in trouble with Margaret Thatcher's government. As he was executive producer of *Heart*, moral dilemmas were clearly his stock in trade.

The series producer was Michael Waterhouse, tall, quiet-spoken, with a less assertive personality than Roger yet as implacable a judge of a story's logic and integrity. Together they hand-picked a team of experienced researchers and producers, individuals of persistent and enquiring minds who would bond into the most effective and supportive documentary team I have ever worked with. We stayed together, making eighteen documentaries a year, for virtually three years, a concentration of experience and skill that is rare in big companies, which shift staff at whim to serve purposes other than the programme in question. Perhaps that was why we won so many awards.

The idea was to sharpen *Heart*'s journalistic edge, and tighten its story-telling. The pace quickened: there was more and faster cutting. We hadn't yet arrived at the fast cutting and many voices of today's programme style but television was already speeding up, and therefore clarifying its narrative. And I was to be more involved on screen. I began to participate in the actual events: I climbed aboard a broken-down bus of travellers as they were evicted from a Gloucestershire field and witnessed the naked hatred Middle England has for the unconventional and non-conforming. I lined up with the defenders of an American abortion clinic as they confronted campaigners who wanted it closed down. And I joined the protesters who marched one summer day in defence of the green fields of Twyford Down.

It was one of those golden mornings when the promise of the day's heat already hangs in the trees and touches the grasses. We came together in a ramshackle shed, half collapsed but good enough a place to distribute the rather ramshackle plans. People were converging from all over, easy-going young people, some with babies, even pushchairs, which would be hard to negotiate across the fields. Some were older, some with memories of landmark causes. A survivor of the famous Kinder Scout trespass, now in his eighties, told how in 1932 six ramblers had been arrested on the highest peak of the Pennines, and gone to jail claiming the right of access to rural Britain. He gave an exhilarating address about that early triumph and perhaps some of us felt heartened, though the odds were against any success this time. Twyford Down was already going under to the diggers.

We were advised to keep to the paths, not to cause damage or leave litter, and when we crossed the trespass barrier on to the roadworks to conduct ourselves correctly. We knew that anyway, but it needed to be said: protests don't police those who join. All protests feel good to those involved: there are shared values, a shared purpose and a sense of doing something about it. People talk readily with each other, share stories and food. To me, so long after Suez and CND, it felt like the 1960s again. A girl in swinging skirts played a guitar and sang a protest song in a thin, plaintive voice; someone helped me across a stile. There was no one to watch us as we wound our way in the growing heat across the downs, the buzz of insects in the long grass. No one until we reached the roadworks. Then there were fences to scale. And police. At this point I addressed the camera, making clear my role as reporter, not protester. I was among but not of them. But I enjoyed their company.

It was why I loved the job I was doing. The broadcaster is in an enviable position: he or she can be among the action, and by some social sleight-of-hand people often speak more openly, more intimately with individuals who are half stranger/half familiar from the television screen. It is almost as if it's a form of confessional. Over the years I have talked with criminals, drug addicts, paedophiles. I have met battered wives, women with AIDS, and heard those seeking euthanasia contemplate suicide. I have heard members of the National Front spell out their sense of alienation, children speak of the trauma of parental divorce, learned from Muslims their specific quarrel with *The Satanic Verses*. It has been my greatest reward to listen and hear directly so many individuals tell their own stories.

I enjoyed the arguments too. At *Heart of the Matter* we were always keen to go against the grain: when the Bosnian war began we argued the case for non-intervention. When the United Nations troops pulled out, we argued the issue of whether they should stay. We followed the stories of a convinced Christian who believed homosexuality could be 'cured' by prayer and of his homosexual son who had committed suicide. We heard transsexuals make the case for having their changed gender identities registered on their passports. We enquired whether vets—in the pay of the farming community—were also alert to the concerns of animal-rights activists. We asked why women shouldn't see active service in the army, or have babies at the age of sixty. And we dissected the claims of the evangelist preacher Maurice Cerullo to cure the sick.

Budgeting was simpler than it had been at the BBC: £800,000 for eighteen documentaries a year, and no more. There was no particular pressure to achieve ratings. There didn't need to be. We were all keen to reach a big audience. I zigzagged frantically between different programmes being made at the same time. While one story was being

369

edited I was often filming the next. Sometimes I was dizzy with tiredness. I recall driving across Florida one evening as a space shuttle was launched, its blazing trajectory in full view, and I was simply too dog-tired to rouse myself in the back of the car and watch it. That tired.

All this was having an effect on my marriage that I didn't allow for. I was caught up in a world of professional highs and lows. When *Heart of the Matter* was on the air I was operating at full stretch, giving it all my energy and concentration. At home trivial things began to matter: the phone calls were too often about my work, cars arrived at early hours to whisk me to airports, I would be called late to cutting rooms to adjust and rework scripts. And I was obviously enjoying it all. Jack, too, was riding the world of professional highs and lows: he had formed a sequence of independent production companies, and they would make good work. One of them, The Drama House, would one day make Hugh Whitemore's account of Alan Turing's life, *Breaking the Code*, and be nominated for a BAFTA. But the financial burdens loaded him with worry. The stress took its toll. Our lives were beginning to run in parallel rather than as one.

And then the BBC moved its entire Religious Department to Manchester.

*   *   *

Broadcasters rarely have any say in policy. It isn't what they do. They are hired and fired to fulfil an on-screen role that is defined by others and sustained, modified or abandoned according to the counsels of people they rarely meet and committees to whose deliberations they never have access. But we could see what was happening. *Heart of the Matter* was moving to the margins.

So it is with institutions. As management proliferates, decisions concerning what is a creative activity become answerable to more pressing institutional imperatives: regional policy, audience numbers, competitive ratings, financial value for money. All of this was happening to *Heart of the Matter*. The Religious Department was moved to Manchester to bolster the output of a BBC region. Stephen Whittle canvassed the support of the churches to oppose the move—putting religion out on a limb rather than its being part of the trunk of the tree—but to no avail. Religion went north. Of some sixty department staff affected, at least a third didn't make the move. A raft of rising young producers—the next generation of talent—stayed behind to nurse their careers in London. Stephen left, and the newly appointed head of Religion, the Revd Ernest Rae, came from radio and had no experience of television.

Then, in 1996, another *volte face*: *Heart of the Matter* was taken back from its independent producer to be made inside the BBC, but this time in Manchester. Well, that was the theory. In the end it was actually made in Barnet, North London. Now I was confronted with an entirely new concept for the programme. At the BBC's interviews for a new editor, Anne Reevell—who got the job—was told that a new format had already been decided, presumably by one of those faceless committees I had never met. The documentary style was to be dropped and from now on *Heart* would be a group discussion preceded by a short, self-contained film.

Its remit would still be to handle moral dilemmas but ones of a more popular sort. Out went the problems of Northern Ireland, and ethnic minorities, in came issues of lifestyle: was body-piercing damaging? Was it OK to be fat? Throughout the late nineties things became increasingly difficult, in terms of money, scheduling and the chase after ratings.

I was now at several removes from the centre of things. I lived in London, but the forward planning and research went on in Manchester. I became a regular on Virgin trains taking a day trip to agree the script and plan the debate. Punctual to a fault, I could always reckon the 8 a.m. train from Euston would get me into the Manchester office by ten forty-five. Now I had no part in the making of the short films that were shot around the world by young trainee researcher-directors—often women—whom I scarcely knew, travelling on their own. I was thrilled by the eager-beaver way they grasped the opportunities, but it was getting ever harder for me to feel at the core of the team or, indeed, to do more than fit into the slot of on-screen presenter. My fears were all too vividly confirmed when *Heart of the Matter* won a prestigious Sandford Martin Award for religious programmes. I wasn't even invited to the ceremony.

Heart of the Matter found itself caught in a pincer movement of falling budgets and increasing demands for higher ratings. The BBC was going through a cost-per-head-per-viewer exercise. Studio-based, we no longer qualified as a documentary. As a consequence we were now classified within the discussion genre, which

372

occupied a lower price band. Even then the BBC no longer paid in full what our programme cost. From now on we had to go out and find extra money from people who would agree to co-produce. What was more, with Producer Choice, a new system of budgeting introduced by John Birt, we now had to pay from our reduced budget for the hire of a BBC studio, and the one studio available in Manchester was too expensive.

All this found a happy solution when CTVC, a non-profit-making production company created from the legacy of the J. Arthur Rank Organisation, joined us as co-producers. That was how *Heart of the Matter* came to be made down a leafy lane in Barnet, where J. Arthur Rank's former home, a rambling 1930s mock-Tudor mansion, now housed—though you wouldn't notice this from the road—a TV studio, canteen, offices. It was in this pastoral backwater that *Heart of the Matter* lived out its years, contributors to our debates coming most often from London, and the entire *Heart* team travelling *en masse* from Manchester to Watford station. And it was with CTVC that we made one of our rare programmes about religion. As the decade had proceeded religion had fallen off our agenda. It was now seen as a minority concern, not one that would galvanise the interests of the public at large. No one then foresaw the way that religion, and fanatical religion in particular, would come to bestride world affairs and all our destinies; no one appreciated how much an understanding of religion would be central to world peace. The hostile reception of our Easter programme in 1996 might have given us a clue.

For Easter 1996, we decided to make one of

those what-if programmes. What if, we asked, Jesus had not died on the cross and then come back to life, but remained dead? Unless you are a believing Christian it is, after all, the more likely result of crucifixion. So we asked, 'What would have happened to the body?' The programme was called *The Body in Question*. I was as surprised as anyone by the story that emerged and the prodigious row that followed.

On 11 March 1996 I flew to Jerusalem to join Ray Bruce of CTVC, a man with degrees in divinity and Islamic studies, who trained for but stopped short of becoming an Anglican priest. His contacts spanned the Middle East from embassies and universities to restaurants and taxi ranks. With him was Chris Mann, a BBC producer of seventeen years' experience, most recently a series called *Ancient Voices*, all involving the search for historical truths and, strangely enough, missing bodies. It had taken him through archives, libraries, catacombs and pyramids. Serious men, and both professing Christians.

In Israel archaeology is a hot topic. Israeli archaeologists are keen to uncover evidence that will substantiate Israeli claims to the occupied territories. At the same time Orthodox Jews condemn any interference with tombs and burials, and wage a war of attrition against the professional archaeologists. It was not surprising, then, that discoveries made by Jews but of prime interest to Christians had not been given much attention. Until the arrival of *Heart of the Matter*, that is.

Back in February Chris and Ray, on a recce in Israel, had found an archaeology catalogue of Jewish ossuaries, published in 1994, listing all those

374

that bore inscriptions. An ossuary, a box of baked clay, was the traditional form of Jewish burial at the time of Christ. This list included seven ossuaries bearing the name 'Jesus'. Two of them bearing the name 'Jesus, son of Joseph'. When we returned to Jerusalem in February we had decided to film these two as part of our story. They were stored with many others in a warehouse, an old factory on a concrete side-street in a run-down suburb of Jerusalem called Romemma, but they had come originally from an ancient tomb brought to light when builders were blasting at a site at El Tapiot beside the Jerusalem–Bethlehem Road. While we filmed the ossuaries Chris nosed around, looking for more. 'Do the ossuaries on adjacent shelves have any relationship to this one?'

'Oh, yes, they were all found in the same tomb.'

This in itself was enough to indicate a family connection. Slowly we examined each of the other ossuaries and found an impressive coincidence of names: beside Jesus, son of Joseph, was the ossuary of Joseph, one of Mary, another Mary, a Matthew, then Juda, son of Jesus. That was it. Nothing more. Everything else was mere speculation. But given our enquiry 'What if . . .' this was exactly the answer we could have expected to find, had Jesus not risen from the dead: ossuaries bearing the names of Jesus and his close family.

The programme told the story straight, explaining our discoveries as we made them, making no religious claims for it. Indeed, we interviewed Jewish archaeologists, who declared all the names very common, and the odds against there being any link with the New Testament story virtually immeasurable. A coincidence, no more? I

375

point out readily that there was nothing conclusive about this discovery. Merely benign speculation, which allowed us to raise issues in a discussion about bodily resurrection.

The programme, broadcast on Easter Sunday, stirred up a terrible fuss. Even before it was transmitted the *Daily Telegraph* gave over Saturday's first leader to it, prejudging it as 'one of the sillier examples of modern questioning', quoting St Paul, and then declaring that the truth of the Resurrection 'cannot be exploded by archaeologists scrabbling in the dust, or textual critics poring over Papyrus, let alone by Joan Bakewell', and then concluding, 'Through faith it becomes clear that not only did Jesus rise from the dead in first-century Palestine, but that he is risen tomorrow, Easter Day.' So that's all right, then.

The Times, too, weighed in before they'd seen the programme, concluding that our speculations— presumably that the discovered names might have something to do with the family of Jesus—were 'absurd' and 'fanciful'. The matter of the names— so common throughout the region—all being together in one family tomb, it dismissed as merely 'a matter of statistics'. Once the programme was transmitted there were further ripples. It was rumoured that even the Vatican had joined in to denounce us.

I might as well have been guilty of heresy. In earlier times I would certainly have been burned at the stake. And I knew then that, even as late as the mid-1990s, to challenge traditional religious belief with reasonable speculation based on actual discovery was to waken irrational and powerful forces. More recently, another BBC documentary, this time about the life of the Virgin Mary, stirred up a similar furore. I fear a world in which certain groups of believers insist on their right to restrain the rest of us from asking legitimate questions. I can see we shall have to remain vigilant.

*   *   *

Our problems continued. Anne Reevell, our tough and resourceful editor, fought valiantly for the programme's values and status. But the odds were too great. We were now hoist on another BBC requirement: 'percentage audience share'. The argument, as it reached me, ran thus: each programme must maximise its percentage share of the total watching audience at the time it went out. We regularly reached 19 per cent, but we were now given a target of 21 per cent. The schedulers worked out that *Heart* could best achieve this by being broadcast later at night, so we found ourselves on air well after ten thirty, and increasingly after eleven. At those times our audience share was easily 21 per cent and so, although our numerical audience was down, we could tick the box that said we were meeting our target. But I was used to real viewers, and plenty of them. Not percentages. I tried to argue the nonsense of all this, suggesting that the *reductio ad absurdum* of such logic was to broadcast at three in the morning when we could perhaps achieve 40 per cent, a success unparalleled in our history.

There were many reasons why a fine and worthwhile programme might not get top rating, but the old assumption that some things were worth doing even if they didn't have a chance to top the charts had now given way to a new one: that television exists to give people the programmes they want and effort must be focused primarily on that objective. Focus groups were operating similarly in politics. We were losing sight of doing something because it was a good thing to do.

For rating reasons we were now ever later on Sunday nights, with smaller budgets and for a mere twelve programmes a year. I decided it was time to go. At my departure, the BBC brought *Heart of the Matter* to an end. *Panorama* inherited what is now called the graveyard slot in the schedules. In 2001 BBC Religion ceased to be a free-standing BBC department and was subsumed into the BBC's Factual and Learning Group. Also in 2001, Islamic extremists brought down the Twin Towers in New York, and set religious divisions at the centre of world concerns.

CHAPTER SIXTEEN

VETERAN

The same story keeps pulling me back. The fact is that what has happened to me has happened because I am a woman subject to the concerns and priorities common to women in the second half of the twentieth century. The story would have had a different shape in Victorian and Edwardian times; it would certainly be different today. The changing role of women—not simply in terms of jobs and careers, but in the very nature of their lives—has been one of the most vivid transformations of my lifetime. My being a woman has always been more important in determining my life than my being a person.

Women have become ever more present in my world, and in the world at large. Those old attitudes of mine, part instinct, part the influence of family, school and church, have been blown away. A new, easy and surprising world-view has taken hold of generations younger than mine. Women students now outnumber men at Cambridge. And because making television programmes is largely a young person's pursuit I have been living in the thick of it. Since their broadcasting breakthrough in the 1980s, women have moved into the centre of things. In 2002, of the twenty-four members of BBC Television's board of management seventeen were women. It is one of the most uplifting and rewarding of all the changes I have seen: women—bright, assertive, intelligent, ambitious, direct, purposeful—making what they choose of their lives. Making mistakes, too. It's all part of being equal.

And my own story has been laced into that history. In choosing what to tell of my life, recalling those early limited horizons, the unresolved struggle between the personal and the public, family life and a career, I seem to have run parallel to a broader historical dynamic. It's what has happened to plenty of women. And it's still going on. The issue now is how to grow old.

*   *   *

By the late 1990s I was being referred to as a

veteran broadcaster. Although it had echoes of wheelchairs at the Cenotaph, it also inadvertently created for me a new role. I could report on the recent past—a subject, especially the Second World War, for which there seems an insatiable appetite— as someone who had been there at the time. I made the series *My Generation* and interviewed those of more or less my age who had made reputations in areas that had interested me—films, television, writing, left-wing politics.

I put to them the suggestion that because we had all been children during the war, did we not share a certain outlook, even a certain cast of temperament? Had not the immediacy of danger, and the collaborative spirit of 'the war effort'— rationing, sharing, unity of purpose—shaped in our childish minds certain accepted concepts of duty, obedience and loyalty while opening our eyes to the inequalities, hypocrisies and false deference that our generation would begin to dismantle? You don't ask thirty or so idiosyncratic individuals to sign up to a consensual view of anything. I got no consensus. But I did alight on other truths.

Rather than the oppressive protectiveness you might expect in wartime, it was the very freedom from constraint by harassed or absent parents that allowed us to roam at liberty, to explore, take risks, begin to define ourselves. And, strangely, the background world in which we did this felt safe. That has been a major legacy in our lives, making us independent, resourceful. Second, rather than be ground down by the grim realities of austerity and rationing, the distress of evacuation and separation, many of us emerged buoyant and idealistic about the world. We grew up on the tide of optimism that greeted the fledgling welfare state. We were grateful for small incremental gains in our standard of living; we applauded the massive rebuilding programmes of tower-block homes and new towns for those who were poor. We grew ashamed of Britain's holding on to its empire and we rejoiced to see our so-called possessions given their independence. Many of us felt confident that we would vote and protest, write articles and march, and in so doing bring influence directly and immediately to bear on government. We believed the state was benign, giving many of us free university education for the first time, an expectation we believed would hold for generations to come.

It is our greatest disappointment that all the fine intentions to extend to others what that first post-war scholarship generation enjoyed have been so thoroughly distorted. Many grammar schools were closed: grant aided schemes have been abolished. And we were guilty of collusion. We believed that a truly comprehensive system was a means of making British society more equitable. But we took our eye off the ball. Somehow those we elected began to dismantle what was good from the past when they should have worked to integrate it into the future. Our ideals for education were high. In practice they failed many of our children.

That might be one reason why many of today's young people are cynical and disenchanted. The rising tide of expectations that prevailed as we grew up—inevitable in a country recovering from war— had prompted our optimism and, to a large extent, been justified. It was only as economic improvements peaked in the sixties and seventies, reaching a plateau of relative well-being, that the public mood swung to disaffection and, as the post-war boom stalled, became a narrative of hopes disappointed. Only since the millennium have the young become motivated once again; disquiet and concern about globalisation are building. The astonishing scale and conviction of the opposition to the war against Iraq shows a public engaging with politics. I watch with interest as a new political awareness is being born. What I sensed in my generation—committed as it was to social welfare and state intervention—was a sinewy resolve, an implacable conviction that your life's shape would primarily be up to you. It would be eased, of course, by the burgeoning improvements we enjoyed in health and education, welfare and travel, but in the end it was for you to fight the illness, poverty, prejudice and tradition that stood in your way. I think the war bred us tough.

My second veteran-reporter's excursion into how things had changed took me to outlandish places indeed: an Amsterdam Internet porn shop, a sado-masochistic club, the set of a porn film, backstage at lap-dancing establishments. The series *Taboo* examined how the limits of sexual display had changed over forty years, the years that included the *Lady Chatterley* trial, Mary Whitehouse and the *Oz* trial, all familiar to me but greeted with gasps of disbelief today. I think I was expecting to be shocked, but in the event shock was inappropriate. Once you've seen a pretty blonde nineteen-year-old open her thighs and heard her boyfriend explain, then demonstrate in detail how they arrange their entangled limbs for the benefit of the camera and which are exactly the best shots, you are beyond shock. The impulse not to look is merely gauche. This is a professional matter and you are into an absorbing discussion of sexual choreography, the outcome of which will decide sales, profits and even awards at the porn Oscars.

My surprise lay elsewhere. The women I encountered were not the hapless victims of vice squads, they were not the drugged teenagers traded across continents by criminal rings. They were bright, feisty women earning a living—paid much more than male porn stars—by what to them was a boring display of their bodies for quick, easy money. It was the men, their clients and dupes, whom they saw as victims. Some of the women were also students; several were saving to set up their own businesses; one, I was informed, was a British police officer on her sabbatical year out. None expected to be judged: the culture is tolerant and permissive. So keep your disapproval to yourself. The porn industry is bigger globally than straight cinema. In Amsterdam it registers as part of the GDP.

But, of course, I was shocked. I was shocked at where my journey had brought me. I have moved from the rigid absolute values of an uptight, repressed society into one that at least pays lip service to equal rights and equal opportunities, only to come up against values so relative, individualism so proclaimed, that almost anything can be justified. Was this the other side of the coin, the seedy expression of a supposed freedom for women, a freedom that has no depth except self-contempt?

Ironically, restraint is arriving from an unexpected quarter, one my generation never anticipated. By the fifties and sixties a broad liberal assumption had gained ground that the world would soon be done with religion, that the need to embrace superstitious beliefs would fall away before the enlightenment of science and humanism. We were wrong about that. Today religions have reasserted themselves. In America, at the behest of its religious right, creationism is taught in southern schools. From the east, religions that control and inhibit the lives of women have entered not only the ethical but the political arena. There has to be a clash. Naked and sexual displays on third-world beaches are deeply troubling for those whose religion requires modesty. It may be time for the hedonistic liberation to take stock. An accommodation may have to be made. It may be that the on-going struggle between dogmatic fundamentalisms and the liberal world will take place over the bodies of women.

*   *   *

Journalists of my generation grew up in a political landscape unique to our particular times. For fifty years we had report, rumour and only occasional glimpses of 'the other side': the Communist world, where things were different and terrible. Already the memory is receding of how absolutely divided the world was throughout the Cold War. The Iron Curtain shut off all spontaneous contact between millions of people, dividing families and sometimes cities. The world was in two halves, each knowing little but speculating extravagantly about the other. We were expected to hate each other. It was almost as if *they* weren't human at all.

384

Thus, to cross from one to the other was to enter a different civilisation, one as strange as an undiscovered tribe might be in the Amazon jungle. The strangeness, the mystery, the treachery informed the fiction of John le Carré and Len Deighton, the films of James Bond. They added a certain apprehensive excitement when restrictions eased. But as, slowly, my contacts with the other side extended, I came to realise it is governments and systems that are corrupt, tyrannies that are evil. The mass of humanity—brainwashed by state or religion though they may be—still lives a life of birth, family, subsistence and death, with the rites attendant on such things. Humanity is a whole: politics and ideologies divide it.

I first crossed through Checkpoint Charlie in August 1967, some six years after the Berlin Wall had been thrown up virtually overnight to stop the flow of refugees from East to West accelerating to a flood. The six-foot-high concrete defence, topped with a cat's cradle of barbed wire, strode through the city, dividing our side—the brightly lit, glittering West, with its shops, goods and geniality—from theirs, the street-dark, sombre East hiding who-knew-what way of life. Guns were trained on the no man's land between, watchful for would-be escapees. I went on one of the few carefully-restricted tourist buses. On our return, as we stopped at the ominous crossing point large mirrors mounted on wheels were trundled out and pushed to and fro below the vehicle, a grim search, but for them as routine as stamping tickets. I recall the crisp West Berlin guide, in slick tight skirt, high heels, her blonde hair breaking from a glossy silk scarf, handing over to a plain squat East German without makeup, a peasant-style cotton scarf tying down her mousy hair. The former warned us not to believe a word the latter said. They were both Berliners.

In the mid-seventies I visited Moscow, passing again through the looking-glass into this most sinister of different worlds. By now there was a pretence of eased tensions in the air and tourist trips were becoming common. I went to report for the BBC's *Holiday* programme. We were there in the week that included Burns night, a major celebration in the USSR where Rabbie is seen as one of the great proletariat poets. More vodka than usual flowed: he would have enjoyed that. There was also a curious episode that demonstrated the paranoia surrounding all exchanges with the West.

The Russians were guardedly keen to promote tourism, so we were received well, given tickets to the Bolshoi and offered a meal in a fine restaurant to follow. During the interval it was hinted to us by some intermediary that there might be a chance to meet the star dancers, who perhaps, but only perhaps, might dine at the same restaurant as ourselves. We were advised not to be surprised to be greeted by them; nor were we to expect it. Rather a convoluted message but we went along.

Alexander Godunov was the star in *Swan Lake* that night, a tall, muscular blond, more sinew than subtlety, but impressive in his leaps and bounds. Afterwards it was indeed he who led a group of friends into the restaurant. Bolshoi dancers enjoyed high profile and status and there was considerable bustle and fuss at their arrival. However, they steadfastly ignored us, making a point, none the less, of demanding the table

386

alongside. Alexander Godunov placed himself on the chair back to back with my own. Half-way through the meal there suddenly erupted a rather stage-managed flurry of introductions, their group finally, and with apparent surprise, acknowledging the BBC visitors. Toasts in vodka followed, in the course of which Godunov leaned his chair back towards mine and managed to ask on the quiet, 'Do you have news of Baryshnikov?' Mikhail Baryshnikov had defected to the West some months earlier while on a state visit to Canada. It had made big news in the West; evidently it had been hushed up in Moscow where he had become a non-person. I told him what I knew, which wasn't much, but, no, Baryshnikov was not in jail, yes, he was dancing, yes, he had been well received, all this muttered between the somewhat forced joviality of vodka toasts and expressions of goodwill in which we joined. In 1979 Godunov himself defected: there was a scene at Kennedy airport when he opted not to go back. He had a subsequent career of only modest success with American Ballet Theater, then went into films: *Witness*, *Die Hard*. He died in 1995 in Los Angeles at the age of forty-five. There were rumours of suicide. I wondered whether he ever hankered for the star treatment I had seen him enjoy in the restaurants of Moscow.

In 1982 I stepped across the frontier again. By then the rigidity of the global divide was softening. Before it changed out of all recognition I had a chance to visit China, crossing again into that mysterious vilified world of Communism. I was part of an official arts delegation, guests of the Chinese government, and thus given the sort of facilities—black limousines, first-class rail travel—

that divided us from the people. China was on the brink of change. Just six years earlier Chairman Mao had died, and the hideous persecutions of the Cultural Revolution had been brought to an abrupt end by the immediate arrest of his henchmen, the odious Gang of Four. The people we met—actors, film-makers, writers—were just the people who had been targeted by Mao's Red Guards as guilty of bourgeois reactionary thinking and been sent into exile to various degrading and demoralising jobs. Now they spoke openly of what they had suffered. It showed on their faces.

Everyone was eager for contact with the West: people stopped us in the street to shake our hands. Their spirit was for change. But they still lived in the old way. Beijing was full of the purr and whirr of three million bicycles. And so many people! Every street, every field, broad avenues, rolling hills . . . always there were people. Yet there was space and calm, no one hurried. Socially, at least, there was none of the stress of competitive capitalism. Everyone still wore the obligatory blue uniform, did identical physical exercises every morning. Differences in hierarchy showed in the finer cloth of the top officials, but otherwise everyone looked the same. Our apparel seemed outlandish to them, and made them laugh. I had a yellow jumpsuit that would have stopped the traffic, had there been any. A few of the street markets were selling produce brought from farms by individual families. It was the first indication that the economy would change. They were delighted it was so. I was delighted to have seen it before their society became more like ours.

In 1989 the most conspicuous divide that now

kept Communism apart from us—the Berlin Wall—was the focus of world crisis. Checkpoint Charlie was a ferment of activity, one of several crossing points where, for a day at a time, the East German authorities were allowing its citizens to pass from one side to the other. There was frantic shopping, poignant reunions, and a febrile expectation of further change. At Tegel Airport I heard one backpacker declare he was here 'to see history'. It was indeed a momentous time: the fall of Communism.

The *Heart of the Matter* team had travelled on impulse, no plans made. The world's press and television crews were converging and the only cars left for hire were a large Mercedes and a stretch limo. We piled the crew and their equipment into the stretch limo, and were promptly stopped at Checkpoint Charlie. East German officials, bemused at the imminent collapse of their power, were unsure how to respond, wanting to be difficult but not knowing to whom they were now answerable. The stretch limo was too much for them. Olga Edridge told me to sit tight and strolled confidently into their office. Handing across a clutch of passports, with a concealed two hundred dollars, she declared, 'Herr Schmidt at the Ministry of Culture said we could get our visas here and now.' Cowering in the Mercedes, I could see the guard bark back in German. Olga was not deterred: she indicated the money. And suddenly we were through. 'Who's Herr Schmidt?' I asked. She had invented him.

The world's media had opted to report from West Berlin: we chose the East. We would examine how the churches and the theatres in East Berlin had, in the previous months, become enclaves of dissident protest, their social functions offering legitimate cover for people coming together to make their subversive plans. East Berlin's hotels were empty. We stayed at the grandest, dining virtually alone in the glittering restaurant, where apprehensive waiters plied us with the best they had. A gauche singer in a red satin dress crooned into a microphone and directed all her charms at a large fat man with a red face, sprawled alone at a table on the edge of the dance-floor. It reminded me of *The Blue Angel*. Full of drunken talk of Germany and its past, Olga and I accepted long-stemmed roses from the manager, reeled together down the empty Unter Den Linden and laid them ceremoniously at the foot of the statue of Frederick the Great. History, indeed.

And so the world turned.

*   *   *

The world turned, too, in my personal life. The balance between my public and private life had always been difficult. Throughout the 1990s it became more so. Since the late 1980s my work had been going with a swing. By the nineties I was on a number of boards—the BFI, Friends of the Tate Gallery, the National Theatre—which brought absorbing interest. I was living a relatively high-profile life, full of decision-making and action, that was challenging and rewarding. I went about my days happy with what I was doing. But at home I was far from happy. Jack and I separated, and I decided to get a divorce.

There were other losses too. Susan's death from

cancer one New Year's Eve took from me the last of our tight little family. She was younger by six years, the one I had called 'our kid' on the streets. She had been a generous spirit, and although we went separate ways, we were held by that powerful umbilical cord of family, and in our case by its particular intensity and pain. Now there was no one who knew what I knew: no one who had so shared with me the long years of our mother's melancholy. I was bereft. It was as though I was losing pints of my life's blood. I was dying with her. My life's witness had gone and the record of what we remembered together rattled around in my head uncomforted. But she had thought of that: she had found time, while dying, to sort and identify the family records and at each of my visits handed to me another clutch of sepia photographs and yellowing pages. There was space to recall the past and lay it to rest. They speak in this book because of her.

My rackety career, late starting and often unfocused, is still that of a freelance. So there is no formal retirement, no contract with employers that ends with brutal finality at sixty or sixty-five. I have a sense that my time is already my own to do what I like with. There is, always has been, a freedom in not having your destiny decided by institutions. I continue to do what I do, subject only to the world's demands. Which, of course, has its limits.

No one has yet designated being seventy as the new fifty. Perhaps it is time to do so now. The culture is at last beginning to be more generous to the old. It has to: not only is the population ageing but the icons of the day—the models, the actresses, the footballers—are ageing too. So are the

391

journalists, the pundits, the image-makers. They need to shape for their own futures an image of being old that doesn't keep them awake at night on every landmark birthday. Wrinkles need to come into fashion.

But this is superficial stuff. More significant for someone of my age is that, as the years pass, I belong to a declining number of those who remember from the 1950s what the true concept of public-service broadcasting was, who absorbed it from the culture of the BBC at that time and whose programme-making has always been guided by its principles. Today there is an assumption that public-service broadcasting derives somehow from the licence fee, and that because the BBC is supported by this unique and obligatory tax, it is therefore under an obligation directly to the public, its funders.

It is the nature of that obligation that lies at the heart of the debate. There is a prevailing view—not mine—that the BBC must seek out, by way of focus groups and analysis, what genres and varieties of programmes the public wants, and then provide them. Within that framework—of popular response—individual programme departments and programme-makers must continue to prove the success with which they are fulfilling this obligation.

Several things follow from this. First, ratings become all powerful, demonstrating to the extent they beat their rivals that the BBC is best, and deserving of continuing licence funding. Second, that any programme that gets big viewing figures is, *ipso facto*, a good programme. This was not how the founders of the BBC saw it, nor how it was understood in the fifties, sixties and seventies. We believed—and I believe now—that the broadcaster's job is to be imaginative and creative to the limit of their talents, to conceive the best ideas of which they are capable, to deliver them in as rich and creative a way as possible and to offer them to a public who, never having thought of such things themselves, can be given insights and pleasures that expand their experience and broaden their delight in life.

The Latin quotation standing proudly in the foyer of Broadcasting House tells how the first governors dedicated 'this temple of the Arts and Muses to Almighty God' and prayed that 'good seed sown may bring forth good harvest, that all things foul or hostile to peace may be banished hence and that the people inclining their ear to whatsoever things are lovely and honest, whatsoever things are of good report, may tread the path of wisdom and virtue.' No wonder Lord Reith hated television!

It is easy enough to dismiss those rotund biblical phrases as laughably out of date and irrelevant. Certainly times have changed out of all recognition. But they can't be wished away. They are where the BBC began and how it proclaimed its duty to the nation. You may reject them, mock them, ignore them, but you cannot say they did not once exist.

Today's programmes have to compete for attention in an entirely different universe. The proliferation of images and abundance of channels has translated mass communication into a universal cacophony. The good gets caught up with the trashy in a whirlwind of notions, ideas, stories, jokes, myths and opinions. Getting noticed is what matters. Programmes seek outlandish ways to catch attention: instructions are issued to put sexy shots within the first few minutes. More explicit sex, more confrontational reality television. We are all shouting together in a wind-tunnel of noise. In such a world, each must inevitably matter less.

The workforce of television has changed too. It has become an industry where loyalty to a single lifelong employer and identification with its aims have given way to a ladder of personal ambition. More television people are, as I have been for so long, part of the casual-labour market. They move between major broadcasting companies, in and out of the BBC, from one independent company to another. They pick up the small change of television style and presentation. Programmes come to look more alike. Certainly they are often slicker, quicker, wittier. Scripts are rewritten and polished according to accepted norms, until either they lose all their originality or, by some fluke, come dazzlingly into focus and surprise us with their talent. But style has come to dominate content. Programmes are seldom more thoughtful, more engrossing as a result of all the time and money spent on them.

And perhaps it was all inevitable.

EPILOGUE

I am in the white room. And it is transformed. It was empty when I began, stark and empty. Full of sorrows. Awaiting developments. It is no longer empty. Or stark. A new life has entered. My relived life.

Slowly its spaces have become home to a drift of papers, some within the grip of giant paperclips, some in the scattered boxes now housed on regular shelves. Stacks of little diaries, a scattering of entries, a few oblique clues. School reports, a clutch of Cambridge bric-à-brac, invitations to sherry parties, a few enigmatic letters—who was Jonathan, who was Ben? And some from people I still know—Karl, Peter, Freddie. Serious boxes house the weightier matters—though just as transient—of a career in journalism and television. Yellowing cuttings, the paper fraying back to the fibre from which it came, remorseless photographs of my younger face forever seeking approval . . . articles by . . . articles about . . . the flotsam of a zigzag life that has brought me to this room.

Indecision sits on every shelf—the public career calling for precise attention to opportunity and self-promotion, and the private life, tracking always the need to love and be loved, men needing my support and encouragement, commanding my loyalty but disposing of theirs elsewhere. And children, whose very existence so quickly came to seem my purpose in life. The wealth and errors of choices made. There was never enough time for it all. Now there is no need.

Time has shifted its perspective. I recall how, once, a single year stretched ahead for ever. Imagining snow when the nights were sunny was a game, conjuring up a foreign country. When the leaves whispered in the trees it was magical to think of them falling into golden heaps. And we wished—how we wished—time would hurry along to bring round the special days, birthdays, holidays, Christmas.

With adolescence came the panic: stop the clocks, don't let this year vanish for ever. What is the past? What happens to it? Does it go on existing somewhere else? The panic subsided, replaced by a busy scurrying of years, plans to be made, objectives, ambitions, friendships to nourish. Soon there were children to bring up, involvement in the lives of others. Time flew without our attending to it. A comfortable rhythm set in. And remains. But is slowing down. Now there is less ahead than behind. A good deal less. And all of it precious. Time is telescoping. I can see the gold in the green bud, imagine snow in the blue sky. I don't any longer want it to hurry by. All is altered and altering still.

My sense of space has changed too, the places I have known. The white room I speak of is at the top of the house I have lived in for almost forty years. In the early sixties, less than ten years out of Cambridge, Michael and I were looking to buy our first home. Like other couples with young families and not much money, who wanted space—space for children, space for books and company, for an au pair perhaps, and a spare room—our only chance was to go for a large Victorian house, then unfashionable, Georgian being the preferred choice, in a run-down condition in a run-down area. At that time the district between Euston station and Camden Town was just such a place. It had that air of Dickensian decay that huddled round the great Victorian stations still belching smoke from steam trains. An area of fogs, sometimes pea-soupers, where soot blackened the windows and the sun that broke through was thin and sickly. This was the Camden of Sickert's brown interiors and Auerbach's dingy views of Primrose Hill.

Yet by the late fifties the occasional olive front door and stripped-pine kitchen hinted that the designing classes—architects and such—had already seen its potential. Potential, not as an investment—we didn't think like that then—but as a place to live. The strong, structural lines, the high ceilings, the flaking balconies provided the skeleton we needed. We would improve it ourselves. Gentrification was on the way.

Chalcot Square was sadly neglected. It has lost its railings to the war effort and the wire netting that replaced them was torn and sagging. The odd broken pram or dumped armchair hung around for weeks. Many houses were multi-lets with a family on each floor. Some were poor, several wayward. After one noisy episode of drunken wife-beating we called the police. But the woman sent them away. A 'domestic', they called it.

The shops along Regent's Park were shabby but serviceable: several small grocers where you were served from behind the counter, a butcher's shop with a jolly fat butcher in a striped apron, a cobbler's, a baker's, a hardware store, a kindly Jewish refugee of great skill who ran an upholstery

397

business and built my sofas. A greengrocer's run by a mixed-race couple from South Africa, whose marriage was illegal in their own country. We thought we were on the up when a launderette moved in. Modern, you see. There were pubs full of smoke with stained patterned carpets and regulars in flat caps. And us.

Now the whole scene has changed around me. The steam trains are long gone. So is the soot and smog. Chalcot Square got its railings back long ago. The houses now sparkle with new paint in myriad different colours. The earlier crowded families have gone, rehoused and resettled as prices rose. The area is known to be home to pop stars and comedians: but you never meet them in the greengrocer's. Plenty of people do meet—coffee shops and wine bars have replaced the family food shops, and restaurants of every kind: Greek, Indian, Italian, Russian. On a sunny weekend it has the air of a resort with strollers meeting and greeting, the dinky shops selling them soaps, smart kitchenware and silken clothes. When Nelson Mandela came to power, the son of the greengrocers went home rejoicing. Only the hardware shop survives unchanged but now film crews use it as a location. They find it 'quaint'.

Beyond what it's now fashionable to call 'the village', the skyline is transformed. Where once St Paul's stood out alone on the horizon, today, from the balcony of the white room, I can see the Post Office Tower, the filigree spider's web of the London Eye and, beyond, a gaggle of towers, Canary Wharf. London spreads out before me, a great, glittering spread of races and styles, of pleasures and pressures. It is at once scruffy and noisy, dynamic and glamorous. I doubt that I shall ever leave it.

*   *   *

There is one new image in the white room. It hangs above the black Victorian fireplace, with its fretted black fender. It is a poster, painted by the Danish artist Vilhelm Hammershøi, and used for an exhibition of his work held at the Musée d'Orsay in 1998.

The painting is of a woman. She sits alone at a table, which has a red cloth and a white bowl. Everything else in the room, the wall, the chair and the woman herself—her hair, her blouse, her skirt—is in shades of brown. The point of the painting is her aloneness and her complete self-sufficiency. She is not sleeping or dreaming like St Ursula. She is upright, alert. She sits facing away from us, looking towards the wall, resting against the ladder-back chair. Her expression is concealed from us, but the set of her shoulders, the angle of her neck, suggest she is relaxed, at ease, occupying with authority her space, which is hers alone and which is at the centre of the picture. It is an image I enjoy, but I am not making an icon of it. It is simply a new presence in a room that is full of old things. But I have a sense that soon she will turn round and look at me.

ACKNOWLEDGEMENTS

I want to thank my many friends and colleagues whose generosity with information and memories has helped this autobiography into being. If the list is long it doesn't mean each one wasn't valued. They include Ann Howard, Elizabeth and Nigel Calder, Karl Miller, Frederic Raphael, Michael Bakewell, Don Paterson, Henry Woolf, Michael Dean, Michael Fentiman, Rowan Ayers, Sheridan Morley, Tony Garnett, Suzanna Capon, Will Wyatt, David Wickham, Bob Greaves, Jim Walker, Jill Evans, Olga Edridge, Roger Bolton, Michael Waterhouse, Anne Reevell, Timothy West, Samuel Hynes, Charles Wheeler, Richard Lindley, and Peter Taylor. Elan Closs Stevens made valuable forays into Welsh graveyards for me. James Codd at the BBC Written Archives Centre has been a tower of strength. The Archive is the source of all BBC documents quoted in the text.

My particular thanks go to my cousins, John Rowlands, Marguerite Devenish and Sylvia Longford; to the poet Harry Guest for his beautiful translation of Lamartine on p.79; to Geoffrey Cannon for his friendship and scrupulous advice throughout; to my meticulous and patient editor Carole Welch; and the best of agents, Ed Victor.

Conversations with my sister, Susan Clarke, in the last months of her life helped my understanding of our early lives together.

I am grateful to Harold Pinter for permission to quote his two poems on pages 182 and 284. Quotations from T. S. Eliot on page 195, and from

PICTURE ACKNOWLEDGEMENTS

Associated Newspapers/Bernard Cookson: 214 bottom right.

Author's collection: 205, 206, 207, 208, 209, 210 top and bottom, 211, 212, 214 top right and bottom left, 216 centre right, 217, 218 centre and bottom, 220.

Copyright BBC Photo Library: 213 bottom, 215 top, 219 top right and bottom.

Clebak: 213 top left.

Glasgow Evening Times: 216 top right.

Granada Television: 216 bottom.

Courtesy James Hancock: 210 centre.

PA Photos: 219 top left.

Punch Ltd/Michael Heath: 216 top left.

Colin Rowe Photography, Plymouth: 213 top right.

The Sunday Times/Tom Kidd: 218 top.

Scottish Television: 215 bottom.

The Sun/Keith Waite: 214 top left.